Readers' reviews from the author of
Love, Life, & Broken Rainbows:

"This book is the best love story since…*Love Story*."

"I laughed and I cried and along the way I fell in love with the people."

"Well written and a good read that keeps your attention, start to finish."

"Kudos to Sheila Carroll for a warm, witty journey through life where we all know, anything can happen."

"The southern style is beautifully portrayed in this true, lovely romance. Hopefully, Sheila will continue to use her marvelous talent in more books."

"Sometimes funny, always brutally honest, an eye-opener for sure… brilliant!"

"I could not put the book down. Can't wait for her next book."

"What a wonderful love story! If you are a Baby Boomer, you will recognize the songs and be reminded of what you were doing at the time of your own youth. Sheila Carroll is a breath of fresh air! Perfect for a book club."

"I loved this book. The author, Sheila Carroll, has a way with words. You feel you are in the room with her."

"Beautiful love story! You will not regret this one!"

"This is a beautifully written, true story that touched my soul. I look forward to reading the sequel!"

"This book touches everything in life with great feeling. …I would love to see more from this author."

Better Things

A Memoir

Better Things

A Memoir

by
Sheila Carroll

For Tom

Ours was a broken road.

Many thanks to those friends and family members who encouraged me to continue my love of writing.

Part one

"Life is like riding a bicycle. To keep your balance you must keep moving."

Albert Einstein

Chapter one

Picking Up the Pieces

Widow. A widow. I was a widow. I hadn't planned on being a widow. Then again, did any woman plan to be a widow, especially at forty-three? I'd accepted my status as such, but the word and its connotations continued to drag pins and needles across my heart. Losing my husband was a painful reminder that our days are not infinite and that regardless of what we believed in the naivety of our youth, we were not invincible. And yet I survived what I thought I would not. Friends and family reminded me that which does not kill us makes us stronger. I didn't know if Barry's death would make me stronger, but I'd obviously taken leave of my senses.

What was I thinking gallivanting off to Mexico with a bunch of strangers? I was a small town girl who was not much of a traveler, an understatement. I had, in fact, flown only twice in my life. Nonetheless, in our last, lucid conversation, my late husband solicited my promise to complete the two quarters of Spanish I lacked in order to finish the college degree I'd been working towards. He was dismayed when I made the decision to put my education on hold after his diagnosis and blamed himself, which was ridiculous. Nobody asked for cancer. It was a disease that made no distinctions among its victims, nor did it need permission to destroy lives.

Though Barry tried to dissuade me from letting cancer sidetrack my plans, my mind was made up. He was my priority, and the decision to postpone graduation was mine to make. I was a nontraditional, part-time student at the University of West Georgia located a few miles south of Bremen, a small town where I grew up and where my late husband and I created a life and raised our two sons, and where I continued to reside—whether by choice or chance, I wasn't sure.

As in most small towns gossip spread like kudzu, and for those busybodies with nothing better to do there were plenty of rumors to fuel the fires of tongue waggin'. Needless to say, everybody kept up with everybody's business. The upside to life in a small town was that many were willing to help when my late husband was diagnosed with cancer—everything from meals to lawn care to free movies from the local video store. Everybody who knew Barry loved him.

I certainly loved him. He was my first and only love, and despite the disadvantages of youth our love withstood the test of time. We'd beaten the odds of a snowball's chance in hell given by our town's meddlers. Barry and I shared a life that included the births of two healthy, rambunctious boys, and the unpredictable ups and downs inherent in any family. However, our dreams and plans for the rest of our lives had unknowingly been as fragile as Waterford crystal, dreams that were just as easily shattered.

Our happy, sheltered life was put on hold with my husband's cancer diagnosis, and though we'd fought with every ounce of strength and energy we had, the battle was lost. His death almost destroyed me, and the process of letting go was by no means easy as I struggled daily with my loss and how to move forward. Most days were like treading water. My therapist assured me that grief was a progression of emotions and that it would take time to heal. Experience had taught her that I would recover, though I was uncertain as to whether or not I would break out of the web of pain. Barry had been my North Star, and each day carried the weight of a broken heart. I was also angry with God for deserting me in my time of need.

My faith was challenged when the many prayers that He intervene and save my husband from Death's harsh grip were unanswered. I felt abandoned, as if I'd been set adrift. In the process of healing I made my peace with God and accepted that His answer had been, "No." Counseling sessions, love, encouragement, and prayer eventually brought acceptance, the last stage of grief. And yet I remained paralyzed by fear of life without

Barry. My husband assured me, three days before his death, that I was strong enough to survive the inevitable outcome and that I had more memories to make. A part of me realized that fresh footprints in the sand waited for me to take the first step, but what Barry hadn't known, or maybe he had, was that I was terrified of taking those steps without him. Regardless, he wouldn't have wanted me to waste my life wallowing in self-pity. Nor did I.

Therefore, it was a godsend that propelled me forward. I'd received a letter in the spring from the university which was brief and to the point: if I didn't complete the coursework for my degree by the end of summer quarter, my diploma would fall under new catalogue guidelines for graduation and would require additional classes. According to the notice, I qualified for a program that would allow me to earn those two quarters in only four weeks at an accredited school in Mexico. Initially I rejected the notion but was advised that my HOPE scholarship would pay the tuition. The remainder of the expenses, such as airfare, room and board, was reasonable. My position as registrar at the high school allowed me a flexible summer work schedule so with very little effort on my part, everything fell into place.

Consequently, the decision was made to take advantage of the lifeline I'd been thrown. I gave the clock one more look and saw that it was not yet eight o'clock, the scheduled time of my departure. I fretfully rechecked my bags and purse, insuring that my passport, a small amount of cash, and several travelers' checks were tucked safely inside, along with one credit card. I made one final walk through the house as I waited for my ride to Hartsfield Atlanta International Airport. The inspection of the thermostat, the doors and windows, and contact info posted on the fridge was disrupted by the honk of a horn.

My oldest brother Jerry (older than his twin by four minutes) and his wife Jerline wheeled into the driveway under the heat of the summer sun, despite the early hour. I grabbed my large, very large, suitcase by the handle, set the security alarm, and locked the door behind me. I walked with resolve towards the back of the car, thankful the luggage had wheels, and questioned my decision for the umpteenth time. Those of us students who'd opted to earn our last two quarters of Spanish in an immersion study program had been told at the pre-trip orientation that we would be responsible for all personal items, including luggage, passports, and jewelry.

My rings were not worth an exorbitant amount, but no monetary value could be placed on their sentimental meaning. The last thing I needed was to lose them or have them stolen. The simple wedding band Barry had slipped on my finger in an uncaring courtroom where we were married by a Justice of the Peace was stored in my jewelry box. I was unsure of what to do with the solitaire diamond ring he'd given me years after our elopement, a ring Barry said was long overdue, and the eternity ring he gave me for our twenty-fifth anniversary.

A friend suggested I leave the rings in a safe deposit box, but I didn't want to put the rings away, as if Barry and I had never existed as one. Instead, the week before I planned to leave, I took the rings to a local, reputable jeweler who had a flair for creating unique new pieces from old ones. Mitch was empathetic as I'd slowly removed the symbols of love from indented fingers. I explained to him that I would be out of the country for a month and didn't want to risk losing them. I gave Mitch a brief description of what I had in mind for the redesign, including the inscription to be engraved, and entrusted the rings, precious only to me, to his capable hands. I asked if he required a deposit, but he understood the significance the rings held for me and answered, "No, no deposit. I know you'll be back to claim the jewelry."

Jerry interrupted my thoughts when he climbed out of the car to help me load the suitcase. "What in the world did you pack? You do plan on coming back, don't you?"

"Yes, but I'll be gone a month, and I'm not sure what the laundering situation will be. Supposedly, students' laundry will be collected once a week and returned to us the following week and swapped for the next batch of dirty clothes. The service costs a few pesos but not more than two or three dollars in U.S. currency. Regardless, I had to pack an assortment of clothes—everything from casual to dress to swimwear."

Jerline leaned out the window and entered he conversation. "Is there a beach nearby?"

"No, but on the last Saturday we'll fly to Cancun for three nights before heading home. It's sort of a reward for our hard work. My friends Cyndie and Martha are meeting me there, which is a hardship, but they're that kind of friends. You know Martha, Jerry's and my second cousin. I hadn't seen her since the funeral until I saw her at Walmart a few weeks ago. When I mentioned my planned retreat in Mexico and that Cyndie would be flying to Cancun for a brief holiday, she jumped at the chance to join our seaside escapade."

Jerline laughed with me over "hardship" and changed the subject. "Where's your camera? I want to take a picture of you as you leave for Mexico. It can be the first of many that you'll take for the photo album you compile of your first trip outside of the United States. By the way, I'm glad to see you found a hat that will shade your face."

"Thanks. The picture is a good idea." I was dressed in white capris, a t-shirt, and Keds—comfy and casual for the hour's ride to the airport and the three hour flight. I'd tucked my shoulder length, blonde hair under the cover of a large straw sunhat with a multicolored hatband. "It was recommended that we have a hat to protect ourselves from sun exposure, along with plenty of sunblock. Even though the climate is mild year-round in Cuernavaca, it seems that the intensity of a Mexican sun will damage the fair skin of '*americanos*'." As I removed the hat and brushed damp, stray strands away from my face, I couldn't imagine that Mexico would be hotter than a Georgia summer.

I dug through the carry-on and mistakenly pulled out the pocket-sized translator my friend BJ had given me as a going away gift. I'd packed extra batteries for the ingenuous device, which would translate English to Spanish and vice versa and would also conjugate verbs. A second search recovered my camera, and I handed it to my sister-in-law to capture my departure from all that was familiar. I looked around the contentment of Treetop, where my husband and children had been happy, and where memories kept me company on those numerous nights when sleep refused to visit. I questioned my sanity, as my older sister Pat had done, in leaving the cocoon of my life behind, but the decision and arrangements were a done deal. Mexico was a chance for me to spread my wings and see where they took me. Inexplicably, I began to cry, and hot tears slid down my cheeks. I removed my sunglasses and swiped at the tears with the back of my hand, careful not to smudge mascara that threatened to melt and mingle with tears.

Jerline put the camera aside. "Don't cry, Sheila, or we won't be able to let you go. We're all worried sick over this trip and don't know what to think of you traipsing off all on your own—and to Mexico! Pat, especially, is having a hard time. And Shelby called me just last week to find out if you still planned on going. She and Donnie don't know why you're hell bent on runnin' off like this. It's not exactly a weekend with friends at Panama City Beach, you know. Florida is not that far away."

With a sense of determination I wiped the last of the tears and handed the camera back to Jerline. I loved my family, and as the youngest of seven I understood their confusion and concern over this educational excursion. Daddy was convinced, as he had been on our family summer vacations to visit relatives in Texas, that the Mexicans would kidnap his fair-haired child and take me to God only knew where. He would have stopped me from going on the trip if he could have and so would Pat, who was ten years older and had been a second mama to me almost from the day I was born. Donnie was the youngest of my three older brothers, and he and his wife Shelby were usually the least intrusive, although they'd both been very supportive during Barry's illness and subsequent death. I appreciated my family's concern, but if I was going to learn to live without Barry, the trip would be a first step towards living again instead of merely going through the motions.

"Ok, no more tears. Now take the picture and let's go. I can't miss my flight, and I have to arrive two hours early for international flights. Besides, I'm anxious to find out who my roommate will be for the next month, and the professor will also be handing out our student visas."

Jerry gave me a hug and opened the car door. "If there's no changing your mind, then let's go. We're early, but I want to get you there on time and there's no predicting the traffic, especially on I-285. Thankfully, the traffic won't the tangled mess it was last summer, when the Olympics were held in Atlanta, and when Barry was..."

To spare my feelings he didn't finish the sentence that when Barry was fighting for his life at Crawford Long Hospital in Midtown. Jerry and Jerline, who had also been high school sweethearts and married right after graduation, chatted during the drive, and I settled myself in the oversized backseat of Jerry's Lincoln with my thoughts. As the sunny scenery slipped by, I reflected on our business, the service station and auto repair shop that Barry had bequeathed to our sons. It turned out to be much harder to manage a business than to work for Daddy, as the boys had done on Saturdays. My sons couldn't agree on how things should be handled, and with resignation Brad found another job and moved on, leaving twenty-one-year-old Chuck in charge.

I didn't blame Brad for his decision. The brothers' personalities were as different as daylight and dark, but I worried as to whether or not Chuck could handle the responsibility at such a young age. I regretted that I didn't listen to my instincts and sell the business right off the bat. I had previously been responsible for the bookkeeping, but decided to relieve myself of that chore, and an accountant was hired. Sherry agreed to keep me apprised of the finances because she was aware that many family businesses failed in the hands of the owner's children.

Not only was the success or failure of the business a concern, my mother's intuition was screaming that Chuck's upcoming wedding was a mistake. I didn't wish any harm to come to Leslie*, but it would have been nice if she'd run off with a truck driver and gotten lost in the landscape of America. But she hadn't, and he was dead set on marrying her despite my many attempts to discourage him. It wasn't that I held any animosity towards Leslie, but she was the wrong woman for my son. Period. Over my protests, Chuck moved in with Leslie, into a house her daddy helped them buy—even though I doubted they could afford the monthly payments. Nonetheless, I did feel sorry for Leslie when Chuck shared with me that she and her two brothers had grown up with a struggling single mom. Eileen* had made a series of bad decisions when it came to men until she'd finally met and married a good man.

On the other hand, Chuck was my child who'd always brought home stray animals for us to nurture. It seemed the habit of rescuing broken souls was one he hadn't outgrown. I dropped those negative notions and shifted to the happier occasion of Brad and Valerie's wedding last month. In contrast to Leslie, Valerie was perfect for Brad; I couldn't have hand-picked a better partner. The day of the nuptials was bittersweet, and I'd willed myself to be led down the aisle by an usher who seated me on the front row, alone. The June wedding went smoothly, and Valerie was a beautiful bride who radiated happiness. Despite the joyous occasion, I almost lost control over my emotions when Brad lit the candle in memory of his daddy. Barry should have been there to share in the blessed event. Sobs loomed like an impending thunderstorm that threatened to disrupt the tranquil beauty of the ceremony.

To curtail my emotions I reflected on my parents' sixty year marriage and their struggles to raise seven children. Added to those hardships was Daddy's drinkin' and occasional womanizing. It was prayer that had finally led Daddy to fall to his knees at the altar of our country Baptist church, to ask forgiveness and to begin his life anew as a born-again Christian. Mama credited his miraculous transformation to the power of her prayers because she'd prayed for Daddy and his unsaved soul every day. Well, almost every day. Some days she'd just wanted to kill him. Theirs was a marriage challenged with an array of trials and tribulations, but they had evidently loved each other—for better or worse—until death did them part. However, two of my older brothers recounted one of many incidents that took place, years before I was born, between Daddy and Mama that was anything but loving and described in vivid detail the scenario…and the suit.

Gene and Donnie were on the back porch with Mama, who was busy doing laundry in a Maytag wringer washer before hangin' the clothes on the line to dry. Daddy strutted out to model his brand new, double-breasted gray suit with its broad shoulders, wide lapels, and loose fitting, cuffed trousers. Daddy was a tall, fairly handsome man, which added to his vanity, and he loved nothing better than to deck himself out in nice clothes, polished shoes, and his felt fedora. He'd related that back in his younger days when going out on the town, he wouldn't sit in his friend's Ford Model T but rode on the sideboard and hung onto the door frame so as not to wrinkle his freshly creased pants. As he sashayed around the porch, he told Mama he was going to the local watering hole for the VFW's weekly dance and for her not to bother waiting up for him.

She gave him the onceover and scanned the last load of what had been a mountain of laundry to be finished. Georgia, an older colored lady who helped out with the washin' and ironin' and takin' care of my siblings while Mama worked in one of the town's manufacturing plants, had been sick with the flu for over a week. So the laundry piled up and had to be done by Mama, and her kids still had to be fed their supper. She had neither the time nor the inclination for gettin' all gussied up and goin' to the honky-tonk, not that she'd been invited.

The brothers reckoned the thought of Daddy all dressed up for other women, smellin' to high heaven of Old Spice, hair slicked back with Brylcreem while she stayed home with chores and children was more than she could handle. Daddy flounced while Mama fumed and said between clenched teeth, "I can't stop you from going out to party on a Saturday night, drinkin' yourself into a stupor, and makin' fools out of us both with some two-bit whore, but you're damn well not going to do it in *that* suit!"

In a fit of anger she grabbed the opened gallon of Clorox and flung the bleach all over his brand-new suit. Daddy was shocked into silence before he found his voice. But find it he did. "Good Godamighty, woman! Have you lost your mind? I bought this suit off the sample rack outta my paintin' money. It cost me damn near fifteen dollars, and you've ruined it!"

Daddy worked in one of the plants, too, and painted houses on the side to supplement their meager household income. As such, he considered some of the extra earnings his and his alone. He raised his hand as if to strike her, and my brothers jumped off the rail to her defense, but she didn't need their help. Mama snatched a garden hoe from the corner of the porch and lifted it above her head with a firm grip. "Hit me, Joe, and I'll split your head like one of my garden watermelons. Bleach won't be the only thing on that suit you're so proud of, prancing around here like a peacock."

Daddy scrambled into the house, dressed in an old suit, and peeled outta the driveway in a beat up Chevy and a cloud of dust. Mama continued doing the laundry and told her sons to wash up for supper, as if nothing had happened.

Theirs was not a marriage made in heaven, not by any stretch of the imagination, and yet it lasted sixty years. Mama was a resilient woman who'd grown up on a farm with nine siblings where they all worked to survive. She had endured more hardship and heartbreak than a rocky relationship, but her strength and her faith sustained her.

Reflections of weddings and marital woes dissipated in a bevy of jets grumbling overhead as we approached the airport. Atlanta was home to one of the busiest airports in the world, and airspace was more than a convenient commodity. Planes squawked their protests like seagulls as they circled the runways, waiting for clearance to land. The deluge of planes landing and departing reminded me of flying pods that transported frenetic passengers to various destinations around the globe. Unexpectedly, there was a knot in my stomach at the thought of boarding a plane for Mexico City where we would spend the weekend. On Sunday a chartered bus would take us to Cuernavaca, where the school was located approximately forty miles south.

I let a nervous sigh escape, and Jerline turned in her seat. "Having second thoughts? You don't have to go, Sheila. It's not too late to change your mind."

"I know I don't have to go, but I want to go. I'm just nervous about the flight, meeting my host family, and being away from home for a whole month." With more confidence than I felt I continued, "I'll be fine." I wasn't sure if I was trying to reassure her or myself.

As Jerry proceeded to the parking lot at the North Terminal, I reminded him that he didn't have to bother parking and that he could drop me off at the curb. He was having none of that. "Nothing doing. We're parking and going with you, all the way to the gate where you're meeting the rest of the students. I can't, in good conscience, toss you out and head for home. I'd be worried sick wondering if you made it to the right terminal and departure gate."

I loved him for his concern, but I was forty-three years old and it was high time I learned to take care of myself. I didn't bother to remind him of that fact as he opened the trunk and unloaded my suitcase. I pulled up the handle and carted it towards the parking lot exit, with both of them on my heels.

As expected, the airport was extremely crowded. The hurry and scurry of fellow travelers was a hodgepodge of disorganized direction as we moved through the throng to the tram that would swoosh us to Concourse D. I checked my ticket to confirm that Flight 703, *Aeroméxico*, would be departing from gate sixteen at eleven o'clock. We were early when we reached the designated waiting area, but I saw Professor Alonso* and other students gathered amid anticipation and luggage. Names were called and checked off the roster, and student visas were distributed when hands shot in the air.

Satisfied that I was where I needed to be, my brother and his wife gave me hugs and made me promise to stay in touch. Jerline reminded me that Pat expected me to call once a week and said she would call periodically from her office, on the company's toll-free line. I'd given my worry-wart sister the address and phone number, provided by the university, where I could be reached.

Jerry and Jerline gave me a final wave and vanished in the crowd among other dispersing family members. My name was called, and I quickly raised my hand. An official document was shoved in my direction, along with a large manila envelope. The sticker in the corner listed a familiar name as my roommate, and my tension was replaced with relief. June was also from Bremen, and her happy-go-lucky attitude was a bonus. We weren't close friends, but Bremen being Bremen, we were acquaintances.

"Sheila! Hey, over here."

At a height of barely five feet, four inches I had to stand on tiptoes to connect a waving hand with a person who was not any taller. "June, I'm so happy to see you! I didn't know you were making this trip, but I'm very happy we're going to be roommates."

She shifted her carry-on and brushed back short, sandy blonde hair with naked fingers. I figured she'd taken the memo about jewelry seriously, too. "Me, too! I hadn't planned on the trip, but two quarters of Spanish are all that separate me from my degree and dream job. I plan to apply at Delta for a position as flight attendant, and the company requires its applicants to have a college education. So here I am." She couldn't stop smiling. "Are you ready for an adventure?"

I considered the past year and a half of my life: Barry's diagnosis, the chemo, surgery, radiation, all futile attempts to save his life. Helplessly watching him suffer was as close to hell as I ever wanted to be. His inevitable death, the heartbreak, and grief that followed conspired to pull me into a black hole of despair and left scars on my soul. As a result, not only was I ready for an adventure, I was ready to begin life again, ready to regain my equilibrium. I smiled and answered emphatically, "Yes, June, I'm absolutely ready."

I was also ready to take the first step on a journey of self-discovery.

*Name changed

Chapter Two

South of the Border

I found my assigned window seat, fastened my seatbelt, and popped a stick of gum in my mouth. Chewing helped relieve the painful ear pressure I experienced upon takeoff and landing, but I didn't have a solution for the butterflies that filled my stomach. I ignored them since there was no turning back. The jet's engines hummed along the runway until the plane roared and soared with the power of a winged dragon. We left the airstrip below, and I watched it fade into a gray ribbon of asphalt.

June and I spent half an hour or so catching up with each other before the "Fasten Your Seatbelt" light was turned off, and she reached for a book she'd packed in her tote. Undisturbed, I napped briefly until the plane hit an air pocket that jarred me awake, and I noticed June had dozed off. I utilized the remaining stint to become acquainted with my host family and opened the packet of information I was given before boarding.

According to the dossier, *mi familia* wasn't Mexican but Venezuelan and had immigrated to Mexico. Thus, they were Latinos whose dominant language was Spanish, but they were also fluent in Portuguese. With the exception of the grandmother, Nieve, the family members spoke English, as well. The head of the household in the patriarchal society was the father, Carlos. He was a soccer coach who operated a school where soccer was taught year-round; the sport was a very big deal in *México*. His wife Marta was a stay-at-home mother, and there were two grown children living in the household, in addition to Nieve. From my two quarters of Spanish I remembered that the word "Nieve" meant "snow" in English, and I wondered if the *abuela* had been born in the winter.

The twenty-year-old daughter's name was Sharon, but the son, who was seventeen, had a more unusual name: Aleho. If pronounced in Spanish phonetically, it was "Ah-lay-ho," but I would have to verify that because I didn't want to insult anyone with mispronunciations. On the other hand, we were there to learn, and I hoped language errors would be overlooked. Especially given that only Spanish would be spoken during the school hours, and we were to speak Spanish as much as possible in the home in which we were guests. I was lost in my interim family's lives and was looking forward to putting faces with the names that were spread across my lap tray. I felt as if I already knew our hosts and wondered what information they'd been given about June and me.

In addition to what I believed was a congenial family, the summer weather in Cuernavaca would be ideal, with highs in the mid-seventies and lows in the sixties. The location had reason to be referred to as "The City of Eternal Spring" boasted in the brochures we'd been given in order to familiarize ourselves with the city. It was the rainy season, and I'd packed a light-weight rain jacket even though the pamphlet guaranteed tourists that the rain would take place at night, usually after midnight, and that we would awaken to sunny skies and mild temps. I'd been so engrossed that I didn't realize the seatbelt sign was on until I heard the announcement to fasten our seatbelts; we were quickly approaching Mexico City. June was still sleeping, and I shook her shoulder to rouse her. "Wake up. We're getting ready to land. Sit up and fasten your seat belt. Incidentally, I reviewed the facts about our family, and I'll fill you in when we get to the hotel."

With a yawn and a stretch, she mumbled, "Ok, thanks. Hope they like us."

It took almost an hour for thirty of us to retrieve our luggage and maneuver to Customs in order to gain entry into the country. We'd been told that a birth certificate and a picture ID, such as a driver's license, would suffice but that it would be easier with a passport. I was grateful I'd immediately applied for and had received my passport. As I reached the checkpoint and placed my luggage on the conveyor belt, the red light came on and the moving band abruptly halted. My classmates had breezed through with a green light, but I was directed to open my bags.

Thanks to two quarters of Spanish and Odette, an amazingly patient tutor, I was able to respond to the command in bits and pieces. "Why have I been stopped for inspection? I am with the other American students, here for a month. I have my papers if you need to see them."

My reasoning was ignored, and the two security guards were insistent that I not proceed with the others. I helplessly watched my traveling companions continue towards the bus that would take us all to the hotel. With a frustrated sigh I opened the smaller travel bag in an attempt to pacify the men. However, one of the men pointed to the large suitcase and repeated, "Abierto."

Compliance was my only option. I stood clothed in embarrassment as my things were ransacked for whatever the men were searching. When they salvaged assorted pajamas and lingerie, my humiliation was complete. I very much wished I could have dug a hole in the ground and pulled myself in after it, and I contemplated what they saw in me that had aroused suspicion. Finally satisfied that I wasn't smuggling drugs or weapons, they allowed me to close my bag and hurry on my way.

Professor Alonso would take a head count, but I didn't want to take a chance on being left in the airport where no one appeared to notice my distress. I was one of the last to board the bus, and when I explained my delay, the professor laughed and told me the process was completely random and not to take it personally. It was easy to be unconcerned when it wasn't your belongings that had been strewn on display for everyone in proximity.

I put the incident behind me and found June, who'd saved a window seat for me. She continued to chat with the person across the aisle from her, and I savored the sights of Mexico City. It was a picturesque city that belonged to a country which had survived centuries that included a number of wars and transformations and whose history and destiny had emerged as one. As the bus hissed along bumpy roads, I took note of the children as young as three years old that stood on street corners or roamed the sidewalks. They were ragamuffins begging for *pesos* amidst the hustle and bustle of the city. Even though the children were smiling the burden of impoverishment was reflected in their beautiful brown eyes. Mexico appeared to be a contrast of splendor and destitution, of many happy people living in hopeless circumstances. I was lost in speculation and was surprised when the bus lumbered over to the curb. The door was unfolded by a friendly driver who assisted us with our luggage and gratefully accepted the tips. We stepped into air that hung heavy with humidity and walked the few feet to our accommodations.

Our hotel was nondescript, nothing brochure worthy, but appeared to be suitable. We checked in and our luggage was taken to our room which was small but practical. The porter smiled and waited patiently for his tip, and I handed him a couple of dollars, which was slightly more than fourteen *pesos*. June had already exchanged fifty dollars for Mexican currency at the airport and handed the porter several bills. His delight turned to disappointment when I snatched the bills from his hand and apologized in broken Spanish for my friend's misunderstanding of the monetary rate of exchange. I gave him one bill that was equal to a five dollar tip, and a jovial smile returned to his dark face.

I closed the door behind him and turned to June. "Did you review the currency exchange chart we were given when we registered for this trip?

She answered nonchalantly, "I skimmed over it. Why?" she asked as I returned the money to her.

"Because you gave that guy more than a hundred pesos for delivering our bags. It's no wonder everyone here believes all Americans are wealthy. Before you throw your money away, you might want to be aware of what you're spending."

"Thanks for the tip, no pun intended. And I promise to study the chart and figure out the rate of exchange. Now let's change clothes and go exploring. I asked Linda, the woman I met on the bus, to join us."

"Good. She seems to be a very nice woman but skittish—more apprehensive than the rest of us. Who's her roommate?"

"Unfortunately, she doesn't have one. She's not actually a college student, but an exception was made for her. She's an emergency room nurse at a hospital somewhere in North Georgia where the Mexican immigration population is growing. Her employer needed someone on staff to learn Spanish, and as a divorcee with a grown daughter, she was the logical choice. It was a last minute decision and she registered late. The rest of us had already been assigned roomies."

Linda's appearance was plain and practical. Her short brownish hair lacked style, and her makeup routine was minimal, at best. Her green eyes were her best feature and reflected her apprehension. I truly felt sorry for Linda and hoped she would make it for the duration of the program. She probably hadn't realized the rest of us had no less than two quarters of Spanish under our belts and that a few were majoring in Spanish and would be in the advanced classes. And if she expected to learn to speak Spanish fluently in a month, then she was in for a rude awakening. Little wonder Linda looked like a deer in the headlights.

The three of us became fast friends as we roamed the streets near our hotel. We'd been cautioned against wandering too far and not to take public transportation to another part of the city where danger could be waiting. I remembered the advice to write down originating addresses, and I'd grabbed a card from the hotel desk in case we got lost and needed to take a taxi. The city was filled with people and vibrant color that hummed along to Latin music that spilled into the streets and combined with the noise of traffic to create a chaotic coherence. The air was infused with the aroma of freshly baked bread and spicy foods from a number of restaurants, along with a scent I didn't recognize. I soon concluded it was the smell of poverty—a faint odor that wafted through the city on the heels of hopelessness.

The sound of a loud truck backfiring broke up my observations as several men riding in the back and hangin' on for dear life called out to us, "Hola, putas americanas!"

June waved and called out enthusiastically, "Hola to y'all! We love Mexico!"

I quickly grabbed her arm mid-wave. "June, don't reply to them. They just called us American whores. Are you sure you've had a couple of quarters of Spanish? Though 'whore' may never have come up for translation in your class."

"Obviously not. You know I'm here to finish the foreign language requirement so I can graduate in August—same as you." Confused she asked, "Why would they be so rude to us?"

"Can't imagine, except that we are Americans."

Linda said, "I read that not all Mexicans welcome Americans to their country, but I'm not sure why they're prejudiced."

I thought about it and replied, "They are united by their shared antagonism, a resentment that has traversed generations. But we're here, and we're going to stay out of trouble." Sunset cast a beautiful, golden glow over the city and created an aura of tranquility. "Let's decide where to eat. We've had a long day and should get back to our hotel for a good night's sleep."

"I agree," said June. "By the way, I noticed a flyer for a concert in an arena not far from here that I'd like to see tomorrow. Are you two game?"

"Sure," we replied simultaneously. A musical matinee sounded like a good idea at the time.

Much to my dismay, I woke up early with a sinus headache from hell and panicked when I recognized that the low-grade fever most likely meant a sinus infection. My swollen, tender glands were another sign that I needed an antibiotic, which I hadn't packed. I swallowed a couple of ibuprofen and told June to meet Linda and go without me as I retreated to my tumbled bed. Three hours later I felt well enough to get a shower and go downstairs to the front desk. I asked the clerk to recommend a restaurant, as well as a *farmacia* within walking distance. The café was on the corner, but the nearest pharmacy was another three blocks. After a light meal I followed the sidewalk towards my destination.

Evidently, my blonde hair attracted unwanted attention, but I didn't feel threatened in the least and wasn't worried about being kidnapped. My only concern was how I was going to convince the pharmacist to contact my drugstore at home and to fill a prescription for Amoxicillin. I was frustrated that despite multiple packing lists, I'd carelessly forgotten the prescription medication as a precaution, which turned out to be something I needed. I located the drugstore but once inside I realized that no one there spoke English.

With the language barrier firmly in place, I did the best I could to explain my dilemma to the pharmacist and how to contact the American pharmacy in order to transfer the prescription. The man's white jacket was as pristine as his smile, and he did his best to communicate with me. He was polite and eager to help *la señorita* as we each struggled with the other's pronunciations in unfamiliar languages. The man's smile crumpled in confusion, and I was about to give up when a striking woman sheathed in a sunny yellow dress and silky black hair interjected, thank God, in English, "You seem to be having a problem clarifying what you need. Can I help?"

I wanted to hug her neck but refrained. "Oh, yes, please." I briefly explained my dilemma but didn't know how to secure an antibiotic because I'd left the prescription behind when packing.

She smiled and said that I had no problem at all as she turned to the pharmacist in an air of confidence and told him what I was there to buy. Genuinely relieved that he could assist the "damsel in distress," he walked from behind the counter and reached for a bottle of Amoxicillin from one of the well-stocked shelves. I was confused that the drug was available over the counter, but the woman told me that many drugs were sold from pharmacies in Mexico without a prescription. My newfound friend waited while I paid for the medicine, which was a mere three dollars, and walked with me to the sidewalk. I put on sunglasses as we stood in the white glare of the afternoon sunshine and thanked her profusely for her kindness.

Gold hoop earrings and an assortment of bracelets jingled as she tossed her hair over her shoulder. "You are very welcome, mi amiga."

We weren't actually friends, but I appreciated the term of endearment. I peeked at my watch and realized that I needed to get back to the hotel and in order to tale the antibiotic right away. "I'm sorry I have to rush off. I would like to become better acquainted with you, but I'm anxious to get back to the hotel and pack so that I'm not late for the bus in the morning."

"I cannot fathom why you Americans are always in a hurry to be somewhere else. Mexico is a beautiful country with much to offer its visitors, if you take the time to enjoy the sights. Perhaps in my country you will learn to relax and to revel in the moment in which you are living. And to also leave your unhappiness here. Si?"

I regretted that my sorrow was apparent to strangers and vowed to smile more often. I genuinely hoped Mexico was where I could leave my shroud of sadness. "Yes, perhaps." With another *gracias* and a wave I dashed down the sidewalk, retracing my route past the familiar pink and orange Dunkin' Donuts logo. The enticement of the delectable aroma lured me inside, and I bought a dozen to share. After all, I couldn't take the antibiotic without food.

I was sleeping soundly when June and Linda got back to the hotel Saturday night, and Sunday morning found our group standing on the sidewalk waiting to load our luggage. I placed a few coins into the outstretched hands of a child, which was met with a look of disapproval from the professor. He didn't elaborate on his noticeable displeasure and continued to check the roster as each student boarded the bus bound for Cuernavaca. We were all adults who ranged in age from the early twenties to the mid-fifties, but we were, nonetheless, the university's responsibility and were expected to touch base with our chaperone daily. June and I found seats next to each other and across the aisle from Linda, whom we'd taken under our wing.

June spoke to me above the noise, "How are you feeling today?"

"Much better, thank you. I'm grateful I was able to get the antibiotic without a prescription—with the help of a kind stranger who spoke English."

As the bus put the city behind us, Linda chimed in. "I'll file that away for future reference. I wonder what else can be bought here without a doctor's prescription."

"I didn't ask." I figured since Linda was a nurse she was interested in the medical differences between America and Mexico. While my fever had subsided, I was tired and not in the mood for idle chatter. I needn't have worried because I had the window seat, which put June and Linda in aisle seats. They carried on a lively conversation while I took in the scenery of Central America's largest country.

Ninety minutes was the estimated time allotted for the route that carried us along rural roads. The bus rumbled and rocked along narrow and sometimes unpaved roads, and the bouncy motion lulled a number of the students into a nap, especially since most of them had partied in Mexico City the night before. I appreciated the break from babbling and noticed with interest the occasional village that interrupted woods and hills. The houses were small and fairly close together, and most all of them were white and boasted red tile roofs. The streets of the villages were cobblestoned, and shops and restaurants were located in the heart of the town for convenience.

While much of the landscape was wooded, the *pueblos* emerged from the shadows and displayed an abundance of brilliant flowers. Blazing orange sunflowers, multicolored zinnias, and assorted dahlias filled pots and window boxes as they danced in the afternoon sun. I'd read that dahlias were Mexico's national flower, and the flowers' vivid rainbow petals and layered heads sang with a life that reflected the vibrancy of Mexico itself. Despite the poor living conditions, the people smiled and handed us cheerful greetings as the bus continued on its cultural and educational expedition. The trip hadn't taken quite as long as we'd been told, and those sleeping were awakened by Professor Alonso. We had arrived at our destination city.

Chapter Three

The City of Eternal Spring

Cuernavaca was as fresh as a springtime rain and embraced her visitors with welcoming arms. I did some research before the trip in order to learn more about Mexico and our host city, the capital of the state of Morelos. Cuernavaca was nicknamed "city of eternal spring" by Alexander von Humboldt in the nineteenth century because of its warm, stable climate and proliferation of vegetation. The city rested on the southern slope of the mountains, *Sierra de Chichinautzin*. As a result warm air flowed up from the valley in the morning, and in late afternoon cooler air drifted down from the higher elevation. Hence, despite being located in a tropical region, the city's temperature remained in the seventies and offered a refreshing change from the clammy climate of Mexico City. It was the pleasant climate that had attracted an eclectic variety of visitors for centuries. The weather would certainly be a nice break from the sticky, steamy July I'd left in Georgia where the heat and humidity of summer were the downside to mild winters.

We hit a pothole, and I noticed the driver was cruising down a residential side street where he skillfully parked the bus at the entrance to *la escuela*. Our first stop was the school because we would have another orientation session, a pre-test to determine class placement, and, most importantly, meet our host "parents" who would take us to our temporary homes. We ambled off the bus, and I surveyed the surroundings. The school sat behind a beige concrete wall with a large, black gate that was opened wide but held a heavy lock. The entrance was further guarded by the thorns of bougainvillea which was contradictorily comforting with its various shades of lavender blooms that tumbled invitingly over the wall. The ubiquitous flowering plant, known as *bugambilia* in Mexico, was unusual in that such beautiful blossoms didn't offer an aroma.

I scrutinized the neighborhood and noticed that none of the homes were visible as they were all protected by walls and gates, which was unusual to me. I reminded myself that I wasn't in "Kansas" anymore and decided to approach my experiences in Mexico with an open mind. However, as I scanned the band of students, I noticed I wasn't the only visitor who was slightly uneasy. Despite our apprehension we had to make the best of things since the facility held our diplomas captive behind its fortified barrier until we earned them.

Professor Alonso clapped his hands and motioned for us to follow him inside. We moved as one unit, with legs of a centipede and were comforted by the beauty of the grounds. To the pleasure of hummingbirds several varieties of Mexican honeysuckle grew abundantly inside the walled garden, and the assorted orange, fragrant blossoms enhanced the mood of the sun-filled afternoon. A small fountain sat in the middle of the flowers and splashed water that provided a sparkling melody.

We shuffled towards the courtyard where a young woman waited behind a table and asked us to pick up our name tags. I located mine, peeled off the sticker, and placed it on my left shoulder. Attached to the name tag was a laminated index card with an address and phone number in bold, black lettering. I tucked the information card into my shoulder bag as our group followed turquoise, tile-topped stepping stones that fashioned a meandering walkway that led to a simple outdoor classroom. The walls of the structure itself were similar to those that surrounded the school, and embraced arched, open windows, and a tile floor that matched the stepping stones; it was similar to a larger version of an arbor. Wooden beams covered with Blue Pea Vine served as a roof and shielded us from the afternoon sun.

The serenity of the setting had a calming effect, and our cluster broke off into separate entities as we walked to waiting benches. As directed we positioned our luggage against the wall and dropped onto pews that were lined neatly in rows. A middle-aged, attractive woman dressed in professional attire, dark hair twisted into a coiled bun, stood at a podium and brought the gathering to order in *Español*. "Soy Señora Sanchez, Director de Escuela. Buenas tardes y bienvenido a México."

We responded as would a class of first graders, our voices a single reply as we repeated her 'good afternoon' greeting and thanked her for welcoming us to her country. "Buenas tardes y gracias."

The director continued her spiel in English. "Some of you are not as advanced in Spanish as others. Therefore, as a courtesy, I will continue your orientation and host family introductions in English."

A young man enthusiastically expressed his gratitude. "Muchas gracias!"

Laughter broke the ice, and there was a collective sigh of appreciation for her consideration. Linda, in particular, looked extremely relieved. I had to admire her for being there. If I'd jumped in the immersion program with absolutely no knowledge of Spanish, I would have been a nervous wreck. Granted, I was uneasy about the month ahead, but I did have a rudimentary grasp of the language. Additionally, all those college courses had taught me the importance of accurate note taking—regardless of the language—and listening.

I directed my attention back to the speaker as she was discussing precautionary food advice. "Most of our restaurants are diligent when it comes to cleanliness, and the water is filtered. But you must always ask if the ice is also made from filtered water, '¿Se filtra el hielo?' Bottled water will be provided for you in your homes but be careful not to swallow water when you shower and brush your teeth. Bottled water is available most everywhere, but never buy anything edible from a street vendor. Your digestive systems are not accustomed to those foods. You may think a cup of chilled fruit is perfectly safe, but let me assure you that it is not." She stopped speaking long enough to mime a person slicing fruit and licking the knife… and then continuing to slice the fruit. No further warning was necessary for me but she continued, "Two summers ago a young man ate burritos he'd bought from a street cart. As a result he contracted a severe case of dysentery and spent a week in one of our hospitals where fluids were administered intravenously. The student eventually recovered and learned his lesson. You have been forewarned."

Señora Sanchez proceeded to our next topic, a review of traffic and taxis in Mexico. "In America you are accustomed to drivers on the right side of the road, but here you must remember that we drive on the left side of the street. To avoid an accident you will need to adjust accordingly when crossing the street. Also, be cautious of the traffic, especially taxis, because a tourist will be no more than a…a bump in the road. Another note about taxi drivers. Regrettably, some of them may take advantage of you and charge you more than what is fair for their services. Seven to ten pesos is reasonable, but you are never to pay more than fifteen—regardless of where in the city the driver takes you. Having covered those topics, I encourage those of you who will be living within walking distance of the city to enjoy a leisurely stroll, along with your roommate, and absorb what Cuernavaca has to offer."

Some of the students exchanged knowing glances as we'd already been warned of price gouging by taxi drivers, vendors, waiters, and bartenders. The preconceived perception was that all Americans were wealthy and, therefore, *gringos* could afford to be overcharged. In fact, a handful of students had not been given the correct change at various restaurants because they had failed to acquaint themselves with the monetary system. I had to budget my *pesos* and had, therefore, become familiar with the rate of exchange. Maybe June had forgotten the proverb about a fool and his money soon parting, but I made a mental note to keep a helpful eye on her when it came to money or she and her *dinero* would part ways.

Señora Sanchez paused to shuffle through her notes before she continued, "No doubt most of you noticed the street beggars in Mexico City, many of them children. I want to discourage you from giving them money as it will be taken home and used by the father to buy alcohol or drugs while his children go to bed hungry. If you want to help them, please wrap your leftover bread from restaurants and give it to the urchins. Or if you are so inclined, buy a meal to be shared among them." She cleared her throat and took a sip of water before moving on to another matter.

"It is important not to venture out on your own. You are advised to always keep the card with your provisional address and phone number with you, should you find yourselves in an unfamiliar location." She smiled and added, "In other words, if you are lost."

We all chuckled, but her reference was an understatement if I ever heard one. I had no intention of losing the card with our home address and phone number, and unless absolutely necessary, I wouldn't call our "parents." Furthermore, nobody needed to tell June and me not to wander off alone in a foreign land, although we had discussed going on afternoon walks instead of a taking a *siesta*. Naps were, after all, for infants and toddlers. Besides, we didn't want to waste time sleeping in the middle of the day.

The director proceeded to wade through her notes. "Some of you may have heard that marijuana is legal in Mexico. Let me assure you that it is not. Should you be approached by a dealer, walk away immediately. The police will do everything to protect you and will more often than not take your side in the event you find yourself in a compromising situation. However, you do not want to land behind bars in a Mexican prison."

Okay, *that* was an understatement. The briefing was concluded, and it was time for the entrance exam to be administered. Based upon our skill level, we were directed to straight-backed chairs and wooden tables that held turned down papers and a small jar of pencils. The Spanish majors were at the top of the food chain, so to speak, and were assigned to the assistant director. The rest of us were lumped collectively with one of the school's bilingual instructors. Linda was placed with our group instead of being singled out as having no basic understanding of Spanish.

I was confident as I began the exam, but not so much towards the end of the test, and I reminded myself not to sweat that small stuff. I was there to learn and to enjoy new experiences. Time was called, and we laid our pencils to the side when the tests were collected. I noticed that Linda was on the verge of tears and consoled her by telling her that things would work out, but didn't add not the way she hoped. Whatever the outcome, the test was behind us, and we would finally be introduced to the people who were unobtrusively sitting on the back rows. I hoped June and I—and Linda—were located with compassionate families. It was feasible that they were also apprehensive, despite the fact that hosting students as houseguests was not novel to them.

June and I rounded up our luggage and scanned the swarm of people as hosts and students connected. I nudged June when I saw a nice-looking woman with chocolate brown hair and brown eyes coming toward us, a woman who easily towered above the shorter Hispanics. She was wearing a blue and olive striped dress that complimented her complexion. A matching cobalt belt and sandals and gold hoop earrings were the finishing touches; her face carried a warm smile. When she was closer I guessed her age to be in her forties, between June's and my ages. The woman noted my name tag and extended her hand. "Hello, Sheila. My name is Marta, and I'm happy to meet you." Next she greeted June, "I'm also happy to meet you, June."

She carried only a trace of an accent and I replied, "You speak English very well. I read that you are trilingual, but I wasn't sure how articulate you would be in my language."

To which June added, "Needless to say, we're very thankful you can understand us. It's a relief to hear English spoken so well by our hostess."

"My husband and I are from Venezuela, where the dominate language is Spanish, but we also learned to speak English. Many of Cuernavaca's citizens speak English but most do not. However, those who speak only Spanish very much appreciate Americans' attempt to communicate with them and will be patient and ready to assist you. Your courtesy is also welcomed."

June spoke first, "Well, that's a relief. Sheila hired a tutor for the first two quarters, so her Spanish is better than mine. She wants to graduate with honors, but I just want to graduate."

Marta continued, "Should you need to ask how to say something in Spanish, the question is '¿Cómo se dice?' followed by the English word or phrase you want translated. My family, as well as your instructor, wants you to succeed in learning our language."

It was prying to ask, but I wanted to know more about Marta and her family. "Why did you and your husband decide to leave your home and move to Mexico?"

She shrugged her shoulders in an offhanded manner. "We came here when my husband, Carlos, was offered the opportunity to open his own soccer school. Soccer is very serious business in Mexico. We've lived here for more than ten years and have welcomed American students to our home for the last five. As part of your study program you are required to speak Spanish when feasible. However, my family also speaks English, and I have learned to loosen the guidelines when necessary. We want your accommodations and your stay here to be pleasant for all of us."

The courtyard was clearing out as students and their families dispersed. Marta reached for one of my bags, but I told her that wasn't necessary. "Please don't trouble yourself with our luggage. We can manage."

"Por supuesto. Of course. Our home is located just down the street and due to the proximity, you will be expected to walk to and from the school. Breakfast is served at seven o'clock on weekdays so that you will not be late for your eight o'clock class, and we eat an hour later on weekends. We'll review the remaining guidelines when you've both had a chance to freshen up and settle in. I am assuming you both are aware of the plumbing situation here. Si?"

We both nodded in the affirmative. The "plumbing situation" to which Marta referred was that the sewage system in Mexico was very old and, therefore, unable to process a lot of paper products that would result in a backed-up toilet. ALL paper products were to be disposed of in the trash can provided and were never to be flushed. It was number three on the list we'd been given at the initial orientation before we left the U.S. Number one on the list warned of traffic and number two cautioned us to stay with a friend and to always be aware of our immediate surroundings.

Therefore, as we ambled down the shady sidewalk, I observed the house numbers posted on the gatepost at the entrance of each home. There was a street sign on the corner, next to a small *tienda*. It would certainly be handy to have a convenience store located half a block away. June and Marta had spent the last few moments in conversation, and Marta brought me into their discussion. "Sheila, you and June are fortunate to attend one of our more prestigious private schools. Your classes will be limited to no more than ten students. Ah, here we are, on the right." Marta unlatched the gate and motioned for us to precede her inside. "Bienvenido a mi casa."

Her smile reflected the sincerity of her hospitality. We were further welcomed by a gentle breeze and a profusion of flowers that applauded our arrival. Dazzling orange Mexican sunflowers and azure Morning Blue Glory were planted along the inside of the wall where they merged in contrast. Two tinted salamanders played a game of chase among the foliage. Beneath large windows at the front of the house, yellow and white Yasmin, deep red Chocolate Cosmos, and fuchsia Asters blended in unison to produce an exquisite masterpiece. To the left was a covered patio where several Bird of Paradise plants rested in a rainbow of clay pots that complimented the flowers' kaleidoscope of colors. The beauty was a blissful display that danced in harmony, and I couldn't pull my eyes away—until I glimpsed the petite figure of an elderly woman watering the plants. She was wearing a faded, floral housedress and practical, black shoes. Her gray hair was pulled into a "cinnamon roll" bun, like the one my Grandma Pearl used to wear.

"Excuse me, Marta, but is that Nieve?"

With a long sigh, Marta pushed back her dark hair and replied, "Yes. She is Carlos' mother and has lived with us for many years, since the death of her husband. She can be stubborn and argumentative, which means some days are harder than others. It's difficult for two women of different generations to occupy a house with one kitchen, but we've learned to compromise. Besides, Carlos is an only child and there was nowhere else for her to go."

June was as curious as I. "What about a nursing home? Can't they take care of her?"

Marta was quick to dismiss the notion. "No. There are no 'nursing homes' in Mexico. Families are expected to take care of their elderly until death. To do otherwise would bring disgrace upon the family, especially the son. But she can be exasperating." With another sigh, she raised her voice and spoke to Nieve in Spanish, which I believed was that the flowers had been watered that morning.

Nieve set the watering can aside and with a shy smile, slipped through the French doors. I very much hoped my Spanish would improve to the point that I could carry on a conversation with her, even one limited by our languages would be interesting. I remembered something I wanted to know. "Marta, was Nieve born in the winter?"

She laughed and replied, "Yes, her birthday is in December, but she was born in Caracas. There is no snow in Venezuela. However, her mother was from the mountains of Pico Bolivar and, perhaps, missed the heavy snows of winter."

As we approached the doorway a dog began barking incessantly and was reprimanded by Marta. June and I smiled at each other; our information hadn't mentioned *el perro*. It was a blond, medium-sized, fuzzy mutt that belonged to no particular breed—a Heinz 57 kinda dog. Fur bangs hung over curious eyes as the family pet barked, jumped, and wagged his tail. Marta introduced us to Buddy, whose name translated to *compañero*. The furry companion appeared friendly, but I was slightly apprehensive as I'd been bitten as a child. June held out her hand to allow the dog to get a whiff, and I cautiously followed suit. We were going to be living under the same roof so we might as well be friends. In addition to the dog, the family had a huge, bright green parrot that wore a red hood over his beak with touches of cobalt blue and canary yellow on his wings. "Charlie" and his striking plumage sat on his perch and gave us an indifferent peek, but patient coaxing from Marta produced an acknowledgement of "Hola."

Marta explained that the bird's name was the same as their first American student whose visit coincided with the parrot purchase. She gave the bird a cracker, ruffled the top of Buddy's head, and said, "You can meet the rest of the family at dinner. If you'll follow me, I'll show you to your bedroom so that you can unpack. You will share a lavatory that has a shower only, but no one else in the family will utilize that bathroom during your stay."

She admonished Buddy to stay, and her sandals clicked down a tiled hallway with June, me, and our luggage close behind. I took note of the large living area that also served as a dining room. I glimpsed a small but serviceable kitchen before Marta stopped at the end of the hall. She opened the door and led us to a large bedroom with several windows draped in venetian blinds topped with tan and turquoise plaid valances. Twin beds were separated by a nightstand and a lamp and wore matching bedspreads that were turned down; fat pillows and fresh linens in coordinating stripes awaited weary travelers. Two dressing tables with large, oval mirrors were positioned on the wall opposite from the beds, and a pair of mismatched chest of drawers waited in two of the four corners. A makeshift desk and a couple of chairs rested beneath the windows. The well-worn furniture had been polished until it gleamed. A variety of potted plants sat happily on a sunny windowsill where the colored pots gave life to beige walls. Marta indicated a bathroom that was small, but as it was located in the bedroom our privacy would be respected. I popped my head in and saw that it was as clean as the rest of the room.

Our hostess opened louvered doors to a double closet and said, "I hope you find your accommodations suitable."

It could have been my imagination, but she seemed a tad nervous as she waited for our reply. She had evidently hosted privileged Americans who had found the living conditions inferior in comparison to what they were accustomed. I attempted to reassure her that the immaculate room was perfect. "I love it! And the beds look so comfortable."

June chimed in. "I can't imagine nicer accommodations." She turned to me. "Sheila, do you mind if I take the bed closest to the windows? I need the sunlight to wake me up."

"Not at all. It suits me to have the bed that's nearer the bathroom."

With sleeping assignments resolved, we hoisted our larger suitcases onto the foot of the bed, and I placed my smaller bag next to the dressing table located on my side of the room. I was tired and anxious to unpack before supper.

Marta agreed, "There's about an hour before supper is served, so why don't the two of you unpack? Essential toiletries have been provided, but please let me know if you need anything else. My family and I want you to feel welcome and happy during your stay in our home. Nuestra casa es tu casa. Te veré en la cena."

June was placing her cosmetics on the dressing table, so I responded, "Yes, see you at dinner and thank you, Marta, for welcoming us to your home. The room is more than adequate."

She smiled, pleased that we appreciated the preparations that had been made for our arrival. "Our larger meal is usually served at one o'clock, and we eat a lighter meal around seven in the evening, but the time may vary. However, I am aware that you had only snacks on the bus ride from Mexico City, and you must be ravenous. Therefore, we are having our big meal to-night. As I said, we will review what is expected of you at dinner, but don't worry. Our expectations are simple." She closed the door and clicked her way down the hallway, and June made use of our private bathroom.

The sound of the flushing toilet was followed by the words, "Oh shit!"

I laughed. "Is that a pun?"

She joined me in unpacking. "No, smartass, it's not. How long do you think it's going to take us to learn to throw the damn toilet paper in the trash?"

"I'm guessing the first time the commode clogs up we'll remember the rule. I get the 'no tirar el papel' rule, but what's up with no washcloths, aka toallitas? There weren't any at the hotel in Mexico City, and I didn't see any stacked next to the towels here. Oh well, when in Rome…"

I was awakened during the night by a thunderstorm that reverberated over the tiled roof. I sat up and was momentarily disoriented until I shook off sleep and remembered where I was. The clock revealed that it was almost three o'clock; June slept peacefully in the bed next to me. We'd closed the blinds, but they didn't shield the room from bright flashes of lightening that bounced eerily off the walls. I sat up, tucked my knees under my chin, and thought about the initial dinner with my host family. June and I remained quieter than usual and listened to the lively conversation carried on among Carlos, Marta, Sharon, and Aleho.

Carlos was tall and tanned, a nice-looking, amicable man with a sense of humor. Sharon was not as tall as her mother but taller than both June and me. She was very slim and pretty and wore her dark hair long and straight. Aleho seemed to be shy and didn't speak to us directly. He mentioned that his summer job would keep him busy and that he had a girlfriend who also occupied much of his time so he wouldn't be around the house much. The teenager stood a head above both his parents, and Marta commented that because of Aleho's size twelve shoes, it was practically impossible to find shoes that fit. She sounded exasperated, but pride and love for her children shone in her eyes. She was especially proud of Sharon, who helped Carlos with bookkeeping at his sports school.

The topic was changed and out of consideration for their American guests, they spoke English but occasionally slipped into Spanish. Nieve, who didn't speak English, ate her meal in silence but sent curious glances towards June and me while Marta went over the relatively simple house rules. She assured us that someone would always be home, but we were given a house key in the event we occasionally came home late at night to residents lost in slumber and who didn't want to be disturbed by a doorbell. The subject of sleep continued: between the hours of two and four o'clock in the afternoon, we were asked to respect the family's *siesta.* June and I had already decided to forego naps and planned to study in our room or take walks and explore the city, but we had no desire to disrupt the family's routine.

We were also expected to keep our room in some semblance of order, but the maid would take care of changing the sheets and general cleaning on a weekly basis. The family had a washer and dryer, but they were not for our use, which I assumed was due to the notorious plumbing problems.

As had been explained during orientation, our laundry would be picked up each Tuesday morning at the school and clean clothes would be exchanged for dirty ones the following Tuesday—for the sum of twenty *pesos* per week. Marta told us the *lavanderas* were dependable and reasonably honest but suggested we make a list of items sent and returned to insure that nothing was missing. Overall, our first family meal was a good beginning.

I lay back onto the pillow with a deep sigh and was overcome with despondency or, perhaps, homesickness. But what I longed for wasn't my brick and mortar home that sat empty in a town that felt like a million miles away. My heart yearned for my high school sweetheart, my lost soul mate. I was well aware of an oncoming grief attack, though they had become less frequent. Unable to suppress the tears, I buried my head in the pillow to muffle sobs of despair. I was so lost in loneliness that I didn't notice June until she sat down beside me and placed a comforting hand on my shoulder. June, like everybody else in Bremen, was familiar with the drastic turn of events my life had taken.

Her brown eyes were filled with compassion. "Sheila, it's okay. I'm here for you. What can I say or do to help you?"

I reached for a tissue from the nightstand and sniffled. "I'm so sorry I woke you, and there's nothing to be said or done. The grief hits randomly, usually when I'm missing Barry the most. Please go back to bed and get some sleep. We have a big day tomorrow, and you need your rest."

She stood and paused before she sat back on my bed. "Sheila, I want you to know that despite whatever pain you're going through, you were blessed more than you know to have had a happy marriage and a husband who loved you."

Lightening darted in the room just long enough for me to see the sadness etched on June's face. "Thanks, June. I know how fortunate I was, but I took too much for granted and regret wasted moments that are lost."

Again June hesitated but said, "Sheila, I'm going to tell you something that I've shared only with my sister. Somewhere along the matrimonial road Ryan* and I lost our way. Through the years we grew apart until one day we both knew the marriage was over, over because we'd fallen out of love. We stay married for the sake of convenience or out of a mutual dependency, but not for love." In the semi-darkness she held up her left hand and pointed to her bare ring finger. "I removed my wedding rings years ago. I gave them to my daughters because they had no meaning for me anymore. They were symbols of love where there was no love left. I don't envy you your loss, or your pain, but I do envy the love you and Barry shared."

I sat up and hugged my acquaintance who'd already become a friend. "Oh, June, I had no idea. I'm sorry for both of us, maybe more so for you."

"Oh, don't be sorry. I've long accepted what is because there's too much water under the bridge for anything to change. Ryan lives his life and I live mine, but we stay together out of habit." She crawled back in her bed and yawned. "Now let's think of more pleasant things and get some sleep. We don't want to be bleary-eyed during class."

"Night. See you in the morning, June." I stared at the ceiling and listened as the pouring rain diminished to a sprinkle and thunder grumbled in the distance. I regretted that I couldn't slip back to sleep as easily as June had been able to do. Dawn slithered through the blinds as I drifted into the cradle of sleep, only to be awakened an hour later by the clang of the alarm clock. I sat up groggily and damned my restless night but threw the covers back and climbed out of bed.

I snapped open the blinds and shook my roommate's shoulder. "June, June! Wake up! It's after six, and we have less than an hour to shower and dress before breakfast is served at seven. I'll grab a shower while you rouse yourself and decide what to wear. C'mon." I felt guilty about disturbing her sleep the night before, but we couldn't be late for our first day of school—or breakfast. "I smell bacon, so someone is already up and fixin' our breakfast. Move your ass!"

*Name changed

Chapter Four

Días de Escuela...School Days

Everyone was seated at the table for breakfast, and I greeted my hosts, "Buenos días, ustedes." "Ustedes" was the closet translation I could find for "y'all." June joined us moments later, and we ate a hearty breakfast of bacon, scrambled *huevos con queso*, tortillas, and an assortment of fruit—some of which I didn't recognize that was indigenous to the region. I watched the others wrap the scrumptious eggs and cheese in a tortilla, and I did the same. I also savored two large mugs of very strong coffee in an attempt to erase the cobwebs of lost sleep that a shower hadn't dispelled. The maid, along with assistance from Nieve, had prepared the meal, and I thanked them both for their time and trouble.

June and I excused ourselves to brush our teeth and gather our purses and school supplies. It was a quarter to eight, and we had to meet in the commons area of the school at eight o'clock for our class assignments. As I waited for June to find something lost among the clutter on her side of the room, I stepped into an absolutely magnificent morning that was comparable to a fresh spring morning in Georgia's Blue Ridge Mountains. Flowers drank in the previous night's rain under a crystal clear sky, and moisture glistened on the lawn in the sunlight of a new day. I was about to yell for June to hurry when she dashed towards me, tucking a pen and pencil into her purse. The only other item we'd been told to bring was a spiral notebook, but I'd slipped the electronic translator into my shoulder bag.

36

We retraced the walk we'd made the day before and were at the front gate of the school in less than five minutes. A small, black car pulled over to the curb on the opposite side of the road, and Linda emerged from the passenger side. She looked like she'd been run over by a truck and dragged along behind it. I cautiously asked, "How are you this morning?"

Tears filled her eyes, but she held them in as she moaned, "I've made a horrible mistake. I live with a divorced woman and her mother. Neither of them speaks English and don't care that I can't speak Spanish. Even the simplest communication is impossible. Added to that difficulty is the fact that the house is located on the other side of town, which means we have to leave almost an hour early so that I'm not late. Maria, my hostess, resents having to get up so early. Another distance downside is that I'm not nearly close enough to hook up with the two of you. I just want to go home. Today."

June and I reached to hug her, and I reassured her. "Once we get our bearings, you can take a taxi and meet us for dinner once or twice a week. On Thursday nights all of us will be going out together with Professor Alonso, and there are field trips scheduled for three of the four Saturdays that we're here. We'll help you get through this." I asked a redundant question, "How is that you're here when you're not enrolled in the university and have had no previous Spanish courses?"

She sniffled and wiped her nose before repeating what June had shared with me. "Due to the language barrier at the hospital where I work, an agreement was made to send one of its employees to a school in Mexico to learn the language. They asked for volunteers, but no one offered to leave their families. Since I'm divorced with only one child, a twenty-year old daughter, I was the logical choice to come here. Nobody else was willing to leave their families for a month, so here I am. But now that I'm here, I regret a decision I was more or less pushed into making."

I don't think she realized that her coworkers had thrown her under the bus. Nobody could learn to speak Spanish in four weeks, and her "friends" damn well knew it. Linda had my sympathy, but I wasn't qualified to tutor her, even if I'd had the time. Nor was I willing to swap housing arrangements. A loud bell interrupted Linda's sob story, and I grabbed her arm. "We gotta go. We can hash this over later."

The three of us entered the school and waited for the assignments to be read aloud. Linda was somewhat happier when her name was read along with June and mine's because it meant we would see each other during school hours. She was ill-prepared for *la clase*, but she did her best to take notes and keep up. I was pretty sure that she didn't ask questions because she didn't know enough to ask a question. Our group was there only to complete the foreign language core requirement. The rest of the students were either Spanish majors or minors and were divided into two advanced classes who were directed to classrooms on the first floor. The rest of us made our way to the stairway that led to the second floor and our classroom.

Opened windows overlooked a small courtyard edged with a well-manicured lawn and a multitude of flowers. The school was clean and airy with a welcoming sense of purpose. It was comparable to any other school, with its tiled floors and concrete walls, both in tan and white. The notable exceptions were the accents of colored pottery displayed randomly throughout the corridors and flamboyant Mexican art that adorned the otherwise drab walls. Eight students gathered around a plain wooden, rectangular table where matching chairs waited for us to be seated. Including June, Linda, and me, there were five women who ranged in age from one who looked to be nineteen or twenty to forty-somethings.

The most notable of the bunch was Barbara, aka, "Big Barbara." She looked like she could wring a chicken's neck and not even blink. She was a large woman who sported several tattoos and wore her pants at least two sizes too small so that her ass resembled two piglets in a sack. Her short, spiked, brassy blonde hair was straight out of a bottle. I was curious about her story, until I remembered that curiosity killed the cat. I'd overheard enough of her conversations on the bus to know she was a woman who didn't mince words. While I didn't plan on being her new best friend, I decided she would be a valuable ally should I find myself in over my head.

The other female, Suzette, was also blonde—a pouty, whiny, typical spoiled daddy's girl who wasn't nearly as gorgeous as she apparently

thought she was. I didn't think she came from a wealthy family, but from what I was able to discern her aspiration as a college student appeared to be to hook a rich husband. She sure as hell wouldn't be the first woman to "marry up" and then promptly forget from where she came. I couldn't help but notice the flirtatious looks she gave Chandler, a young man who reeked of old money. The "preppy" appeared not to notice her, and I figured he wouldn't give Suzette the time of day unless he thought she might be easy.

Rumor was that Chandler was on academic probation and that this sabbatical was his last chance to redeem himself before being bounced out of yet another college. I didn't care for the air of arrogance he wore and decided to have as little to do with him as possible, which shouldn't be a problem. The other two young men in our group were Political Science majors, studious roommates with full scholarships who had aspirations of attending law school. Regardless of our individual goals, we were all in the same boat.

We fell silent, and heads turned as our instructor entered the classroom. He looked to be in his early forties and was very neatly dressed in tan trousers, a pressed, blue shirt that complemented his dark complexion, and a matching striped tie; his brown loafers were well-worn but freshly polished. He was a reasonably handsome man, slightly taller than average, and fingers of gray touched an abundance of black hair. The man greeted his class, "Buenos días, estudiantes. Soy Profesor Garcia y estoy feliz de conocerte."

With the exception of a petrified Linda, we politely repeated—in Spanish—his good morning and that we were also happy to meet him. He quickly dispensed with roll call, making notes next to our names, and proceeded to hand out textbooks and accompanying workbooks. He told us the workbooks were ours to keep, but the textbooks were to be returned at the end of the month in the same condition in which they were received. Should we lose or damage our book, we would have to pay for the *libro* before our final grades would be released to the university.

As we'd gotten a late start, the first hour and a half of class was pretty much a review of masculine and feminine nouns and which article defined them as such. According to Professor Garcia, we would review the remaining parts of speech during the course of the next couple of weeks. The rudimentary review was critical in learning the language. I jotted down a few notes and noticed that Linda sat stunned. Her notebook was opened, but she was holding her pen in midair as if she didn't quite know what to do with it. I decided it would be a good idea to stop by the front office and find out the cost of utilizing the copy machine. I could take very good notes and for what was sure to be a nominal fee, offer to copy them for her. Our instructor verified the time on his watch, and right on cue the bell rang indicating our fifteen minute morning break. The break was much needed after sitting for almost two hours. I stretched the kinks out of my aching back and followed the others downstairs.

We all headed to the courtyard where the snack bar was opened for business, but due to my large breakfast I wasn't hungry and bought only a bottle of water. The younger students, who must've been famished, bought everything from cokes and chips to taquitos and tacos—much to the gratitude of the *cajero*. The cashier was counting *dinero* faster than she could make change for the *americanos*. The headmaster entered the feeding frenzy and loudly clapped her hands. "Atención, por favor."

We fell silent as she explained that our break would be extended an extra ten minutes in order for us to meet the women who would be doing our laundry. We were required to sign our names to the list so the laundresses could become familiar with us before picking up next week's dirty clothes. We were introduced to Abril, Elisa, and Danita, the oldest. The women sent shy smiles in our direction but gave the impression that they wanted to please us because, as was brought to our attention, tips would be met with appreciation. Danita folded the roster and carefully placed it in the pocket of her apron as the trio left with a farewell wave.

A second bell summoned us back to class where I listened attentively and took notes in Spanish, careful to make notations in English for clarification. During break I'd mentioned to Linda that I would be happy to copy my notes if she wanted to use them as a study guide. She was desperate for help and she readily agreed to pay the cost, which was ten cents per sheet. The final bell of the day dismissed us at one o'clock, and June and I proceeded to the sidewalk that would take us home while Linda reluctantly climbed into the same car that had brought her to school.

We were both happy to make the short walk home, especially given Linda's circumstances. When we entered the front door, we were greeted by Buddy's barks and appetizing aromas from a dining room table laden with food. Given the large breakfast we'd been served, I was surprised to see such a huge meal for lunch. Marta and Nieve were busy in the kitchen, so we went to our bedroom where we dropped our belongings and washed our hands. We returned to the dining area to find a smiling Marta waiting for us.

"Ah, there you are. How was your first day at school?"

June answered, "It was good. Our professor is very nice lookin', but the women noticed that he wears a wedding ring. Well, I don't think Sheila noticed."

"No, I didn't notice. He's very thorough and was pleased to answer whatever questions any of us asked. I think it's going to be a productive minimester." I didn't add that we had four weeks ahead, weeks filled with course requirements. I decided instead of worrying about the class, I would heed the advice of the woman who'd assisted me in Mexico City to slow down and appreciate what her country had to offer.

Marta motioned for us to have a seat. "Carlos has invited a friend to join us for lunch. Daniel is his assistant coach and has never been married. He is a good man, Sheila, and I am certain you will like him."

"What? I'm sorry I wasn't paying attention. My mind was somewhere else."

June kicked me under the table, and I gave her an angry look. She smiled like the Cheshire cat and whispered, "Listen, honey, I know your experience with men is limited, and it's been decades since you were in the dating pool, but I think you're about to be thrown into the deep end. Time to sink or swim."

Carlos and Daniel walked in, and Marta excused herself to greet them. I took the brief interlude as an opportunity to reprimand June. "You're out of your mind! What in the hell gave Marta the impression that I'm interested in meeting a man?"

She was taking pleasure in my discomfort and laughed out loud. "You may be upset by her assumptions, but I'm tellin' you this is a fix up." She smoothed the lace tablecloth and waved her hand over the table. "I guess the way to a man's heart really is food—even in Mexico."

Her laughter faded when Marta, Carlos, and the dark stranger approached the dining table that accommodated eight. Before introductions could be made, Aleho, Sharon, and Nieve joined the party. Daniel, however, made a point of circling the table to where I sat and introduced himself as he bowed, took my hand and kissed it with lips that loitered. I blushed and pulled my hand away, which didn't deter him from saying, "Eres una mujer hermosa."

My blush deepened at the bold man's compliment that I was a beautiful woman, but I was a guest and Daniel was a family friend. As a courtesy I thanked him. "Gracias."

Daniel seated himself across from me, but I kept conversation to a minimum. Assorted serving dishes were passed around, but I'd lost my appetite and only nibbled. Marta encouraged me to eat more because *la cena* would not be enough to sustain me until tomorrow's breakfast. I assured her that I was used to eating a light meal for supper and that I would be fine; nonetheless, she insisted that I have a slice of flan for dessert. The baked, caramel topped custard was delicious, and I wished I could have enjoyed it without Daniel's unwelcomed scrutiny. I was grateful when Carlos pushed his chair away from the table, which indicated the meal was finally over. I cringed at his suggestion that I join Marta, Daniel, and him on the veranda for a visit in the afternoon shade before retiring for *una siesta*.

I was fuming with indignation and promptly, but politely, refused. "I apologize, Carlos, for not being able to prolong this gathering, but I have homework and need to review my notes from this morning's class."

Daniel reached for my hand, but I yanked it away before he could plant another kiss and hoped my underlying message of dismissal was not too subtle as I said in a chilly tone, "Buenas tardes." I turned on my heel and almost fled down the hallway to the bedroom where I found June rolling in laughter.

"'You are a beautiful woman'." June mimicked in Daniel's deep, flirtatious voice.

"Give it a rest, June! It's not funny, not one bit, and if you were single he would have fed you the same line. Nice man my ass. Did you notice how brazenly Daniel stared at me? The man was practically inviting me to crawl into his lap."

"I don't think his lap is where he wants you to crawl. Most likely, his bed." She couldn't stop laughing.

"You can laugh all you want, but as soon as I hear that man leave, you and I are going for a long walk to clear my head, which is pounding with humiliation. I can't imagine why Carlos and Marta would be so presumptuous, especially on my first full day as their houseguest. When we get back here, Marta and I are going to have a talk, woman-to-woman."

I let out a sigh of relief when I heard "adios" exchanged. The front door closed, followed by the sound of Daniel's departing car. "He's gone. Let's put on our walking shoes and sneak out the back door. I don't want to run into anybody until I've had a chance to cool down."

The household slid into its *siesta*, and we were careful not to disturb the family. Thankfully, neither pet bothered to acknowledge our exit. The afternoon was perfect for a walk: blue skies, mid-seventies, and a city that slept, which meant less traffic. We had no idea which direction we should go, but since the school was to the left, *a la izquierda*, we agreed to go right, *derecho*. We walked down the sidewalk, noted the sleepy store on the corner, and made another right. In less than twenty minutes we were in the heart of the city, the central plaza, where we discovered that not everyone napped.

Street vendors lined the square and busily bartered to get the best price for their wares. Unless occupied, they called to June and me to *echar un vistazo* and since it cost nothing to have a look, we obliged. June had experience in bartering as she'd been to Cancun on a vacation with her family a few years earlier, where she'd learned the phrase, *es muy caro*. She didn't know directions in Spanish, nor could she remember the currency exchange, but she damn well knew how to say, "It's too expensive."

While she bartered over the cost of a lovely silk scarf, I wandered around the piazza and took in some of the sights of Cuernavaca. I was surprised to see a number of Americans who didn't appear to be students or tourists but residents for who wore the city as comfortably as an old shoe.

My attention was drawn to a few beautiful cathedrals, many built in the seventeen hundreds that reflected the country's predominantly Catholic faith. They beckoned parishioners to seek solace behind heavy wooden doors and stained glass windows. My eyes traversed the outskirts and rested upon a palace, which I was sure was the Casa de Cortés that I'd read about. Several statues honoring the city's history were also visible. While oddly out of place in a setting of antiquity, I spied the infamous "golden arches" of a McDonald's one block down the street and could almost smell those "World Famous Fries." I pulled out my translator to see if there was a Spanish word for the fast-food restaurant, but apparently "McDonald's" was "McDonald's" in any language.

June interrupted my survey when she tapped me on the shoulder. I noticed she was wearing the blue scarf and asked, "So did you get the scarf for what you wanted to pay?"

She smiled and brushed her cheek with the soft silk. "Yes, I did. And before you say anything about dinero, I used my calculator to make sure I paid exactly what he and I agreed was fair." She glanced at her watch. "We should probably head back. The last thing we need is for Marta to send out a search party."

"You're right, and I feel much better about the "Daniel situation." Even so, I need to have a candid conversation with Marta before she lines up a procession of men to meet me." We both laughed at the thought of their home's entrance becoming a revolving door for potential suitors.

We walked the direction from which we'd come, and when we reached the *tienda* I suggested we stop by and pick up some munchies. I hadn't been interested in eating lunch and was famished after our outing. The owner and his wife welcomed us to their well-kept establishment with a friendly greeting, "Buenas tardes."

They offered assistance, but I didn't think they spoke English and asked, "Hablas Inglés?"

They shook their heads in unison. The man replied, "No, no, lo siento."

There was no need to apologize for not speaking a second language, given that I was an American who scarcely spoke Spanish. To the couples' relief I answered, "No es un problema."

June and I made a few nonperishable food purchases, including several bottles of water, and were about to leave when I thought of Nieve. I walked to the chest freezer and retrieved a container of vanilla ice cream and hoped the elderly lady was not diabetic. I would ask Marta before giving the treat to her mother-in-law.

We returned home to Buddy's happy barks, who had apparently decided we were his best friends. He wagged his tail in appreciation for the pats on the head we gave him before June took our purchases to our room while I sought out Marta. She was in the kitchen with Nieve, preparing supper, and I asked in English if it was all right for Nieve to have the ice cream I'd bought for her. "Yes, and thank you for your thoughtfulness. She loves ice cream, but treats are an indulgence we can't always afford." She smiled affectionately at her *suegra*. "Her favorite is strawberry."

I gave the ice cream to Nieve, and her smile brightened the tiny kitchen. Next time I would bring *helado de fresa*. June entered the cramped space and offered to help, but Marta had everything under control. She did, however, accept our offer to set the table.

June and I chitchatted until Marta and Nieve brought in the evening meal, and Marta called the rest of the family to come and eat. We made light-hearted conversation around the table, and I asked if there were a lot of Americans who lived in Cuernavaca and why they had chosen to do so. Carlos said the city hosted hundreds of American residents and gave several reasons. Many Americans had discovered the beauty of the location, and the mild weather suited older adults. They also realized that their retirement funds would allow them to live a more lavish lifestyle in Mexico. Additionally, the city hosted thousands of tourists each year that fed the local economy. Carlos added that there were many, many wealthy Mexican residents of the city, which is why Cuernavaca was sometimes referred to as the "Beverly Hills of Mexico."

The discussion segued to the sights June and I would see on our field trips until Sharon began to clear the table. The rest of the family dispersed, and I asked Marta if I could speak with her in private—and in English. Nieve retrieved a spoon from the *cocina* and carried the ice cream to the veranda, and June followed her to unwind in the twilight.

Marta and I sat on the sofa, but I wasn't sure how to begin the candid conversation. Marta sensed something was troubling me and asked, "Sheila, are you upset with Carlos and me for wanting to introduce you to Daniel? You hardly touched your food, and I heard you and June leave shortly after Daniel left. Did he do or say something to offend you?"

"No, absolutely not. It's just that I'm not interested in meeting a man right now, especially one who's interested in a romantic relationship. It's entirely possible that I won't ever be in the market for a man. My husband died less than a year ago, but my love for him didn't."

Marta was baffled. "But you did not die, and you can love him without sacrificing your life to mourning. You are alive, and life is for the living. You must free yourself of yesterday and live your life before it, too, is gone. You are much too young to be alone, and Carlos and I thought we were helping by inviting an old friend to meet you. Would your esposo want for you to be happy again?"

"Yes, he would very much want me to be happy." Describing the loss of my much-loved husband and the black pit of pain that followed was going to be more difficult than I thought. Marta was a woman who climbed in bed each night with her loving husband, so explaining my heartache to her was comparable to explaining a tsunami to the nomads of the Sahara. I swept my hair from my face and tried again. "I appreciate your good intentions, but please accept that I'm not interested in becoming involved with another man." I reached for her hand and implored her to understand my position. "When my heart heals I may be more receptive to the idea, but right now I need time to adapt to being a widow instead of a wife."

"I cannot relate to your situation or pretend to know your heart, but I will respect your wishes." She gave me a hug and smiled. "The matter is closed."

With a sigh of relief that I'd nipped Marta's matchmaking attempts in the bud, I thanked her for allowing me to be honest in sharing my feelings with her. Dating was on the back burner, and I planned to focus on my studies and my status as a single woman. I was in Mexico to learn, to leave anxiety behind, and to smell the roses.

Marta usually stayed busy with household chores, but one afternoon she treated us to a trip to the open-air market where one could buy everything from fresh fruits and vegetables to homemade bread to live chickens and goats. Sombreros from black to rainbows weaved through the crowd in search of a bargain. The market of stalls was a bevy of activity filled with sounds of price haggling, children laughing, and the horns of delivery trucks. Drivers hedged their way along dirt paths, through the throngs to deliver more goods, and we all coughed from the dust and exhaust fumes left in the wake. Smells varied and were an assault on the senses. The pungent aroma of food prepared with spices, peppers, and onions mingled with the unmistakable odor of livestock. The marketplace was a Norman Rockwell painting come to life, if the artist had been Latin American.

That experience was the first of many as June and I settled into a routine and adjusted to Mexico and took in the sights. We continued to walk in the afternoons, and it was on one of those walks as we strolled along the tree-lined sidewalks of the city square that we came across a person who claimed to be a fortune teller. The woman held up a stack of tarot cards and gestured for me to take a seat in front of her stall. She resembled a box of crayons in that her clothing and scarves included almost every color. Her lips were covered in red, and eyeshadow in shades of purple and fuchsia could have given Tammy Faye a run for her money.

I wasn't interested and thought the scam would be a waste of time and money, but June encouraged me. "What are a few pesos, Sheila? It'll be fun. C'mon, I'll sit with you and may even have her foretell my future."

Reluctantly, I allowed June to coerce me into paying the "psychic." The woman randomly selected a few cards that she flipped over one by one and proceeded to read them in English. In the first card she saw much misery, which was followed by the death card. She spoke without empathy in a matter-of-fact tone. "You are very sad because you have lost someone close to you, perhaps your lover or your husband, someone you loved very much died not so very long ago."

I remained silent and didn't bother to point out that anyone with any sense of perception could know I was *muy triste*. The stranger I'd met at the pharmacy in Mexico City wasn't a fortune teller, but she'd recognized my sadness. Regardless, I was a good sport about the whole thing and let the woman continue as she pointed excitedly to the next card. "You will not be always alone! This card, the one with the bearded man, he is the one. You will meet him somewhere close to you, in your pueblo, when your heart is ready to love again."

It was time for me to finish this charade. "I thank you for the reading, but this time your cards are mistaken. It's true that I lost my husband last year, but you took a shot in the dark. As for your ability to predict my path, it's not likely there's a 'bearded man'—or any other man—waiting for me."

I stood to leave, and the woman's placed her hand on my forearm. "It is true. The cards never lie to me. You will fall in love again when the time is right."

There was no reason to argue with her certainty that love would one day find me. I kindly removed her hand from my arm and tipped her a few extra pesos before June and I walked to the curb to hail a taxi. We usually walked everywhere, but we'd agreed to meet Linda at *La Cocina Mexicana* for dinner, which was located several miles from the center of town. We'd chosen the restaurant based upon our instructor's recommendation and because it was a midway point between our homes. When the driver delivered us to the restaurant, June opened the cab door into the oncoming traffic and was sharply admonished by the driver. He lamented in broken English that he feared a speeding car would take the door right along with it and to always exit away from the street, *siempre.*

Linda was in slightly better spirits as we ordered a glass of wine from our attentive, albeit non-English speaking waiter. Linda recognized some of the menu items, and June helped her make her meal choice for the patient waiter. We unwound in the ambience of soft lights, melodious music, and a second glass of wine. Since the three of us were anxious about our first exam on Friday, we made plans to spend the next afternoon studying together before Thursday night's outing to one of Cuernavaca's more exclusive nightclubs, The Crystal Palace.

I wasn't sure what the dress code was at the swank nightspot, but when it came to the question of what to wear, the rule of thumb was to overdress, especially for women raised in the South. I'd packed semi-formal attire: an ivory, knee length chiffon layered dress and matching heels, along with a fake pearl necklace and earrings to compliment the dress. June planned to wear a navy dress and cubic zirconia earrings since she'd left her diamonds behind. Linda had brought a green satin outfit she felt would suffice, and she planned to add a touch of makeup.

As the night wound down, we paid our tabs and left what were more than fair tips. Per Señora Caro's suggestion, we wrapped up our leftover bread and gave it to the children who begged for money but were happy to have something to eat. Sadly, as Marta explained when I questioned her about the children begging in the streets, there were no social programs, such as welfare and food stamps, offered by the Mexican government to provide assistance to the poor. The prevailing consensus was that one must work if one wanted to eat and provide for their *familias.* I shook my head over the injustices suffered by the youngest victims as we signaled for taxis to take us home.

I reminded Linda to tell her house mother not to pick her up after school the next day since she would be studying with us for a few hours. She planned to take a taxi back to her place and dress for the nightclub before meeting the rest of our troupe in front of the school. Previous arrangements were made for us to ride together in a minibus, and Linda's host would drop her off at eight o'clock. Afterwards, the bus driver would take her home, as well as the others who needed transportation home so as not to inconvenience their families at a late hour.

June and I both slept soundly and woke up early on Thursday morning to a breakfast of coffee, bagels, and fruit. We told Marta we wouldn't be home for lunch as we didn't want to invite Linda to a home that wasn't ours. Instead, the three of us walked a few blocks to a sidewalk café for our midday meal where we lingered over our food. June and I did our best to help Linda prepare for the test, but she was lost in a language that was *muy difícil*. However, it was Mexicans who found English to be a very difficult language to learn, and it was nice to help them in return for their assistance. I grew up in a large family and was outgoing, which made it easier for me to meet people and work together to bridge the communication gap. Linda, on the other hand, was shy and too intimidated to initiate a conversation.

It was almost four o'clock when we parted ways so as to have ample time to primp for our first big night out in Cuernavaca. June and I each took a quick, refreshing shower and applied fresh make-up. I put a few rollers in my hair while June dried her hair and added gel. Her simple, yet elegant, blue dress flattered her trim figure; pumps and a matching clutch completed her ensemble. She touched up her lipstick while I slipped my cream-colored chiffon dress over hair rollers and let it fall gracefully over matching pantyhose. I straightened the see-through, short sleeves and ruffles that brushed the top of my knees and set free Velcro rollers. I fluffed my tumbled hair and splashed on a dab of perfume and mauve lipstick. We scanned over each other and figured we were as ready as we would ever be. But, apparently, there was an opinion we hadn't considered.

We walked through the family room on our way out the door where Marta gave us an appreciative glance and said, "Eres una mujer muy hermosa, y quiero hacerte el amor hasta que salga el sol." She crossed her arms and waited for our response.

I caught a few of the words but didn't fully comprehend what she'd said, nor did June. We smiled and answered, "Sí," as if we knew precisely what our house mother had said to us.

Marta startled us when she slammed her hand onto the coffee table and said, in English, "No! The answer to everything in Spanish is not 'sí'. I told you each that you are a very beautiful woman and that I want to make love to you until the sun comes up. You both smiled and readily consented to my proposition." She stood and yelled for Carlos and Sharon, who scuttled to the den. "Carlos, Sharon and I will be joining our houseguests tonight. They are like lambs to be thrown to the wolves, and I cannot allow them to be taken advantage of when we are responsible for their well-being."

I was still processing what she'd said in Spanish and wondering how I'd get out of a predicament such as she described. June spoke first, "Marta, we may not have understood what you said to us, but we're grown women who know how to handle ourselves in a nightclub. Besides, Professor Alonso and the others will be there, and we can keep an eye on each other."

I agreed with June. "Yes, Marta, we'll be fine and should be home no later than midnight."

It was Sharon's turn to add to the debate. "I want to go! When my friends and I go out, we're often turned away because the doorman suspects that we have no money for drinks. But when we go to a club in the company of Americans, we are welcomed as if money were no object. Mi madre is right that you need her to chaperone. Professor Alonso may have plans of his own, and the younger students are likely to have too much alcohol to be useful in watching out for you. Please allow us to go with you. It'll take ten minutes *solamente* for us to change."

The wall clock announced that we were twenty minutes early. I looked at June and shrugged. "I'm sure it will be okay for y'all to join us, and there should be room on the bus."

"Yippee!" shouted Sharon as she scampered to her room to dress, followed by Marta.

Marta, Sharon, June, and I sashayed into the nightclub as if it any other ordinary Thursday night. Linda trailed behind, and I summed up her hesitancy as shyness. Once inside, our swagger was halted as we took in the opulence of *El Palacio de Cristal*. The centerpiece was a crystal chandelier that subtly illuminated a huge, parquet dance floor where merrymakers swooned to romantic music supplied by the orchestra. The musicians' backdrop was a waterfall that flowed from the ceiling to a "river" that encircled the band. It was an actual waterfall—not one of those blue, shimmering foil imitations used at high school proms. Strategically arranged, dimly lit, mock street lamps provided a moonlight radiance that enhanced the surreal setting. The band members wore black and silver costumes that coordinated perfectly with the flattering, black-sequined dress worn by the sole female singer. She was stunning, and the dress sparkled in the subdued lighting as her velvety voice crooned to the crowd in a sensuous shadow that floated throughout the club. Couples were lost in *la música* and, from what I could see, each other.

We remained mesmerized and allowed our senses to be overwhelmed until the professor shooed us towards the curved stairway where tables overlooking the balcony had been reserved for our group. I followed along but continued to revel in the lavish surroundings. My only frame of reference for such a place was the ballroom settings in those old Fred Astaire and Ginger Rogers musicals from the forties. I inhaled the essence of the nightclub and was glad I'd packed a fancy dress. I touched the faux pearls and decided I should have packed my real pearl jewelry. It was impossible not to stare at the women who sat at tables that served as a perimeter for the dance floor. They were draped in elegance and were adorned in a lavish display of jewels. The only thing fake about those women were services purchased from a very good, very expensive plastic surgeon.

We split from the herd and found tables to accommodate our individual cliques, and a waiter appeared seemingly out of thin air to take our drink orders. Sharon leaned over so I could hear her whisper, "See what I mean about Americans? You are walking dinero in Mexico." She was undoubtedly relishing her night out at such a grandiose club, and I was pleased she and her mama had come with us.

The waiter held pen to pad and encouraged us to start a tab, but Marta was quick to dismiss him. She explained to us that it would be better to pay per item ordered so as to avoid confusion at the end of the night when the total might be less than accurate. The waiter left in a huff but had no choice but to oblige Marta's demand. The tab wouldn't be a problem for me because I rarely drank and wouldn't have more than one glass of wine. But she was watching out for us, and I didn't want to argue over a discrepancy in *el cheque* that could spoil this magical evening.

Students began to mingle on the dance floor, and I was approached by a middle-aged man who exuded a hefty dose of cologne. He tapped me on the shoulder and asked, "Te gustaría bailar?"

Marta sized him up as harmless. "Sharon, this man wants to dance with Sheila. If she agrees the two of us will dance, too." Sharon hopped up from her chair, ready to party.

I was content to sit and watch the eclectic crowd, but I didn't want to spoil Sharon's fun. I accepted the man's offer of a dance, and he escorted me down the stairs to the swarming dance floor. He carefully but deliberately led me away from Marta and her watchful eye to *la música* that was an upbeat tune and required no body contact. Even so, the man clasped me tightly to his chest and in heavily accented English murmured, "Señorita, be mine for one night only, sí?"

I practically screeched a word that was the same in both English and Spanish: "No!" I struggled to free myself from his grasp, but the man had the grip of a python and the limbs of an octopus. As he attempted to move in for a kiss, I stomped my heel onto his foot. Undeterred, his hand connected with my ass, and I was fixin' to slap his face when Marta intervened and yanked the man up by his shirt collar. He lost his hold on me, and I backed away from the fire. A couple of bouncers stepped into the scene, hoisted the man up between them, and showed him the exit.

The music continued, but I was too gun-shy to accept any other requests to dance. Marta and Sharon decided the best thing to do was for us to dance as a group. So we, along with June and Linda commandeered a section of the dance floor, kicked off our shoes, and proceeded to dance to the Latin beat. Barbara, who didn't seem to give a rat's ass that she was underdressed, joined our ensemble and was surprisingly limber for a big girl. To cheers of "¡Arriba, arriba!" we danced under the luminous chandelier until euphoric exhaustion sent us to seek solace in the coolness of the night where our chariot awaited our return.

Chapter Five

Memories Made in México

Friday's alarm alerted us way too early that it was time to rise and shine. I hit the snooze button more than once and then remembered that it was the day of our first test. I wanted to go over my notes *una vez más,* even though one more time probably wouldn't make a difference. I shoved back the covers and swung heavy feet over the side of the bed. June was oblivious to the clock and the sunlight that sneaked through the blinds and announced another day. I made my way to the windows and yanked open the blinds, much to June's dismay. "What are you doing? Close those damn things and go back to bed. Or did you forget that we don't have to be at school until nine o'clock today"

School was delayed an hour on Friday since we had only to take the exam, followed by a field trip. "No, I didn't forget. But wake up Sleeping Beauty. It's exam day, and we promised Linda we'd meet her in the court-yard at the usual time to review together. She's worried sick about how she's going to do on her very first Spanish exam. To tell the truth, I'm worried for her."

June pulled the covers over her head and burrowed into the mattress. "Can't you meet her without me? I'm beat and need the extra hour to sleep. Please?"

"All right, sleep. I'll get a shower and let Marta know you're sleeping in today because you are understandably too old to party until midnight."

My comment hit a nerve. I would be celebrating my own birthday on Saturday, but I saw no reason to share that information. June had recently hit the big 5-0 birthday and was hell-bent on proving that fifty was nothing more than a number. She flung the covers aside and climbed out of bed with a grumpy, "I'm up!"

Hot showers and hotter coffee did wonders to restore our energy, and we dashed out the door and scurried up the sidewalk to school and found Linda waiting. She looked like hell in a handbag, with dark circles that revealed her sleepless night. June and I ignored her obvious fatigue and greeted her with a cheerful "Buenos días."

"'Buenos días'," she mocked. "The two of you may have crashed after dancing until my feet screamed in protest, but I couldn't sleep for worrying about this damn test. I got up and reviewed my notes but was too tired to focus. I've been up since the crack of dawn and let me tell you, my house mother was none too happy about getting me here at the usual time. She'd looked forward to an extra hour's sleep. I guess I should have called a taxi."

"We're sorry, but we did come to school early to help you study," said June, who was trying not to begrudge Linda the extra hour of sleep she'd sacrificed.

Our conversation was halted when Profesor Garcia deftly parallel parked his car at the curb, and we watched as he put a Lo Jack in place to secure the steering wheel. He hopped out of the car, boot in hand, and proceeded to place the device onto one of the front wheels. He then double checked to make sure all the doors were locked. We stood dumbfounded by his meticulous efforts to safeguard a Volkswagen van that was almost twenty years old.

Before we could ask he answered our curious stares, "On average seventy cars a day are stolen in Cuernavaca, and while my car is old, it is the only means of transportation my family and I can afford." Briefcase in hand, he sprinted through the gate with a smile on his face and as an afterthought added, "Buena suerte en el examen."

Good luck my ass. It was going to take more than luck to make the "A" I wanted, and I'd studied diligently. The three of us gathered at a table under the shade of a big oak tree and went over the week's notes until the bell called us to class. I don't know if everyone was subdued because of the late night or if they, too, were worried about the test our instructor was handing out. He cautioned us that anyone caught cheating would receive an automatic zero on the test, which none of us was willing to risk. Most finished the exam in half an hour and were excused. I finished in forty-five minutes but used the remaining fifteen minutes reviewing my answers and changed only one. At the end of the hour the tests were gathered, and we were excused to make our way to the bus that sat in the midmorning sun. I was looking forward to the tour of the city's various *panaderias*, and I'd promised Marta that I would bring home a loaf of fresh baked bread for lunch from one of the bakeries.

Everyone was in high spirits as we boarded the bus, relieved the exam was behind us. I was sure I'd made a good grade. The test wasn't as tough as I'd expected—or my hours of studying had paid off. June was certain she'd made a "B," but Linda knew she'd blown it and looked like someone who'd crapped in her Easter basket. She didn't even want to go on the field trip with us, but we convinced her that a break would be good for her. Our advice didn't stop her from asking me answers to various questions on the test and obsessing over the ones she'd missed while she chewed her fingernails to the quick. As soon as I had a few minutes alone with June, I pulled her aside and expressed my concern. "I'm worried Linda is on the verge of a nervous breakdown."

"No she's not. She's just upset about the test, but she'll do better next week. I'm sure she's fine and looking forward to the big Fourth of July party tonight for us Americans at whatever the name of that place is."

I pushed aside my concern for Linda and accepted that she'd made her bed and would have to lie in it. I would be pleasantly surprised if she made it through the next three weeks.

June interrupted my contemplations. "Did you hear me? What's the name of the club we're going to tonight, and what are you wearing?"

"The name of the place is Sundown Party, and according to Sharon it's a bar that's nothing as nice as The Crystal Palace. I'm wearing a skirt, a t-shirt with a sequined USA flag that I packed for tonight, and sandals."

She agreed casual dress would be the best choice, and I took in the sights of the city as the bus chugged along and stopped at several bakeries. With each stop, we were met with the scrumptious fragrance of freshly baked goods and warm greetings from the owners. It was impossible not to choose something from each *panaderias*, so in addition to two loaves of bread, I bought a variety of pastries I thought Nieve would enjoy.

At the end of our outing when I handed the elderly woman the assorted *pasteles*, delight filled the crevices of her well-worn face, a roadmap of her life's voyage. Between the purchases June and I made, there were plenty of sweet treats to share after the midday meal. Instead of our usual walk, June and I opted to join the family in napping. We'd been up very late the night before and had plans for going out again to celebrate America's independence. The house was deep in peaceful sleep when the jangle of the telephone jarred us awake, followed by a tap on our bedroom door and Marta's voice. "Sheila, there is a telephone call for you. It is your sister."

I followed her down the hall to the phone and apologized for the caller disturbing her rest. She waved my worry aside and said she'd been reading and that no one was awakened. She handed me the receiver and retreated to her bedroom.

In a lowered voice I asked, "Hello? Is this Pat?"

"Yes, stranger, this is Pat. What took you so long to get to the phone?"

"I was asleep. Everyone here takes a siesta after lunch, so please don't call between two and four o'clock when we're napping." The prospect of a daily nap was an enticing concept that June and I had dismissed in haste.

"A nap! Are you sick? Do you need to come home?"

"No, I'm fine."

"Then why in the hell haven't you called to let me know you're all right? Nobody has heard one word from you since Jerry left you at the airport a week ago, and we've been worried sick. Now that I know you're safe, have a happy birthday tomorrow. We'll go out for lunch when you get your ass back home where you belong."

"Thank you. I don't want you to worry, but I've been very busy. I have school from eight until twelve and then my roommate, whom you know, and I nap or study for a while before taking a walk. Tomorrow we have a field trip to the mountains, and I'm looking forward to hiking."

I felt her frustration when she hissed, "While you're gallivanting all over the place, the very least you can do is take a few minutes to call and let me know you're ok. So, princess, if you don't want me to disturb your beauty sleep, I damn well better hear from you once a week. And let me remind you that I don't speak Spanish, so stop switching back and forth between English and Spanish."

"Lo siento. I mean, I'm sorry, but this is an immersion program that requires us to speak Spanish almost exclusively. Sometimes I forget to speak English only. I made the same mistake when Valerie called a few days ago to confirm that I'd arrived at the home of my hosts. I forgot to ask her to call you, but I promise to call one day next week. Please start the communication chain and let Daddy know I haven't been kidnapped."

"I'll call him first." We chatted for a few more minutes before "I love you" and "happy birthday" and "goodbye" were exchanged. I carefully replaced the receiver onto its cradle and crept back to my nap.

Once again, the alarm announced morning way too early. It was Saturday, but there was no sleeping in as field trips had been planned for all but one of our Saturdays. I kicked off the covers, hauled myself to the floor, and stretched life into my weary limbs. I called to June that it was time to get up, whether she wanted to or not. June mumbled her protest, "I'm too tired. Remind me again why we have to go on this trip."

"Because attendance is mandatory, and we can't miss the bus. Now get a move on."

The last thing I wanted to do was hike up some mountain, but I hit the shower while June pulled the covers over her head. I grabbed a clean towel, but had learned to bathe without a washcloth. Apparently, *toallitas* were not considered necessary for personal hygiene. The skimpy spray washed away my grogginess as I thought about the celebration of the night before.

The tavern was decorated with red, white, and blue banners and balloons, along with a huge American flag that hung over the bar. Even the music reflected a culture not their own as the place was hoppin' to the sound of the DJ's aptly chosen, "Born in the U.S.A" by Bruce Springsteen, and other classic American rock music. They were certainly catering to the *rico americanos*; there was no comprehending that we weren't all wealthy. That fact wasn't a concern, and my fellow students danced with a variety of partners.

I, on the other hand, declined several offers to dance. I'd learned my lesson about dancing with strangers in a foreign country. I much preferred hanging out with those who danced as a group—except for Suzette who wrapped herself around a young, handsome *hombre*. I hoped she wasn't going to stir up trouble, but security was tight and there were no incidents that disrupted the partygoers. Barbara was holding court at the bar, and some of the guys were taking swings at a piñata when Professor Alonso rounded up his charges and counted heads as we boarded the bus. We returned to the school where host families waited for their "children." June and I, and a few others who lived within walking distance, enjoyed a moonlit stroll and a soft breeze.

Contemplations of last night dissipated in the shower. While June showered I put on a minimum of makeup and slathered on sunscreen before getting dressed in shorts, tank top, and walking shoes. I pulled my hair into a ponytail and tucked it through the opening of the baseball hat I retrieved from my small backpack where I packed a couple of bottles of water and a granola bar. I knocked on the bathroom door to hurry June along before I joined the others for breakfast. By the time June was ready to go, she barely had time to gulp down a cup of coffee. We rushed to the school to board the bus, and I was thankful to find a vacant seat close to the front of the bus. I was prone to carsickness and didn't want to ride in the back on what were sure to be curvy roads. We dropped onto the seat, and June dug a bottle of water and a pack of peanuts out of her backpack. She was still pilfering around in her bag when she let out a frustrated "Damn it."

"What's wrong? Did you forget your camera?"

"No, my sunscreen. Do you have any with you?"

"Sorry, but I applied mine before I got dressed and left it on the dresser. Maybe Linda or one of the others has a bottle with them." Unfortunately for June, nobody had thought to bring along sunblock. I wasn't surprised she'd forgotten her sunscreen. She spent half her time searching for misplaced items on her side of the room we shared. I did my best to keep my things in order, but June's clutter didn't bother her in the least. Nor was she worried about the lack of sunscreen. She was asleep before we left the city behind us for the hour's drive.

I was thankful I'd taken Marta's advice to carry a lightweight pullover as the temperature dropped about ten degrees in the higher altitude. The hike was less than two miles but very steep and made me grateful that I walked daily, although the thin air made it difficult to breathe. Once we reached the summit, I forgot about the strenuous climb. The views from the top of the Tepozteco Mountains were magnificent, and we could see Cuernavaca lounging like a mirage in the distance. A small, Aztec pyramid rested atop, and the majestic mountains supposedly held mystical powers. We roamed the mountaintop, took pictures, and appreciated a snack under a cloudless blue sky before we began the descent. The bus chauffeured its occupants to the valley where the village of Tepoztlan and its abundance of shops and cafes welcomed her visitors. The centerpiece of the mountain town was a church that more closely resembled a castle and an adjacent monastery. Businesses sacrificed *siesta* in favor of tourists, and we spent the afternoon over a relaxing lunch and browsing the various shops until the sun sagged against the skyline.

An hour later June and I arrived home to a surprise party for me. There were balloons and streamers and a pink and white birthday cake that sat in the center of the dining room table. As everyone sang *feliz cumpleaños*, Nieve patted my hand and said, "Si eres joven de corazón, siempre serás joven."

I hugged her fragile frame and thanked her for reminding me that if I was young at heart, I would always be young. I was overwhelmed by their simple act of kindness and wondered how they knew it was my birthday.

As it turned out, the school had supplied Marta with informational files on June and me—just as they had given us background info on our host family. They wanted to celebrate my birthday to ease any pangs of homesickness.

I wasn't nearly as homesick as I'd expected, and neither was June. However, she was distraught over the red welts that covered her body and prompted Marta to call the doctor on Monday. June stayed home from school because the doctor made a house call, which was inconceivable to us. He diagnosed her with sun poisoning, gave her a steroid injection, and left a tube of hydrocortisone cream to help relive the itch—all for the sum of fifteen dollars. Nieve offered an aloe plant to cool the sunburn, but June suffered the consequences of her carelessness.

She'd learned a painful lesson and so had Linda, who was ready to pack up and go home after she failed her second exam. Through tears she admitted, "This trip was a horrible mistake. According to the headmaster, it takes a minimum of six months to learn the language. And that's if I lived here and completely immersed myself in the lingo. I'm a miserable disappointment and don't know how I'm going to face my boss and friends at work. They were all counting on me to come back rattling off Spanish like the employee they need."

She was beating herself up for nothing. "You mean those 'friends' who sent you as the sacrificial lamb? Not one of them was willing to do what you volunteered to do, so screw 'em. As for going home, I seriously doubt if that's possible unless it's a family emergency."

"You're right. The school is not going to give the hospital a refund, given that an exception was made for me, and I don't have the gall to ask them to pay to fly me home early. On a more positive note, I have a meeting with both professors and Señora Sanchez in the morning to reassess my foreign language challenges."

"Well, that's something. I'm sure the three of them can find a solution."

The way out for Linda was that she would stay in our class two days a week, and on the remaining three, Marta would work one-on-one tutoring Linda. The goal was to teach her some basic phrases in Spanish that would be useful in a medical setting; she would be excused from the exams.

Linda was relieved not to be tested and to have Marta's assistance, but she couldn't shake the feeling of a failure. To cheer her up, we decided a trip to Acapulco would be a perfect weekend getaway on our one free Saturday.

June and I agreed to purchase the tickets while we took care of other errands. We stopped by the post office where we each dropped a handful of postcards in the mail on our way to the bank to exchange traveler's checks for Mexican currency. The money would be used for bus tickets, tips, and other incidentals. We fell silent when we entered the somber setting of the bank. I paused at the entrance and took note of the rigid line where customers waited their turns to see the proficient tellers held behind bars. Two guards with automatic weapons were posted at the door and the gate where the vault was locked; another armed guard roamed the lobby. I was by no means fluent in Spanish, but June's Spanish was definitely sketchy. I cautioned, "June, don't say a word. Not one word. And don't make any sudden moves. The guards are locked and loaded, and I have a gut feeling they shoot first and ask questions later. So let's quietly ease our way into the line, take care of our business, and slide out the door."

"Okay. I'll let you handle the transactions here, and I'll handle buying the tickets at the bus terminal so I can practice my Spanish. Linda gave me the money for her ticket at school this morning."

I agreed, and in theory it was a good idea. As luck would have it, the teller I approached spoke English, and in less than ten minutes we were outside and hailing a cab to the bus terminal across town. June attempted to buy round-trip tickets, but the employee spoke no English and made no effort to assist her. My friend made the classic mistake of speaking louder and slower, "I NEED TO PURCHASE THREE TICKETS FOR ACAPULCO ON SATURDAY."

She was met with frustration. "No entiendo ingles."

I believed the woman when she said she didn't understand, but I also believed she could have been of more assistance had she wanted to help two blonde *mujeres americanas*. I intervened and between us, June and I managed to buy three tickets for Acapulco. According to the schedule the bus would leave from the station at nine a.m., and we would arrive at the beach three and a half hours later. Our return bus would leave at two o'clock on Sunday afternoon. With our mission accomplished, we hailed a taxi and gave the driver the address.

Once home we shared our plans with Marta, and she offered to make our reservations at the Copacabana. We declined but were grateful for her assistance in securing the phone number. The desk clerk spoke English and was happy to book the room for us as he readily accepted my credit card. June called Linda to tell her arrangements had been made for our weekend at the shore, and I washed up for supper.

I was pleased Carlos and Marta were eating with us because I wanted to discuss our visit to the bank. Marta and June were conversing about their events of the day, so I turned to Carlos. "I would like to know why there are armed guards at the bank. It was a nerve-wracking experience, and I can't imagine why they are necessary."

Carlos gave me an incredulous look before he threw his head back and laughed until he had to wipe tears away. Marta stopped in mid-sentence to ask Carlos what was so funny. "Sheila and June are confused as to why there are armed guards at the bank."

It was Marta's turn to laugh. When she was composed enough to speak she said, "It should be obvious that without guards with guns the bank would be robbed every hour of every day. There are guards to protect the money in American banks. ¿Sí?"

I attempted to clarify, "Well, no. There may or may not be a security guard on the premises, but he does not carry a semi-automatic weapon."

Carlos and Marta shook their heads in amazement as the topic changed to the soccer championship to be held in California. Carlos and his team would be leaving at the end of the week, and he was certain they would return with the first place trophy. The prestige of winning an international competition would be a feather in Carlos's cap and would, undoubtedly, increase the enrollment at his training school. He was very self-assured as he proceeded to elaborate on the ins and outs of soccer, and I struggled to stay alert. I feigned interest, but I was excruciatingly bored with his bottomless well of soccer strategies. When there was a brief lull I politely excused myself with the pretext that I needed to pack a weekend bag; June was quick to follow suit.

Friday's exam was behind us, and the field trip to one of the city's several beautiful parks was a good way to unwind. There was a treasure hunt with clues, in Spanish, planted throughout the park, and the teams into which we'd been divided had fun searching for the prize. No one was surprised when two of the Spanish majors claimed the "treasure" of dinner for two at a local *restaurante*. Afterwards, most of us rented paddleboats and lazily drifted along the stream under cottony clouds before we were shuttled to a restaurant on the outskirts of town, an old farmhouse that had been converted. We were served at colorful tables on the large, shady, porch where a mariachi band wearing traditional attire serenaded us. It was a perfect afternoon, and we reluctantly returned to the school. As we parted ways June reminded Linda not to be late meeting at the bus depot for our fun-filled weekend.

At the last minute, Suzette invited herself to join us on the outing to the beach when her brief affair with Jesús had come to an abrupt end. The train left the tracks when he'd foolishly introduced her to his parents, his extremely wealthy parents. His mother had seen through Suzette's pretense and recognized that she was nothing more than an *Americano de excavación de oro* who was not nearly worthy of her only son. I'd already surmised that Suzette was a gold digger, but I'm sure it hurt her when Jesús' *madre* referred to her as such and tossed her out of the villa like she was white trash. Jesús hadn't even attempted to intervene and instead remained tightly tied to his mama's apron strings. I could have told Suzette that she was nothing more than a childish act of defiance, Jesús' equivalent of a two-year-old's tantrum, but there was no reason to interfere in her high hopes. To her credit, Suzette shrugged off the ill-fated romance, bought a bus ticket, and made the decision to crash with us for the weekend to lick her wounds.

We figured the more the merrier, and as June and I followed the sidewalk home we chattered like excited squirrels about our upcoming beach trip to Acapulco. Our carefree mood changed from anticipation to bewilderment when we entered the house filled with Sharon's shouts. She had a rolled-up newspaper and was hitting Buddy while screaming obscenities in Spanish. I didn't have to be fluent in Spanish to comprehend that Sharon was mad as hell and that *el perro* was the source, but I couldn't imagine what the dog had done to provoke her anger.

To his credit, Buddy didn't seem to mind the abuse and even appeared to be smiling as he slowly turned over onto his back. Marta put an end to Sharon's tirade. "That's enough! Go to your room, Sharon, and calm down. The dog meant no harm, and you are the guilty one in this matter. We will deal with this situation when your padre comes home."

Sharon flung the newspaper across the room and hurled one last, "Damn you!" at Buddy as she stormed down the hallway. Her door slammed so hard the windows rattled.

The two of us found a seat on the sofa, and I asked, "¿Que pasó?"

Marta brushed her hair back and seemed to be debating as to whether or not to tell us what had happened. With a shrug she replied, "Sharon was growing a pot plant on the windowsill in her room, which was almost ready to dry and smoke. Buddy innocently knocked the plant to the floor. Sharon couldn't salvage the marijuana because by the time she came home the dog had eaten the plant." Her stern face revealed the gravity of the circumstances. As we all knew, marijuana was illegal in Mexico.

Despite that fact June and I burst into laughter, and June said, "Well, that explains why Buddy doesn't have a care in the world."

I added, "Kinda gives a whole new meaning to 'potted plant'." We tried to stifle our amusement over the stoned dog but to no avail. Marta lost her composure, and school girl giggles sprang from her tightly drawn lips as she wiped away tears. Sharon may not have seen the humor, but the three of us laughed until I had the hiccups. Other than eating everything in sight for the next day or two, Buddy didn't appear to suffer any ill effects from the marijuana—or from Sharon's wrath.

The four of us met at the bus station where we boarded and stowed our bags on the rack above our seats. Acapulco was approximately a four hour ride to the coast, so we were thankful to find the bus clean, comfortable, and air conditioned. Suzette cried for the first twenty miles—until we told her that was enough time to waste over a two week affair with a man she'd just met. She dried her tears and lost herself in a book, and I lost myself in the scenery. We traveled through Cuernavaca, and I saw parts of the city I'd missed, including a large shopping mall. The city faded into the background as the driver skillfully merged onto México 95, where I grew bored with interstate travel. I didn't realize I'd drifted off to a sound sleep until the bus began to jostle over cobbled streets. Awakened, I returned to the landscape and noticed the beautiful Sierra Madre del Sur Mountains.

Mexico's largest and oldest beach resort boasted a skyline that stretched itself majestically under the noonday sun and painted a picture of abundance. However, another portrait of the city was one of destitution viewed from the bus window. Ragged clothes hung on lines strung between rundown apartment buildings, beggars were on every corner, and barefooted children played with sticks in the street. It was the same contrast I'd seen in Mexico City, a contrast between the haves and the have-nots that could be found in almost any city in the world.

As the bus continued towards the coast, it was as if the veil of poverty was lifted, a curtain drawn to reveal city streets lined with grand hotels where the Pacific Ocean slapped the sand and encouraged tourists to frolic in the surf. Our driver, Juan, pulled into the conveniently located terminal, and taxi drivers rushed to assist us with our luggage, hoping to secure the fare to our hotel. Juan brushed the con artists aside as he chose one taxi, loaded our bags in the trunk, and told the smiling driver to deliver us directly to the Copacabana.

We arrived less than fifteen minutes later and were welcomed with cocktails, complete with tiny colored paper umbrellas. We glanced around the lobby before we were ushered to the registration desk, and the clerk offered to make dinner reservations for us at the El Mirador Hotel's restaurant where we could watch the men dive from the iconic La Quebrada cliff. Despite the misconception that all Americans were rich, we readily held credit cards in hand. We were more than willing to pay to watch professionals dive into the ocean a hundred feet beneath the jagged cliffs. Reservations were made, and we were given room keys and directed to the elevator. Our room was large, with two double beds, and a balcony that overlooked the beach. The room itself was nondescript, much like any hotel room on any beach, but the view was one that convinced us we'd landed in a tropical paradise. Palm trees surrounded the kidney-shaped pool where guests lounged lazily on floats or around the perimeter in brilliantly cushioned patio chairs. Breakers beckoned us to swim in the sea. Bikinis abounded and svelte, bronzed bodies glistened with suntan oil, but faces were protected from the unforgiving sun by large, colorful hats.

Suzette spied a couple of hunks she was sure would help restore her wounded pride. "Let's change into our suits and hit the beach! I don't want to waste a minute of this trip in a room."

"Neither do I," said Linda.

We quickly changed, applied sunblock, threw a few necessities in our beach bags, and headed for the pool area where we were just in time to connect to a Conga line. The music ended, and we crashed onto empty chairs and ordered frozen margaritas from the tiki bar. I was content to relax in the sun, stroked by the ocean breeze, but June and Suzette spotted a banana float being towed behind a boat. They enthusiastically coaxed Linda and me to join them on the wild, wet ride. There was no holding on when the boat began to jump the surf and sway with the waves, and we plunged beneath the salty sea. Each of us spit and sputtered our way to the surface where the boat had stopped to wait for us to climb back onto the banana shaped inflated towable, not an easy feat.

The ride ended with us tumbling onto the shoreline. I thought I was too exhausted to do anything but collapse until I spied a young man offering parasailing rides. "I've always wanted to go parasailing, how about y'all?"

Linda and Suzette were already halfway to the pool and waved me off, and June thought I was as crazy as a Betsy bug. "Sweetie, if you want to strap a parachute on and run on the beach behind a boat pulling you across the sand until you're airborne, then go right ahead. If you're sure about this, I'll get the camera from your beach bag while you're paying and getting harnessed up. I'm sure you'll want pictures. Otherwise, who's gonna believe it?"

"June, wait. Didn't you ask me in Atlanta if I was ready for an adventure? Well, parasailing definitely qualifies. Please come with me. They have a double harness."

"There's a fine line between adventure and suicide. If you want to strap your ass in a harness and fly above the ocean behind a boat, then by all means have at it. But there's not enough tequila in Mexico to get me drunk enough to go with you."

June waved as I embarked on an exhilarating experience. When I landed safely on the shore, there were more hands loosening the harness than necessary. I thanked one of the men, in Spanish, for a thrilling ride and told him the view had been amazing. He answered in English, "Speak English, please! I need to practice speaking your language for to talk better to tourists."

I laughed and replied, "Necesito practicar español para un examen oral." A portion of our final would be to converse briefly in Spanish, and I needed all the practice I could get.

We laughed together, and I gave him a few extra pesos for the new memory before June and I made our way to the pool. Linda was napping under a canopy, and Suzette was making the acquaintance of a couple of men who looked to be about her age. The afternoon zipped by much too soon, and we had to hurry so as not to be late for the show provided by brave cliff divers. Four women sharing one bathroom had to be as choreo-graphed as a ballet, but we arrived at the restaurant in time for our reserva-tion—wearing sundresses that highlighted sun-kissed shoulders. Several men turned in their chairs to give us admiring looks and flirtatious smiles, much to the chagrin of their dark-haired ladies. We nodded but didn't en-courage the male attention, except for Suzette who flipped her long, straw-colored hair and handed out come-hither smiles.

I couldn't believe she wanted to pull at that thread after her last Latin lover dumped her or, more aptly, allowed his mama to do his dirty work. I firmly guided Suzette in the opposite direction. "No you don't chica. We don't need that kind of trouble, so lose the Scarlett O'Hara perfor-mance. We came together, and we leave together. You'll thank me in the morning."

She yanked her arm away and pouted but reined in the coquettish charm as we were seated on the terrace, adjacent to a large wooden plat-form where spectators could gather at the cliffs. I took in the beauty of our surroundings and felt like I'd stepped into that Elvis Presley movie from the sixties, *Fun in Acapulco*. Not only were the views of the ocean and vi-brant colors picture postcard perfect, a mariachi band crooned to the crowd while we enjoyed a tasty meal.

The "oohs" and "aahs" of the crowd alerted us to the arrival of the mus-cular men in tight swim trunks who would provide the evening's entertain-ment, at risk of serious injury or death. Several boats were anchored just outside the forty foot channel, a prime viewing spot. The boats dipped in waves that collided against the cliffs. June and Linda were not as interested in the divers as Suzette and I. They lingered over sangrias and watched from a less crowded distance while the two of us hurried to find a spot near the front of the platform.

One by one the divers approached the edge and assessed the mood of the sea, which made timing critical. Satisfied with conditions, they saluted and smiled at the group as we cheered them on. Each one of them made the sign of the cross on his chest before plunging into crashing waves that waited in the depths below. There was a communal sigh of relief as the diver surfaced and waved to signal all was well and deftly ascended the cliff.

After the last of the performers waved goodbye, I added another memory to my expanding catalog. Suzette joined the others and the crowd thinned, but I remained on the deck until the golden orange sunset melted into the horizon. A lavender twilight brought with it an overwhelming sense of melancholy, and my heart yearned for the past—or for whatever waited on the other side of limbo.

We arrived from Acapulco to a house where the disposition had shifted from one of anxious anticipation to one of dismal disappointment. Carlos' soccer team had made it to the final round of the playoffs, but the Americans defeated Mexico for the championship. Carlos was visibly disheartened, but I couldn't offer insincere sympathy when I was proud of the American team and their win. Neither June nor I mentioned that fact and chose instead to remain silent. We followed the cue from the rest of the family and ignored the elephant in the room. Neither did we acknowledge the spot Marta had cleared from the china cabinet for the trophy—a space that stood silent…and empty. The devastating loss was simply swept under the rug, and June and I focused on finishing the course we needed for graduation.

The last week of school arrived and brought with it an aura of carefree relaxation of rules. Class bells were turned off, break time was extended, and class time was spent reviewing notes for Friday's final. Linda hadn't learned nearly as much as she'd hoped, but Marta taught her as much as she could in the limited timeframe. Suzette finally caught Chandler's eye and, for the time being, reveled in his attention. We were all in high spirits and decided to go out as a group on Thursday night, party night in Cuernavaca. Linda opted to pass because she wanted to get a jump on her packing. June and I planned accordingly and packed before studying for the final exam and heading across town.

The downside was that we had to arrange our own transportation to the disco bar on the west side of the city where the majority of the students agreed to meet. Some of the younger students had stumbled upon the happening venue, El Almacén, a week earlier and convinced us that we "old people" would feel right at home at the discotheque. Barbara reminded them that their young asses would be old one day, although none of us considered ourselves "old." I didn't pack a pair of bell bottoms, which were a popular fashion throwback from the seventies. Instead, I wore acid-washed, slim-fit jeans and a white t-shirt while June dressed in tan Bermuda shorts and a blue blouse; we both opted to wear flats. We took a minute to tell everyone goodnight, and mother hen Marta cautioned us to be careful and to enjoy the evening. As we walked to the corner to hail a cab, I realized I would miss Marta's motherly concern. Then again, I had worrywart Pat waiting at home for her baby sister.

Our taxi dropped us off at the entrance of a large, orange and yellow building, aptly named "The Warehouse," and we stepped into the seventies. As my eyes adjusted to the bouncing, multi-colored lights, I was sure I spotted John Travolta on the translucent tiled dance floor doing the Hustle across a sea of lights that captured his every move. Of course, it wasn't John Travolta who moved to the beat of the Bee Gees' Spanish version of "Stayin' Alive" but a wannabe who was wearing a paisley, polyester shirt, opened to his navel, revealing several gold chains. A white suit completed his disco look, and the flamboyant dancer was almost certainly grateful for the platform shoes that added a couple of inches to his short stature. June and I found the others at a large table close to the dance floor but declined to order drinks and settled for seltzer water with lime. Taking heed to be selective with whom we danced, we proceeded to "Bump" the night away under the silver disco ball that glimmered from the ceiling.

I left the crowded dance floor and was downing a glass of refreshing water when June ordered a glass of wine. I squinted in the semi-darkness to see the face of my watch, a face that screamed it was after one o'clock in the morning. I reached across the table to get June's attention. "June, we have to go! It's later than we'd planned to stay, and Marta will be worried about us. C'mon, we gotta get a taxi."

June said, "I'm going to stay a while longer, until I finish my wine. You go ahead without me, and I'll share a taxi with Barbara or one of the others."

I snatched her arm and set the glass of wine on the table. "Let me remind you of our deal that when we go somewhere together, we leave together." I reconsidered. "You're a grown-ass woman so if you want to stay, then stay. Enjoy your wine."

I claimed my small bag from a pile of others and stood to leave when June changed her mind. "Okay, you're right, it's time to go. We have to get up early, and I don't want to blow the final. I just need to visit the ladies' room first." Women never passed up the opportunity to pee while men, on the other hand, had a bladder the size of a watermelon.

"Good idea. I drank lots of water to stay hydrated and don't want to pee my pants if we get a reckless taxi driver. Oh, hell, they're all reckless. Let's use the facilities and get out of here."

We exited the club, and rain met us. I regretted that we hadn't grabbed a raincoat or an umbrella but we'd planned to be home before the nightly cloudburst made its appearance. As we joined dozens in summoning a cab, I retrieved the plastic-coated card with our home address to have in hand for the driver. Fifteen minutes later a taxi halted in front of us, and I showed him the card. "¿Conoces esta dirección?"

"Lo siento, pero no." He was sorry but wasn't familiar with the address. He pulled forward to collect another passenger.

By the time the third taxi stopped to pick us up, we were soaked to the bone. Thankfully, the driver acknowledged that he knew the location but forewarned us the cost would be thirty *pesos* to drive such a distance at the late hour. I readily agreed and found enough Spanish to answer, "Sí, pagaremos la tarifa."

To my surprise, June protested. "Did you agree to pay this rip-off artist thirty pesos?"

"I did. Of the three taxi drivers who bothered to stop, he's the only one who has a hint in hell where our place is located. So, yes, I told him we would pay the fare."

"Well, I'm not going to be held up like that. We were told that seven to ten pesos is fair and that we should never pay more than fifteen for *any* taxi ride, regardless of where we're going." She crossed her arms and stood her ground as rain continued to drench us.

While I understood her not wanting to be taken advantage of, it was not the time to argue over a few dollars. My clothes clung to me like Saran Wrap, and I shivered in the rainstorm. I yanked open the door and shoved my friend into the backseat. "To hell you're not. And divided by two, it's only fifteen pesos."

I gave June a look that let her know I was dead damn serious, and she scooted over to make room for me. I cautioned her to not offer the driver advice regarding directions because she still got a little confused on her Spanish for left, right, and straight. Even so, the ride took longer than it should have, but eventually the driver found the house, collected his fee, and discarded us on the sidewalk. The gate was locked, and the house was dark. I found my key, and we slinked into the house with the stealth of cat burglars so as not to disturb the sleeping family. I'd never been so grateful to be home as I hung my wet clothes over the shower rod, donned cotton pajamas, and crawled into a bed that cradled me in comfort.

In a blink it was morning, and we hauled our tired asses out of bed. June assessed the damage in the mirror. "Oh, hell, I look fifty years old!"

I hated to remind her of her age. "June, you *are* fifty years old."

"Damn! Then I look sixty years old." She laughed good-naturedly.

Despite our late night a shower and several cups of coffee revived us so that we were wide awake for Friday's eight o'clock final. The two hour written exam—plus the half hour conversation in Spanish—was challenging, but I didn't doubt that I'd made a good grade. Linda was given a separate test designed for what she'd been learning and wouldn't be given an unnecessary grade. We were all relieved our last test was behind us and looked forward to the last field trip.

Linda, June and I, along with the rest of the students, met in the court-yard before boarding the bus for our tour to Taxco, in the state of Guerrero. Taxco was known for its wealth of silver mines and for its silver jewelry and other items crafted from the metal. It was an hour's drive, and we would be having lunch there, with plenty of time allotted for shopping. I was beginning to feel like the *americanos ricos* had been pimped out during our visit. It seemed the expression, "spread the wealth" was taken literally, and without comprehending we were not all rich.

Nonetheless, it was a magnificent drive through the countryside to a picturesque city that huddled in the valley of the Atatzin Mountains. Narrow streets wound upward through the city, and in the center was the Santa Prisca Cathedral, built sometime in the seventeen hundreds. At the highest point of the city there was a statue of Jesus, known as "Cristo," who watched over the people. The chime of the church bells was a reminder that it was lunchtime.

Sightseeing aside, we savored a meal at a small upstairs café where we were seated on the balcony and could inhale the sights, sounds, and smells the town offered her tourists. We reluctantly pulled ourselves away from the café's relaxing atmosphere and the warmth of the mid-day sun to pursue the best bargains we could find. After much bickering over prices June and Linda bought necklaces for themselves and their daughters, and I purchased a pair of eye-catching earrings as a souvenir. We all made one last pit stop at *el baños* before we boarded the bus for the return trip.

A few of us fell asleep as the bus glided along the curvy road that led us back to Cuernavaca, but the younger students were pumped about cel-ebrating our last night at a local bar, The Lazy Lizard. June jostled me and asked, "Are you up for going out one more time before we leave tomor-row? Suzette said it's a local watering hole with a salsa band that also plays a few American hit songs. Sounds like fun."

I stretched my arms above my head and yawned. "Well, if someone would let me get in a catnap, I might be willing to go out tonight. I finished most of my packing on Tuesday, when our laundry was returned. What about you, Linda? Do you want to go out tonight?"

"Might as well follow the crowd. Besides, we can sleep a bit later in the morning since the bus doesn't pull out for the airport until ten. But I sure as hell want to be home before midnight. June told me about the two of you getting caught in the rain last night."

I admitted, "Not our finest hour. Ok, count me in, but let me get some rest."

I finished my nap in the solace of the bedroom I shared with June, who opted out of a nap in order to hand-wash her silk blouses and hang them to dry. I woke up refreshed and looking forward to our last night out. I took a second shower, did my hair and makeup before getting dressed for the group's final party in Cuernavaca. I pilfered through my clothes and chose a short white skirt and navy t-shirt that matched navy espadrilles. June skipped the shower but retouched her makeup and changed into a denim skirt and white blouse. We accentuated our outfits with the jewelry we'd bought in Taxco and decided we didn't look half bad for a couple of women wearing a few decades. June tousled her short, blonde hair, and we left on a cloud of excitement to meet friends at The Lazy Lizard, better known as "El Lagarto Perezoso."

Except for the neon signs in Spanish, as well as the band singing in Spanish, the bar could have been any bar anywhere: wooden floor, dim lighting, loud music, and alcohol. It wasn't a large tavern, but it was packed; Barbara and her friends monopolized the horseshoe bar. As my eyes adjusted to the semi-darkness, I saw a few people from our group on the dance floor gyrating to the rhythm of Santana's "Oye Como Va," an older hit song of the American rock group. Even in the muted lighting I was able to read the back of one the waiters t-shirts that boasted: "We won't make fun of your Spanish if you won't make fun of our English." I pointed out to Linda that someone had a sense of humor.

"Seems like a fair deal," said Linda, who was exuberant she survived the month in Mexico. She'd already contacted her boss to inform him that she wouldn't be returning as a bilingual employee. The band cranked things up and Linda joined June on the dance floor, who was boogying to the beat of Ricky Martin's "Livin' la Vida Loca." A waiter walked by balancing a tray of sizzlin' fajitas, and the tantalizing aroma of steak, peppers, and seasonings wafted in his wake.

I maneuvered my way over to the bar and ordered a wine cooler. Barbara laughed at my choice and teased, "What's the problem, little bit? Can't hold your liquor?"

"No, I can't. I rarely drink, so it's best that when I do, I stick to wine or wine coolers—and limit myself to two of either."

She laughed a boisterous chuckle and scanned the bar. "I know you're radar is off, or broke, but there's a good lookin' man checking you out from across the room."

"What? Where?"

"Easy, girl, you'll spook him. On second thought, he doesn't look like a man easily put off. He's been sitting at a table in the corner by himself, but he's on the move, headed in this direction. Don't turn around. My advice is to play it cool and act uninterested."

"That won't be a problem. I'm not interested."

"I wouldn't be too quick to toss him over. He's a handsome hunk, slick dresser, and oozes money. If I could get his ass drunk enough, I'd have a run at him myself. Just remember if he starts any shit with you, I'm right here."

Before I could answer, Mr. Suave sauntered over and wedged himself between Barbara and me. He was tall and very attractive, with blue eyes accentuated by his suntanned face. His thick dark hair was rippled with a few gray waves. He appeared to be somewhere in his late forties and was, indeed, a 'slick dresser'. His light tan, tailored slacks and white silk shirt showcased his trim physique. Although he carried an accent, his English was impeccable. "Allow me to introduce myself. My name is Miguel Ángel, and I've been admiring you since your arrival. It's a shame your beautiful legs are not on the dance floor so that every man in the bar can appreciate them." He extended a bended arm. "Shall we…I'm sorry, I don't yet know your name."

I may not have dated in almost thirty years, but I recognized a player when I saw one. "It's Sheila, and thanks for the offer to dance, but no thanks. I'm here with friends, not to pick up a man."

He tilted his head and gave me a dazzling smile. "Aah, you are from the South in America. I adore your southern drawl, the way your words drip slowly, like honey, from your supple lips." His laugh was warm and sincere. With a bit of mischief he chided, "I do not wish to whisk you away to a deserted island. I want only to have a dance. ¿Sí?"

Don Juan's cologne was intoxicating, and his slow, sexy smile was disarming. I leaned over the bar to look at Barbara, who shooed me in the direction of the dance floor. The handsome stranger guided me through the crowd with a hand that rested on the small of my back and attempted to pull me closer as we stood facing each other. I resisted his advance and maintained a gap between us as we chatted about nothing. When the music stopped he took my hand and escorted me to his corner table. "It's too noisy to talk on the dance floor, and I want to know more about you. How is it that you are here, in Cuernavaca? I detected a southern brogue. From which American state are you?"

"Georgia. I, along with my classmates, am here as a student from the University of West Georgia in order to complete the Spanish requirement I need to graduate in August. Tonight is my last night in your beautiful city. Tomorrow our group leaves for Cancun before returning to the United States."

"No! It cannot be that we have only just met, and you are leaving already." He scooped up my hands from the table and kissed the palms of both with soft, sensuous lips. His penetrating blue eyes were filled with desire. "Stay. Stay in my country, and I will show you a Mexico the tourists never see. We will go to the mountains and visit secluded beaches and dance under the stars. Please stay here with me." He noticed the absence of a ring and commented, "You are a single woman?"

From the warmth of his touch and the lust in his eyes, I didn't think dancing under the stars was what Miguel had in mind. I reclaimed my hands and planted them securely in my lap before I answered, "Yes, I'm single. As for staying in Mexico, that's out of the question. I have to return home, to my family and to my job responsibilities." There was no need to mention that cancer had made a widow of me almost a year ago because it was irrelevant. We were nothing more than two ships passing in the night.

"As you have no husband waiting for your return, it is a simple matter to resolve." He held his hand to his ear, pretending to hold a telephone. "You call your family and your place of employment and tell them you have been delayed in Mexico and will be home in another week or two." He shrugged nonchalantly, as if there was nothing else to discuss.

I changed the subject. "Tell me about yourself. Are you married? Do you have children? Where did you grow up? What is your occupation?"

"All right. Though I wear no wedding ring, I have been married for ten years, and I have an eight-year-old son. He and his mother left last week to visit her family in France for a month, until school opens in September. I grew up in Venezuela, born to a mother who was a native in my country and to a European father. I moved to France as a young man and met my future wife there. After my son was born, I relocated our family to Mexico because I had the opportunity to expand my import business by opening souvenir shops for tourists. Now that you know more about me, will you consider extending your stay?"

The man had revealed that he was married and had a child, although his wife and son were out of the country, tucked far away somewhere in France. "I'm sorry, but even if I were willing to postpone travel arrangements and was interested in a brief affair, you have a wife. Or do you believe that out of sight means out of mind? Otherwise, you would be wearing a ring."

"You Americans are so hung-up on marital status. Latin Americans have a more casual attitude toward 'faithfulness', especially men. I have never worn a wedding band, and yet I have been faithful to my wife for almost five years. She forgave me the two previous dalliances as they were nothing more than that. Does a gold band on a man's finger guarantee his fidelity in your country?"

I thought about my friend Joann* and how she'd confided in me that her husband of twenty-six years had an affair with a coworker. From the outside looking in, she and her husband had the perfect marriage: great jobs, three healthy children, and a large home in a prestigious neighborhood. Like Barry and me, they'd married as high school sweethearts and seemed to have it all, but the façade was an illusion, there house one of cards. A few days after Barry's death, Joann stopped in to check on me and told me about her husband's betrayal. Divorce was complicated and messy, so they'd sought counseling to work through Keith's* unfaithfulness. Apparently, mine was not the only fairy tale without a happily-ever-after ending.

Miguel tapped my shoulder. "Are you so bored that you didn't hear my question?

"No, I heard you. You're right in that a wedding ring doesn't insure vows won't be broken." I pushed my chair away from the table. "If you'll excuse me, I need to locate el baño."

He stood when I left the table and pointed me in the direction of the ladies' room. When I exited the facilities, Barbara motioned me over to the bar. "So what does James Bond have on his mind?"

"As you pointed out my radar is really rusty, but I think he wants to screw my eyes out."

She took a long drag off her cigarette, flicked the ashes into her empty beer bottle, and looked over her shoulder to get another gander at the man who waited for my return. She tilted her head and blew several smoke rings. "You're a bright girl, Sheila. I bet you could learn to read Braille in a few short weeks."

"Barbara! I'm not about to climb in bed with a man I just met. Trust me when I tell you that I'm not going to be any man's one-night stand. Although, he did ask me to postpone my trip home and spend the next week or two with him sightseeing."

"'Sightseeing'? Is that what they call it here? You don't have to speak

Spanish to see 'horny' written all over his face. I can't think of a better time to test the waters. Stay in Mexico, have a fling, and then go home. It's not like you're gonna bump into each other at Kroger."

I sat shaking my head at her blasé attitude. "That's not gonna happen, Barbara. Not only would my family call the CIA if I'm not on the Atlanta flight, he's a married man. His wife and son are in France."

"She's an ocean away. Besides, it apparently doesn't make a difference to him."

"Maybe not, but it makes a difference to me."

Miguel approached and casually inserted himself into our conversation as he began to methodically kiss each of my fingertips. "Will you extend you visit and be my guest?"

Much to Barbara's annoyance I answered, "Sorry, but no. I'll be leaving in the morning, as scheduled, for Cancun. I'm meeting two of my girlfriends there, and they'll be frantic if I don't show up."

He let out a disappointed sigh but accepted my decision. "Very well. But please let me drive you home tonight." He retrieved his wallet to settle the tab and handed me his business card. "If you should change your mind…"

Before I could say anything June was standing next to me and propped her elbow on my shoulder. "Did I hear somebody offer us a ride home?" She gave Miguel the once over and smiled. "You're certainly good-lookin' enough, but Sheila and I have a pact. If you're taking her home, you'll have me taggin' along. I think I can accept your offer for the two of us. Right, Sheila?"

Miguel's eyes meandered over me from head to toe, and I avoided his scrutiny by tucking the card in my bag and turned my attention to June. "Yes, June, that's right. Then again, the offer may not be for two. If not, we can catch a cab."

His reluctance was replaced with a smile. "I will be delighted to drive both you and your friend home. Do you know the address?"

I'd memorized the address by then. The three of us left the bar, and he led us to the parking deck across the street where he opened the door of a silver Mercedes and said with a wink, "I trust your ride will be more comfortable than a taxi."

I sat down in the passenger's seat where luxurious leather caressed me with softness. June climbed in the backseat and mumbled, "Nice ride."

Her comment was lost as Miguel hurried around to the driver's side and slid under the wheel. We rode in silence as none of us seemed to have anything to say. Miguel adjusted the radio, and I recognized Selena's voice singing "No Me Queda Mas" and began to hum the tune, even though I didn't understand all of the words. His voice intruded. "Do you like Latin music?"

I composed my response in Spanish. "No entiendo las letras, pero la música es muy bonito."

"Muy bien. It is not necessary to fully understand the lyrics to appreciate the beauty of the music. She is singing about a lover who has abandoned her for another, of love lost. It is a poignant tale of heartbreak."

I was all too familiar with the heartbreak of love lost but said nothing as the car turned onto our street. I was about to thank Miguel for his kindness in delivering us safely home, but he'd already put the car in park and held the door open for me. June let herself out and headed to the gate; she waited patiently on the porch. I slung my bag over my shoulder and could feel the weight of approaching rain, as well as the warmth of Miguel's arm around my shoulders. I'd planned to shake the good-looking stranger's hand and tell him that it was nice to have met him, but his kiss caught me by surprise as his lips landed lightly on mine.

He reminded me, "You have my card, and nothing would please me more than to hear from you in the morning, after you've had a chance to sleep on my proposal. Promise me that you will consider the proposition."

I pulled myself from his arms. "There's no reason for me to lead you on, Miguel. I won't be contacting you, but it was nice to meet you. Thank you again for the ride home."

With a tinge of regret, he stroked my chin. "The city of Cuernavaca will weep rivers of tears over the loss of your beauty."

Oh, he was good, a real Casanova. I was grateful the night sky hid the warm blush that colored my cheeks. Miguel was handsome and debonair and was offering me a romantic escapade, but it was clear that the need to move on with my life came with limitations. With a final wave goodbye I went inside and wondered why our paths had crossed. I climbed in bed and accepted that our meeting was nothing more than a chance encounter to be forgotten.

Morning came and brought with it a flurry of activity—last-minute packing, multiple room scans, and goodbye hugs passed around the porch. I'd called Pat collect to remind her that I was leaving for Cancun and would be home on Tuesday afternoon. She said it was about damn time and confirmed that Kim would pick me up at the airport. We gave Marta our home addresses and telephone numbers because we all promised to stay in touch, but we each knew we wouldn't. June and I had fallen in love with our host family and the city itself. We decided that one day we would go back and stay in one of the city's luxury hotels, with plans to visit Marta and her family. But we both knew we wouldn't, just as we knew we wouldn't continue our daily walks together once we returned home to our separate lives.

My days in Mexico were peaceful and structured: class each morning, with exams and field trips on Fridays and Saturdays, afternoon *siestas*, study sessions, occasional nights on the town, and long walks through a beautiful city. Several people along our route recognized June and me and addressed us by name. We took time to stop and speak to them, and they were delighted to assist us with our Spanish. We were rarely home for supper because we'd stumbled upon several eateries along our walks, both Mexican and American. Our last stop was always at the corner store where a carton of ice cream or some other sweet was purchased for Nieve, who waited on the veranda like an excited child. I would miss them all and waved from the window.

The bus lunged forward, and I shifted in my seat to find a more relaxing position. The driver followed signs that pointed us in the direction of the airport in Mexico City where we would embark for Cancun. I was pleasantly surprised by how many more of the billboards I was able to read than I had when I'd arrived a few weeks ago. My hiatus in Cuernavaca had ended, but I would hold in my heart the experiences and the people I'd met. I wiped away tears and realized I was nostalgic for a time in my life that was already a memory. I thought about a song from the sixties by the Byrds, adapted from the Book of Ecclesiastes: "To everything there is a season...a time to weep, and a time to laugh; a time to mourn, and a time to dance."

*Name changed

Chapter Six

"Sheee-la, Sheee-la, Sheee-la"

The flight was uneventful, and our group gathered our luggage, exited the air conditioned airport, and strode into a tropical breeze and glaring sunshine. There was a passenger van waiting to take everyone to the hotel, everyone except me. Professor Alonso had agreed to allow me to join friends Cyndie and Martha at the Hyatt Regency where the three of us would share an ocean-front room at the ritzy resort. His stipulation was that I couldn't change my flight and that I would reconnect with my party at the airport for the return trip to Atlanta. Fair enough, especially given that the other students would be staying at a modest hotel located further down the beach, away from the more popular restaurants and clubs.

June gave me a hug. "I'll see you at the airport, unless our paths cross before then. Have a good time with your friends and be careful."

"Thanks, June. I hope y'all have a wonderful time. And remember to count your pesos twice." She laughed and gave me the thumbs up as she hurried to find a seat on the van.

I hauled my luggage along the sidewalk to where a line of taxis waited for fares, hailed the first one, and gave him the address. He hoisted my suitcases into the trunk and proceeded to speed through traffic, seemingly oblivious to caution lights and pedestrians. My first few taxi rides in Cuernavaca had scared the hell out of me, but I'd gotten used to impatient, reckless driving and horn blowing. In less than fifteen minutes the driver wheeled into the circular drive of the Hyatt and slammed on his brakes. I gave him the correct change, plus a tip, and climbed out of the cab. I walked to the back of the car to find the doorman waiting to assist me with my bags. He barely had time to unload the luggage before the cabby screeched into the steady flow of traffic. The porter secured my suitcases onto a trolley and escorted me to the registration desk where I was greeted with "¡Buenas tardes! ¿Cómo puedo ayudarte?"

I wiped sweaty hair from my face and asked, "¿Habla usted inglés, Señor?"

His smile broadened with pride and he replied in a heavy accent, "Sí, si, claro. Welcome to our resort. How can I help you, señora?"

"It's señorita." His smile grew wider until he was all teeth, and he resembled a hungry alligator ready to devour me. Latin men were certainly bold. I continued, "I'm meeting friends here who should have arrived this morning." I gave him their names and asked him to call the room, hoping they weren't on the beach soaking up the magnificent day. As luck would have it, they were in the room unpacking when they got the message that "Señorita Sheee-la" was waiting for them in the lobby. I sat in an oversized chair, away from the busy desk, and thought about Cyndie and Martha.

I couldn't imagine the two of them deciding to go to Cancun together. Like everybody else in Bremen, they knew each other by name, but they weren't friends and didn't have anything in common. Martha and I were connected by our family's DNA and could recall a few mutual memories. Life had not always been kind to Martha, but she was a survivor and an eternal optimist. She'd graduated and married by the time Cyndie and I entered our first year of high school, and the two of them didn't have any shared experiences. No doubt they'd taken books to occupy their time on the plane. Nonetheless, I was sure the three of us would get along well and have fun relaxing on the beach. The elevator doors opened, and I was jolted from my reverie by joyful squeals of "Sheee-la!"

I stood to welcome their hugs and didn't realize how much I'd missed home until I saw old friends. Curious about their flight I asked, "How was your trip? Did you spend the entire flight reading or did you become acquainted with each other?"

They both began to jabber like those Disney cartoon chipmunks Chip 'n' Dale who often spoke simultaneously, talking about everything and nothing. The two of them laughed together and Cyndie proceeded to tell me how they'd intended to read, but once they began talking, neither of them bothered to open a book. I was genuinely happy that two of my friends had fallen into a new friendship. The three of us carted my luggage to the elevator for the ride to the fourth floor, but a bellhop intervened.

Cyndie said, "We were just about to put on our bikinis and go down to the pool for a few hours before it's time to get ready to go out. Let's get you upstairs so we can all change."

I answered, "Spending the afternoon by the pool with both of you sounds great. You'll have to catch me up on what's been going on at home. I've had a good time and made several new friends, but I do miss my family. What time is your flight on Tuesday?"

Martha replied, "Four o'clock. What time is yours?"

"Eleven o'clock. I would love to switch flights and fly back with y'all, but I don't want to push my luck. My professor was reluctant to let me stay here instead of with the rest of our group, but I promised not to miss my flight."

Martha was impatient to make the most of our brief trip. "Then let's hit the deck! We don't want to miss another minute of this gorgeous day."

"I agree," said Cyndie. "You can unpack later, Sheila."

After depositing my bags and changing into swimsuits, the three of us tossed hats, sunglasses, and Coppertone into a beach bag. We found lounge chairs near the pool and grabbed oversized towels from a huge stack provided for guests. My friends had had lunch in the hotel's café, but I was starving and motioned for a pool waiter who was standing near the bar. He promptly appeared at my side and handed me a menu. "May I help you?"

"Yes, please. I'd like water with lemon. When I've had a chance to look over the menu, I'll order something to eat."

Cyndie cautioned, "Don't order a big meal. We plan to eat out in a few hours, and then hit one of the clubs. Martha and I thought we would have a good time at Señor Frogs. We passed it on the taxi ride from the airport, and I don't think it's very far from here."

Martha added, "There's a Hardrock Café located across the street and down a block." She turned to me. "I thought you might like a good old-fashioned cheeseburger for a change."

"Sounds delicious. I'll just order nachos and cheese or something else from the appetizer offerings to tide me over. Do either of you want anything?"

They nodded in the negative, and I gave the waiter my order. When he returned with a tray, I noted his name tag and thanked José before signing the ticket. Martha and Cyndie acknowledged José with "Hola."

Jose returned the greeting, "Hola, senoritas. ¿Cómo te llamas?"

I laughed and replied to his inquiry, "Lo siento, pero mis amigos no hablan español."

Martha was quick to ask, "What did you say to him? What was he asking about us?"

"Because you both greeted him with hello in Spanish, he mistakenly thinks you speak Spanish and asked what your names are. I was merely telling him that you don't speak Spanish."

José read my signature and asked, "What is your name, señorita? My English lacks many pronunciations of our guests' names."

"It's Sheila."

He looked as if he were mulling over the enunciation before he spoke. "Sheee-la is a delightful name!"

I didn't bother to correct the drawn out vowel and simply said, "Gracias."

The friendly waiter motioned to Cyndie and Martha and asked, "What is your name?"

Cyndie smiled and said, "Sheee-la."

Martha answered, "Sheee-la."

The waiter was dumbfounded and held up three fingers. "Tres Sheee-las?"

My friends were having too much fun for me to amend their names for the confused waiter, so I went along with them. "Yes, three Sheee-las."

José shook his head in amusement as he left to wait on another sun-bather soaking up the rays. After my midday snack I relocated to the cover of the cabana and must've dozed off. Cyndie roused me to wake up. "Hey, are you okay?"

I propped myself up on an elbow and drowsily mumbled, "I'm fine. It's siesta time in Mexico, and I've adopted an afternoon nap."

Martha snapped her fingers. "Well wake your ass up. It's after five, and we all need to shower before going out tonight. Round up your stuff and let's go back to the room."

The walk through the lobby was comical. Several staff members addressed us with smiles and "Buenas tardes, Sheee-la, Sheee-la, Sheee-la."

We laughed in the confinement of the elevator as we realized we were each known as "Sheee-la." The waiter didn't waste any time spreading the word. I good-naturedly scolded my friends, "We've evidently all been la-beled 'Sheee-la' by everybody who works here. Why in the world did y'all give him my name when he asked for yours?"

Cyndie snickered. "Because we really like how he pronounced 'Sheila'."

Silly laughter carried us down the hallway until we were welcomed by a cool, clean, and tastefully decorated room that I didn't have time to appre-ciate it when I arrived. The large room boasted two queen beds and a sofa bed that rested next to sliding glass doors that opened onto a balcony where a white wrought-iron table and three chairs cushioned in bright green sat invitingly. I couldn't resist the invitation and marveled at the beauty of the Caribbean. The crystal colors ranged from pale turquoise to a deep sapphire and were accentuated by the white crest of breaking waves. Umbrellas in an array of vivid hues and patterns dotted the beach, and the hint of a breeze whispered over blinding, white-hot sand. Children scurried like sand crabs to run into the refreshing surf. I deeply inhaled the salty waft and realized that I was completely content and yet—

My reflective contentment was intruded upon by Martha's frustrated shriek. "There's not one damn washcloth to be found. Not a single one. Do you think housekeeping forgot to leave them?" she called across the room to me.

I left the solitude of the balcony and entered a room that echoed the soothing cerulean colors of the sea. "No, Martha, housekeeping didn't forget. Toallitas are not commonly used in Mexico, but I'm sure if you call the front desk, they'll send us a few."

"Not used here? Then how am I supposed to wash my ass without a, what did you say, toallita? Sounds like something you'd eat instead of bathe with."

I ignored her comment about eating washcloths. "Yes, toallita. Call the front desk while I unpack and decide what to wear tonight."

Cyndie instructed Martha to ask for a bunch of washcloths to get us through the next few days. I overheard Martha on the phone, repeating her request. In exasperation, she handed me the receiver. "I don't speak Spanish and can't understand a word that man is saying, and I don't think he's even trying to understand me. Can you please tell him to send up some washcloths so I can take a shower?"

I rolled my eyes and hoped my Spanish would be sufficient. "Por favor envíe varias toallas a la habitación cuatro dieciocho. Gracias."

I may have mispronounced a word here or there because the man on the other end of the line replied in English, "Of course, at once. Do you think twelve washcloths for the three Sheee-las will be sufficient during your stay?"

I covered the mouthpiece and glared at Martha. "The man is speaking English! What part did you not comprehend?" She shrugged, and I explained to the desk clerk that the washcloths were for the duration of our visit and thanked him for his tolerance of the three Americans.

Martha jumped in the shower and told me to toss her in a washcloth when they showed up. I was sorting toiletries when Cyndie answered a knock on the door and found a woman from housekeeping standing on the other side with a mound of washcloths. The woman was clearly put out that three women should expect to be pampered and sarcastically mumbled something to that effect in Spanish. She thanked the maid and gave her some money that promptly erased her irritation. Cyndie interrupted Martha's shower to hand her a washcloth before she spoke to me. "Do you think that woman was mad at us because we expect to bathe with a washcloth? I'm pretty sure she made some kind of smartass remark about spoiled Americans, but my tip put a smile on her face."

"I don't care what she thinks of us or if she was inconvenienced. The request for washcloths wasn't unreasonable. By the way, exactly how much of a tip did you give her?"

"I don't really know since I don't understand the money exchange. Martha and I cashed traveler's checks at the airport for Mexican currency, two hundred dollars each."

"You and Martha have got to get a handle on how much you're spending. You can't throw money around like a Rockefeller, or you'll be broke before you know it and wonder what the hell happened to your cash. From now on don't pay for anything or handout tips without checking with me. Please." Lord, it was going to be like monitoring June, times two.

It was only a block to the restaurant and the sun had not yet set, so we walked the short distance—much to the delight of the men who drove by in cars or on bicycles. I was dressed in fuchsia and turquoise silky shorts and a matching hibiscus patterned shirt and strappy sandals, while Martha and Cyndie opted to wear brightly-colored sundresses. There were whistles and cat calls of *mujeres calientes*, or as I told my girlfriends "hot women." A few of the men were brazen enough to slow their vehicles and drive along beside us in an attempt to attract our attention. I ignored them all, but Cyndie and Martha smiled and waved. Martha elbowed me and asked, "What gives with these men? They're giving us all the once-over, but I get the impression that it's you they want to meet."

"Don't be ridiculous. They'd be happy to pick up any one of us, which is going to happen if y'all don't disregard them. C'mon. I see the Hard Rock sign from here."

Martha looked over her shoulder and watched as a good-looking young man on a bicycle rode past the others and stopped in front of me. He smiled and did his best to charm me, but I let him know I wasn't interested and to move on.

"See what I mean, Sheila? That man didn't notice either Cyndie or me. They're all like moths drawn to a flame, and you're the flame. What gives?"

I put my hands on my hips and brushed my hair away from my face. "Okay, here's the deal. While I'm not any more attractive than either of you, you're both brunettes. What my roommate and I figured out is that many of men here prefer fair-haired women. Don't ask me why because I don't know, but June, who is also a blonde, and I were accosted on numerous occasions but were careful not to engage or encourage unwanted attention."

Cyndie said, "I've considered going blonde to find out if blondes really do have more fun, you know, like the Clairol ad from the sixties. But then again, I'm having a good time already!"

Martha was like a dog with a bone. "Or the ad that assures women that 'gentlemen prefer blondes'. I tell you one damn thing. The next time I come to Mexico I'll be wearing a Dolly Parton wig. To hell with being blown off by all these men just because I'm a brunette."

"Martha, you're a married woman. Did you really come to Cancun to have an affair?"

"No, and hell no, but that doesn't mean I wouldn't appreciate the attention you're getting."

"Stop whining. You've always gotten more than your share of male adoration." I held the door open, and we signed in for a table. We waited at the bar, and I hummed along and tapped my fingers in rhythm to *la música*.

Cyndie was lost in the party-like atmosphere that permeated Cancun. Martha pulled out a stool, took a step back, and stared at me. "There's something different about you. You're absolutely radiant."

"It's probably due to all the time I've spent in the sun. June and I walked almost every afternoon, and we spent a weekend in Acapulco with a couple of other women, students who became friends."

"No, it's not your suntan. You're glowing from within. There's definitely a difference, but I can't quite put my finger on it." She ordered a glass of wine and continued to study me. Her eyes opened wide and she said, "You're happy! That's what's changed. The depression that threatened to suffocate you has vanished." She hopped off the barstool and hugged me. "I don't know what happened here in Mexico but whatever it was I'm relieved to see you've lived through losing your husband. We all had our doubts as to whether you would make it out of the dark hole you'd crawled into."

Cyndie leaned over and asked, "What's going on? What are y'all celebrating?'

Martha beamed. "Look at Sheila, really look at her, and you'll see she's changed."

"Now that you mention it, I did notice the way she interacted with the waiter at the pool and how she laughed with us about giving him her name as ours. She almost seems like her old self, a happier version of the woman she left in Georgia."

I smiled at my friends. "It's true that I've changed from the sad, grief-stricken person I was, which can be attributed to time and prayers. And what I was reminded of in Mexico is that life is a gift, to be appreciated and lived to the fullest every day, never to be taken for granted. Despite sometimes living in cruel circumstances beyond their control, the people here, for the most part, are happy and many have hope that tomorrow will be better. That positive outlook and accepting that sometimes life is just not fair has helped me over the hurdle."

Martha agreed. "Hmmm, it's true that the people I've met here are always smiling. This experience has been good for you, and it's high time you get on with your life."

We scooted down two stools to accommodate a young couple, and I continued, "I need to do more than just breathe and put one foot in front of the other. I've had to resign myself to the fact that he died, and I didn't—something Marta tried to point out when I was a guest in her home." I omitted Marta's attempt at matchmaking. "I will love Barry for the rest of my life because I don't know how not to love him. Even so, I can't rewrite the ending to our love story, so it's time I learn to be me without him, without us. It's time to let him go." For all my bravado, I didn't realize those words would prove to be easier said than done.

Her eyes glistened with tears as Cyndie reached to embrace me. "Oh, Sheila, we would never think you could stop loving Barry, and neither would anyone else."

Cyndie was living her own love story, although the road that brought her and her husband together had been a long and twisty path. While I'd married my high school sweetheart as a teenager and remained in my hometown, Cyndie's journey led her out of Bremen to Auburn—into a good university and a bad marriage. After a messy divorce she packed up her baby daughter and returned home where she eventually reconnected with Larry, her first and only love.

Thoughts of the lovebirds were interrupted when I heard my name called, signaling our table was ready. "Enough about me and the emotional roller coaster I've been riding. We're here to have fun, not to dwell on the past. Let's eat and then find our way to Señor Frogs."

The subject was changed, and we chatted and laughed our way through the meal. By the time we found ourselves outside, the sun had slipped beyond the horizon. We didn't realize our destination was only a few blocks away, so Martha found a taxi that whisked us to the trendy bar where music blared its way onto the sidewalk. I cautioned my friends not to start a tab and to pay for each drink when it was ordered. Cyndie said, "Not a problem for me. I'm sticking to bottled water."

Martha and I decided to have no more than one drink as she reminded me, "Don't forget, Sheila, we plan to take a bus over to Playa del Carmen in the morning for a day trip to do some shopping. I want to buy a few mementos." She winked. "And maybe jewelry from my husband."

"I remember. Cyndie got the brochure in the lobby, and I said I'd go with y'all. Don't worry about me having a hangover because I'm not a lush, but I should be able to handle one margarita without dire consequences."

I was wrong. When Martha and I ordered our "one drink," the waiter offered a souvenir glass for only a dollar more. Martha declined, but I figured I wouldn't be in Cancun again and ordered the larger drink that arrived in a tall, curvy glass with the club's logo on the front. The bartender was generous with the alcohol, and it wasn't long before I was dancing the Macarena with a bunch of strangers on a crowded dancefloor. The Latino dance was a rhythmic pattern of five strokes that was easy to follow. The song of the same name and dance were popular everywhere, including America.

I'm pretty sure we all had a good time at Señor Frogs, but some of the night was a little foggy. I heard one of the waiters tell a woman "no bailes en la mesa," but I don't think I was the one dancing on the table. Wrong again. It was close to midnight when Martha and Cyndie helped me out of the club into the fresh night air. It was clear that the walk back to our hotel would do me some good. They sang Cyndi Lauper's old hit "Girls Just Want to Have Fun," and I envied them because I couldn't even remember the lyrics. I don't even think I could have found my ass with both hands. We stumbled along the sidewalk, and the ocean breeze did slightly help clear my head.

There was a man on a bicycle with a cooler strapped on the back fender calling out, "¡Tamales! ¡Tamales! Tamales calientes para la venta. Solo dos dolares."

Cyndie turned to Martha and said, "Do you think that man is selling tamales? I could eat something. I'm sure it's too late for room service, and the hotel café is closed at this late hour. We should have enough cash if we can figure out how much they cost."

"They can't be expensive. I know 'dos' is two so I'm guessing a couple of dollars. Sheila, do you want a tamale?"

The very thought of anything to eat gagged me and sent me hurling my supper onto the grass. I may have been drunker than Cooter Brown, but I had enough sense not to let my friends buy anything edible from a street vendor in Mexico. I wiped my face with a tissue I pulled from my pocket and warned, "No! Don't buy tamales from a cart on the street. Trust me on this. I noticed a vending machine in the lobby, and the night clerk can give you change. Please get me back to our room before I barf on the side of the road again."

"Okay, okay. We're almost there."

Food was forgotten as they helped me to the bathroom barely before the next eruption of nausea. Cyndie held my hair out of my face, and Martha rinsed a cloth in cold water to wash my face. Together they tugged me into my gown and tucked me in bed. I must've passed out because that's the last thing I remembered.

Morning brought sunshine and coffee—and a helluva hangover. I felt like I'd been run over by a Mack truck, and my mouth was as dry as cotton. I lay still and watched sunlight dance around the ceiling fan. I regretted my choice of a *muy grande* margarita and wondered why anybody would get hammered on a regular basis when the aftermath of alcohol was so awful. I could hear the shower running but had no idea what time it was or how long I'd slept.

Cyndie was flitting around the room like a butterfly when I stirred. "Good morning, Sheee-la. Rough night? Martha and I had breakfast in the café so you could sleep in, but I ordered coffee and toast from room service. Better get a move on. It's after ten, and according to the schedule, the next bus leaves in less than hour for Playa del Carmen. You still have to shower and put on your makeup. I'll find something for you to wear. Do you want shorts or a sundress? We're wearing shorts and comfortable sandals."

I pulled the covers over my head to block out the sunshine and her sunny disposition, but she yanked them right off the bed as I protested, "I don't think I'm up to the trip. Maybe we can postpone it until tomorrow and hang out around here today."

"Suit yourself, but we're going. I showered first thing this morning, and I'm dressed and ready to roll. Martha should be ready in about half an hour, but I can close the curtains and let you sleep through this dazzling day if that's what you want. Although it would be a shame for you to miss the outing. The pictures in the brochure are charming."

I stuffed my head under the pillow and wanted nothing more than to sleep the day away in the peace and quiet of a cool, darkened room. But if I let my friends, the same friends who took care of me last night, strike out on their own, I might as well throw them to the sharks. They didn't know any Spanish beyond *hola* and *gracias*, nor did they have a clue how much cash they had in Mexican currency or how much they were paying for anything. I slid the pillow off my head and slowly sat up. A hammer was pounding from somewhere inside my head, and rubber legs dangled from the side of the bed. "I'm up, Cyndie. I'll get in the shower as soon as Martha is out of the bathroom. Could you please pour me a cup of coffee, and do you have any ibuprofen?"

I swallowed the ibuprofen she fished from her bag and finished the cup of much needed caffeine. Martha exited the bathroom and looked me over. "Honey, if you can't hold your liquor you should stay away from the hard stuff, especially tequila." She towel dried her hair and offered another tidbit of advice as she refilled my coffee cup. "You'll need to drink lots of water today. Now get your ass in gear, and I'll find a pair of shorts and a t-shirt for you."

"Yes ma'am." I gulped down the coffee, climbed in the shower, and let the warm spray rinse away the remnants of poor judgment. I couldn't disappoint my friends and hurried to make myself presentable for the forty-five minute bus ride to the beach in Carmen. Hats, bags, and cameras in tow, the three of us painted a pretty picture of exactly what we were: American tourists…or suckers, depending upon one's perspective.

The short taxi ride dropped us off at the bus station where several bus lines competed for passengers. I spotted one that boasted air conditioning and pointed Cyndie and Martha in that direction. I dragged my weary ass aboard, paid the fare, and motioned for my friends to do the same. We found three seats together and proceeded to discuss plans. Martha said, "I definitely want to do some shopping, especially in a jewelry store. A friend of mine was here last year, and she bought a stunning diamond necklace for about half of what it would have cost her at home."

I put in my two cents worth, based on my Taxco experience. "I'm sure there are several jewelers vying for American dollars. However, you should be careful that what you buy is the real deal. Most of the retailers are honest, but I'd hate for you to get back to town and have the jewelry appraised only to find out that you were burned a new ass. At the very least, I would use a credit card so you can dispute the charges if you pay for something that turns out to be inferior."

Cyndie added, "I don't plan to buy jewelry unless I find something really pretty, but I'd like to browse the shops for souvenirs."

I squinted at my watch. "Before we spend the day shopping, I want to eat lunch. The dry toast I choked down wasn't much of a breakfast, and I'm starving."

Martha opened her wallet and replied, "I hope I have enough money to pay for lunch, or we'll have to eat at a restaurant that accepts credit cards."

"I know what you mean," added Cyndie. "The pamphlet said the bus ride was inexpensive, but I'm broke now that I paid for the ticket."

I did a few calculations if my head, beginning with the sum they'd each had in cash at the Hard Rock last night after we settled the check. "There's no way y'all can be broke. Other than two bottles of water and a margarita, you haven't been anywhere to spend that much money."

Cyndie said, "You're right. We even charged breakfast to the room so we would have more cash to spend at the beach. The bus driver took the rest of my money."

Martha vouched for Cyndie. "Mine, too."

I'd paid approximately six dollars so was confused. "How much did the driver charge you for a one-way ticket?"

They were also confused. Cyndie was the first to answer, "We don't know. We pulled all the money we had, including coins, from our wallets and held it out to the driver. He smiled and raked all of it into the money bag and didn't offer us any change."

"That scamming sonofabitch." I was livid as I marched down the aisle to where the driver sat bouncing happily along the road, grinnin' like a possum. In my best, and angriest, Spanish I let him know that if he didn't return my friends' money to them immediately, I would report him to the police the minute we arrived at the bus station. I don't know how much of what I said was accurate, but he understood "policía" and "tiempo en prisión." He slowed the bus, eased it to the side of the road, and reached under his seat to retrieve the money bag. He handed me some cash, which I counted. "¡Todo esto ahora!"

The grin was replaced with a scowl when I again demanded, "All of the money, now!" He was unmistakably disappointed at having been caught, but he dished out the rest of Cyndie and Martha's money. I returned to my seat and divided the money, to the best of my computations, between the two of them and admonished, "We need to establish some ground rules before we begin this shopping trip. If you're interested in an item and want to know the cost, then you will ask, '¿Cuánto cuesta?'

I made them repeat the phrase before I went on with the lesson. "NEVER pay the first price you're quoted. Instead, reply 'es muy caro' and walk away. You've told the salesperson that the item is too expensive, and he will undoubtedly drop the price. You have to keep us the charade until he makes his very final offer, which will be 'Oferta final'. If you want to make the purchase after negotiating over the price, then pay what should be a fair price. It's a bargaining game played by the merchants."

Martha considered my recommendation. "Maybe it would be better for you to stay with us while we're spending money."

Cyndie readily agreed, and I continued, "Then remember what I told you about not spending any money unless you talk with me first."

I was glad we'd had that discussion before the bus pulled into the station. As we walked off the bus, I took a minute to give the driver a scathing, go-to-hell look and couldn't resist telling him, "Bésame el trasero."

Martha asked, "What did you say to him?"

"I told the thief who took advantage of my friends to kiss my ass."

Cyndie was worried. "Oh no, Sheila. How are we going to get back to Cancun if he refuses to let us board?'

I sighed with relief that I hadn't let them make the trip without me. "Cyndie, do you see all of these buses waiting for passengers? We'll take another bus when we leave. In the meantime, let's find a good restaurant and enjoy the rest of the day."

Taxis lined the curb like ravenous cats waiting to pounce. I hailed a cab, and we slid across the back seat for the ride to the beachside village. The driver recommended a sidewalk café for lunch, and I asked him to drop us off at that location. He most likely got a kickback from a family member. Nonetheless, the food was delicious. The relaxing ambiance created by soft music and ocean breezes served as the perfect setting. Cyndie and Martha ate everything on their loaded plates and were tempted to unbutton their shorts. They both agreed the meal was the best Mexican food either of them had ever had anywhere. They pushed back from the table with groans of satisfaction as we paid our checks.

I suggested a walk along the cobbled streets to work off some of the calories we'd consumed, and we perused several shops along the sidewalk. I stopped in my tracks when I saw a large souvenir store with a sign I recognized. It was the same logo on the card Miguel had given me a few nights ago. I noted the pair of azure angel wings with the letter "A" in the center and the words "Miguel Ángel" written below in calligraphy.

I casually said to my friends, "Hey, y'all, I'm gonna browse around in that store across the street, the coral one on the corner. Why don't you both locate a jewelry store so Martha can find a token of her trip?"

"Nothing doing," said Cyndie. "Given the look on your face, it may be an interesting pit stop."

"She's right. What's wrong with you?"

"Nothing, really." I hesitated but spilled the beans. "I met the man, on my last night in Cuernavaca, who may own that store. I'm gonna stroll over and ask someone if Miguel Ángel is the same person who sauntered up to me at the bar and introduced himself."

Cyndie spoke for both of them. "We're in!"

We waited for a break in traffic that clogged the streets of the small resort town before one of the drivers motioned for us to cross in front of him and Martha remarked, "It's that blonde hair of yours."

"Give it a rest, Martha."

We entered the store and were immediately greeted by a sales clerk. "¡Buenas tardes! ¿Como puedo ayudarte?"

I smiled and requested that he speak in English, if possible. "Si es posible por favor habla ingles."

"Certainly. How may I assist three such beautiful Americans?" He made a sweeping gesture and continued, "We have many fine items for you to purchase today."

I removed a business card from my purse and handed it to the zealous salesman. "Is this person the owner of this shop?"

He examined the card. "Sí, sí. Es la misma persona Señor Ángel posee muchos, muchos tiendas. Perdón, yes it is the same person who owns many, many shops in México." He returned the card to me and asked, "Are you a friend of Señor Ángel?"

"No, not a friend, more of an acquaintance. Thank you very much for your time and the information. "Buenas tardes."

He was disappointed that we bought nothing, but I was anxious to leave the shop before Martha and Cyndie could give me the third degree. No such luck. By the time we were out the door the interrogation began. Cyndie got the ball rolling. "So you met a man who owns souvenir shops all over Mexico?"

"Yes, on Friday night he approached me in the bar where we were celebrating and asked me to delay my trip home so I could spend a week or two with him. Not only was that unthinkable, he's a married man."

It was Martha's turn. "So you didn't even consider it? As for his marital status, have you forgotten that old song by Stephen Sills, 'Love the One You're With'?" Where exactly was the man's wife while he was out on the prowl? Was he handsome?"

"That seventies song has nothing to do with me. As for his wife, she and his son are in France for the month, but he's still married. Furthermore,

I have a plane to catch on Tuesday. Or have you forgotten that I have a family and a job, not to mention Chuck's wedding in August? And, yes, he was very handsome."

Cyndie put her arm around me and said, "You made the right decision, Sheila. Besides, we would have been worried sick if you hadn't shown up yesterday."

Martha smacked me on the shoulder. "Do you mean to tell me that you rejected a good-looking millionaire when you don't even have a husband?" She waved her hand towards the ocean. "We could have spent these sun-drenched, lazy days on a yacht out there! You might have considered us before you climbed on your high horse and refused his offer."

"'We' could have been on his yacht? I believe his invitation was for one, which is not the point. He's married, I have to go home, and I'm not interested in a sexual dalliance. Believe it or not, I've made love with only one man in my life. Besides, Miguel never mentioned that he owned a yacht."

Cyndie interrupted Martha's rant, "Well, you know a man with his money has a yacht tucked away somewhere. I've never been on a yacht before."

Martha was still fuming. "Yes, 'we' could have hung out with you and what's-his-name for a few days. I'm confident that if millionaire Miguel had gotten you in his bed, he wouldn't have minded if you brought a couple of friends along on a Caribbean excursion. I mean, hell, you're practically a virgin."

"Ok, that's it! I've heard enough about the affair that wasn't. Time to move on." I looked around town and spotted a jewelry store that rested on a triangular lot. "Isn't that the jewelry shop our waiter recommended to us?"

Cyndie was ready to change the subject, too. "Yes, he said it was in the triangle a few blocks down the street. C'mon Martha. You said you wanted to look at jewelry."

Martha was still miffed that I hadn't reeled in a millionaire for "us," but she knew the argument was lost before it began. "I guess I could look around and see if anything appeals to me."

We crossed the street and entered the store, where two armed men stood guard. Cyndie and Martha were startled by the security, but the shop was a visual paradise that dazzled us and distracted them. If diamonds were a girl's best friend, we were in the right place. Glass case after case was filled to the brim with an array of jewelry in a wide variety of precious stones and every imaginable design, from classic to whimsical. I wasn't much of a jewelry person, but even I couldn't resist the opportunity to appreciate such stunning pieces of handcrafted jewelry. We separated and gravitated towards individual tastes. I was admiring a collection of antique pendants when I overheard Cyndie ask one of the clerks on the next aisle, "Kunta Kinte?"

The clerk was polite but puzzled as he replied that he didn't understand the question, "¿Perdón? No entiendo la pregunta."

Cyndie repeated, "Kunta Kinte is this necklace?"

The clerk responded in fragmented English, "I apologize, señora, pero, uh, but no comprendo 'Kunta Kinte'."

I slipped up behind Cyndie and asked, "What are you asking this nice man?"

"I want to know how much this necklace cost, so I asked him in Spanish in case he doesn't speak English. He seems to be having trouble comprehending the phrase you taught me. Do you think my southern pronunciation is the reason he can't understand what I want to know?"

"No, Cyndie, I don't think it has anything to do with your accent. I think it has to do with the fact that Kunta Kinte was the main character in an Alex Haley novel that was published about twenty years ago." A light came on as Cyndie recalled the television miniseries. I sighed in frustration but continued, "You can't just spit out words that sound similar in Spanish no more than you can make up your own words in English and expect to be understood. The question I told you to ask when inquiring about the price of an object is '¿Cuánto cuesta?'"

She repeated the phrases and shrugged. "'¿Cuánto cuesta?' 'Kunta Kinte?' Oh well, I just want to know the price of this necklace."

I shrugged at the merchant who was then aware of what my friend had asked and gave her a price for the necklace. The quoted cost was much more expensive than the prices I'd seen elsewhere. "How much is that in American dollars?" she asked.

I held up my hand to end the exchange. Unlike me, Cyndie had been born into money and had, consequently, grown up accustomed to having pretty much whatever she wanted. No wonder she was willing to pay the first price given for an exquisite silver and turquoise necklace. I pulled her aside and reminded her of our agreement that she wouldn't buy anything until the purchase was discussed with me. "We're going to walk away and act completely uninterested in the necklace or anything else in the store. I'll tell him the jewelry is overpriced and that we're going to shop elsewhere."

I didn't get the chance to say anything because the vendor was immediately ready to negotiate a better deal. After a few minutes of haggling, we reached an amount that was comparable to some of the necklaces I'd seen in Taxco. Cyndie handed the man her Visa card and was delighted at having saved almost two hundred dollars. "Let's find Martha. I can't wait to show her what I found and how much money you saved me. I hope she hasn't already bought that bracelet I saw her drooling over."

We needn't have worried about Martha. She took to bargaining like a duck to water and bought a twelve hundred dollar bracelet that she negotiated for eight hundred. She used her credit card and planned to have the bracelet appraised when she got home. However, I didn't think she would be disappointed because the bracelet was gorgeous. Emeralds and sapphires intertwined in a braided gold setting. The stones were small but appeared to be flawless.

Martha said, "I chose this one because the colors are the same as those of the Caribbean, and every time I wear it I'll remember this girls' trip."

They were happy with their purchase, and we left the store. I suggested we head back to the bus station. "If I remember correctly the last bus for Cancun leaves at seven o'clock, and it's almost six-thirty."

"Suits me," said Cyndie.

We easily found a taxi and another bus line for the trip back and were seated across the aisle from a delightful young couple, the same couple I'd spotted in the café where we had lunch. They hadn't noticed me because they had eyes only for each other, but during the bus ride we became acquainted with Isabella and her fiancé Mateo. He was as handsome as she was beautiful, and they glowed with happiness. They were college students who worked part-time and planned to be married as soon as they could save enough money. We chatted the whole trip, and by the time we reached the bus depot in Cancun, it felt like we were old friends instead of new ones. Martha mentioned a taxi, but Mateo was quick to offer us a ride to our hotel.

I asked, "Are y'all staying at the Hyatt or near there?"

Mateo laughed aloud. "No, we can't afford anything so luxurious or expensive as the Hyatt or anywhere else in the vicinity, but I'm happy to drive you there. Besides, I like to hear you speak. I forgot to ask, but are 'y'all' from Allyboma?"

It was my turn to laugh over his mispronunciation of Alabama. "No, but close. We're from Georgia. Please don't put yourself out. We can take a taxi."

Isabella insisted, "It's no bother at all. Our car is old, but it is dependable, and there's room for all of you in the back seat."

We accepted their kind offer and clamored into the accommodating back seat of a Buick from the seventies. Cyndie continued to talk up the young couple, and I poked Martha in the ribs with my elbow. "Barry used to tell me that I was way too trusting and naïve, and it has occurred to me that we may have made a very stupid decision. After all, we don't actually know these people, and I think I heard Barry rollover in his grave. Pat would have a hissy fit if she knew I'd willingly gotten in a car with strangers who could be planning to kidnap us for ransom. Just wanted to share that happy thought."

Martha mocked, "Thanks, Sheee-la, but that's something we should have thought about before we piled our asses in the car. All we can do is pray that our next stop is at the Hyatt Regency. I really think they're completely trustworthy, and Cyndie doesn't look worried."

Cyndie was laughing at something Isabella had shared, so I answered, "I'm not overly concerned, but for future reference I probably need to be a bit more cautious about situations like this."

I shouldn't have doubted my first impression because Mateo dropped us off in front of our hotel, safe and sound. We exchanged goodbyes and addresses and promises to stay in touch, which none of us planned to do. We waved to the disappearing Buick until fatigue lured us to our beds.

I was wiped out from balancing an exhausting schedule over the past week and totally crashed on Sunday. I hated to bail on my friends, but I slept for hours while Cyndi and Martha enjoyed each other's company and Cancun. But Monday was our last full day in the glorious arms of Cancun, and I didn't want spend it sleeping. The three Sheee-las spent it lounging around the pool, soaking up the sun, and enjoying the relaxing atmosphere that defined Cancun. We read, talked, and people watched the morning away, but after lunch the lure of the ocean summoned me to the shore. I stood and stretched. "As much as I would love a siesta, that's a habit I've got to break before I get back to the real world. I'm going for a walk on the beach. Anybody want to join me?"

Cyndie rolled over onto her back and shielded her eyes from the sun as she reached for her sunglasses. "A walk sounds heavenly. I can cool off in the clear, blue water."

Martha yawned and said, "Oh, what the hell. I might as well go with y'all. Give me a few minutes to go upstairs and grab my camera."

She returned with her camera bag, and the three of us donned sunglasses, straw hats, and another layer of suntan lotion, a smell that brought back memories of childhood trips to Panama City Beach. We walked around the tiki bar and through the gate to the footpath that led us to the scorching sand where the heat seared my flip-flops. Frothy whitecaps disappeared on the shore where multicolored beach towels were a striking contrast against the white sand. While most of the beachgoers preferred the sun, a woman and her infant dozed on a colorful patchwork quilt beneath the skimpy shade of a palm tree.

Men smiled and nodded their admiration as we strolled along the beach under a cloudless, blue sky. A balmy breeze waltzed over lazy waves and lifted a delighted child's kite into the air. Several sailboats that bobbled in the distance boasted colorful sails. Pelicans gathered on a weathered dock that stretched its wooden fingers to touch the turquoise sea. I don't think even Monet and his palette of watercolors could have captured on canvas the perfection of the day.

But Martha gave it her best shot as she took pictures, with their parents' permission, of beautiful, bronzed children building sand castles and playing in the surf. Sunlight played in the varied blues of the ocean and invited me to join in the fun, an invitation I couldn't resist. I kicked off my flip-flops and rushed to the shoreline where refreshing breakers swarmed around my ankles. I called back to my friends, "I'm going for a swim. Come on, y'all!"

Martha asked a woman who was sunbathing to keep an eye on her camera, kicked off her sandals, and splashed her way towards me. Cyndie was right behind her and commented on how shallow it was considering how far from shore we'd waded. "I'm only waist deep, but we're several yards from land. Can y'all believe how clear the water is? There's not even a strand of seaweed between us and the sandy bottom."

Martha couldn't resist teasing her. "Then it will be easier for you to see the shark right before it takes a bite out of your ass!"

"Damn it, Martha. Did you have to put a damper on the day?"

I motioned them towards several large rocks that protruded from the ocean floor. "Hey, let's see if we can walk over to those rocks and then we'll swim back to the beach."

The suggestion seemed harmless, and they both willingly followed me down the rabbit hole. I hadn't considered that rocks above the ocean's surface were comparable to an iceberg in that the bulk of the mass was unexposed and lurked dangerously below.

We were chest high in the salty sea as we approached the rocks when Cyndie cried out in pain. "Stop! I'm stuck! My foot is caught in a crevice."

Martha and I swam to her aide and freed her foot from the rock's vise-like grip. I asked, "Are you okay?"

"Yes, I think so. It doesn't feel like anything is broken, but my ankle is beginning to throb."

I put her arm around my shoulder. "We need to ease you back to shore. I'm so sorry, Cyndie, for my stupid suggestion."

"It's not your fault. We all agreed to walk out to the rocks, and I'm the one who accidentally stepped in the gap. I'm sure I'll be fine, but I do need to take the weight off my foot."

Martha slipped Cyndie's other arm over her shoulder and together, along with the buoyancy provided by the water, we managed to make it to shore. With our help Cyndie hobbled back to the pool area where she collapsed onto a chaise. Martha stacked beach towels under the injured foot to elevate it, and I rushed to the bar and explained the need for an ice pack. I immediately applied the ice to Cyndie's slightly swollen ankle while Martha dug through her bag and retrieved a bottle of ibuprofen. She handed a couple to our injured friend, and I suggested we find a doc in a box, better known as an urgent care center.

Cyndie moaned but objected. "No, that's not necessary. My ankle seems to be only sprained, and the pounding pain has subsided. The ice and ibuprofen are probably what any doctor would recommend. I'll just keep it propped up for the next few hours, and if it worsens we'll find a clinic before the end of the day."

Satisfied that we'd done all we could, I apologized again and spent the next few hours keeping her comfortable. Martha unpacked several new magazines to occupy our time while Cyndie rested. Thankfully, she was much better by late afternoon and able to shower and dress for dinner at a nearby restaurant recommended by the poolside bartender, who was fascinated with the "tres Sheee-las." Cyndie's slight limp was barely noticeable.

By morning she was almost back to her old self, and the three of us enjoyed breakfast at a sidewalk café close to the hotel before we set about packing for the trip home. Checkout was at eleven o'clock, but I got up early in time to pack and make it to the airport where I would reconnect with my fellow travelers. My concern was that I'd be leaving Cyndie and Martha to fend for themselves for a few hours, and I couldn't help but worry about them.

When everything had been crammed into suitcases and we'd all done a room check to see if we'd forgotten anything, we called for a porter to assist us with the bags. The desk clerk was kind enough to oblige my request that he allow my friends to store their luggage in his office until it was time for them to catch the shuttle to the airport. He, too, had been captivated by the three Americans all named Sheee-la.

Cyndie and Martha walked out of the hotel with me, and before hailing a cab I said, "Thank you both for meeting me here and letting me stay with you at this beautiful resort. I've had a great time." I furrowed my brow. "By the way, how much money do y'all have left in Mexican currency?"

Each of them pulled bills and coins from their wallets. "I have no idea," said Cyndie.

"I've spent most of mine," replied Martha.

I counted the money they held in their hands, and they each had a few *pesos* more than thirty dollars. I pulled out four dollars from each of them. "Put this aside for tip money when your luggage is loaded and unloaded. You both have enough cash to pay for lunch and tips, so don't let the waiter jerk you around about the bill. There should be several other Americans around who can help you if you need assistance. You've already bought and packed your souvenirs, but if you're browsing and are approached by a salesclerk, just say 'No tengo dinero', which means you have no money. Unless you want the item enough to use a credit card and if—"

Martha interrupted my instructions, "Shelia, we'll be fine, so stop worrying about us. Thank you for letting me tag along with Cyndie. I can't tell you how much I've enjoyed myself." She hugged me and elicited a promise to stay in touch once we were home, but that was doubtful as our paths seldom crossed. She would step back into her life, and I would step back into mine.

Cyndie embraced me and added, "I can't remember when I've had so much fun on a girls' trip, despite the sprained ankle. Don't worry about us. Just be careful and find your way back to the other students and have a safe flight." She hugged me again. "I'm so proud of you for finishing your degree! I'll see you at work next week."

"I'll be there with bells on."

An attendant flagged a taxi and loaded my luggage. Time had gotten away from me, as often happened in Mexico, so I scrambled into the back-seat and directed the driver to take me to the airport, pronto. I glanced out the window and waved one last farewell to my friends who had become friends themselves. Martha and I were family but had never been close. Cyndie and I had been in school together since kindergarten but hadn't been friends as we ran in different social circles and definitely different cliques. However, our working relationship had spilled into friendship over the last few years. I was grateful God sent Cyndie into my life when He knew I would need her unwavering compassion and support.

The driver left the ocean behind us, and I realized that I was ready to go home. I was homesick and anxious to see my family. And I had a newfound confidence that I was strong enough to cope with whatever challenges were waiting in phase two of my life.

Part Two

"Grief is in two parts. The first is loss. The second is remaking of life."

Anne Roiphe

Chapter Seven

Home Sweet Home

I made it to the airport with a few minutes to spare, and I was happy to see my friends. The flight passed quickly as June, Linda, and I caught up with each other and shared stories of Cancun. Their hotel wasn't nearly as swanky as the Hilton, but they'd made the best of it and spent most of their time on the beach or browsing the open market where June bought rainsticks for her grandchildren. The carved, long, hollow tubes with sealed ends were filled with pebbles and when toppled, they made a sound similar to that of rain. June was going to tell the kids that the rainsticks were a reminder of the nightly rains in Cuernavaca and about the night she and I had been all but stranded in a downpour. The cumbersome souvenirs wouldn't fit in June's suitcase, so she had to carry them onboard and stash them overhead, much to the annoyance of the flight attendant.

Other than that minor inconvenience the trip was uneventful, and the "fasten seatbelt" light alerted us to buckle up for landing. Goodbyes were shared among us as we retrieved our carry-on luggage and lined in the aisle, anxious to get through U.S. Customs and to waiting family members. Thankfully, I wasn't subjected to a search as I'd been when I arrived in Mexico City. Having never been out of the country, I didn't realize how good it would be to hear, "Welcome back to the States" from the Customs Officer at the checkpoint as he smiled and returned my passport. I was blessed to be a United States citizen, something I was guilty of taking for granted. I promised myself to be more grateful for all the blessings in my life.

My family was one of those blessings, and I'd missed them more than I thought. My niece and her lovable toddler were smiling, and Kim motioned me towards them. She wrapped her arms around me, and the sting of tears surprised me as I returned the bear hug. She pulled away and looked me over from head to toe. "You look great! I'm so relieved you're finally home. We've all missed you and worried over you, but Mama kept everybody posted after her weekly conversations with you. I'd hoped you would gain a few pounds, but your skinny ass didn't pick up an ounce. Did you eat enough?"

There was no need in pointing out that I was a healthy weight. I laughed and reached for Macy, who readily came to me, and I savored her sweetness. In our large family babies were considered community property. "Yes, Kim, I ate plenty, but June and I walked almost every day so I guess that offset the calories. I wish all of you would stop worrying about me."

"Hey, that's what we do best. Let's catch a tram and pick up your luggage. I plan to swing over to Cumberland Mall because I need to exchange a pair of shoes at Macy's. There are several restaurants in the area where we can eat supper, unless you're too tired."

"That sounds good. I'm not going to unpack until in the morning, and I don't have to be back in the office until Monday. I'm going to invite my kids to supper tomorrow night so I can touch base with them and catch up on what's going on in their lives. I'm anxious to see them and my new daughter-in-law, but I dread having to include Chuck's fiancé." With a sigh of disappointment I attempted small talk." When Brad and Valerie returned from their honeymoon last month, I made two trips over here to pick them up. They were bumped from their flight due to overbooking and flew in the next day. They'd volunteered to give up their seats when Delta offered them a night in a Denver hotel, a meal voucher, and a fifty percent discount on their next flight."

"I can't say as I blame 'em."

We made our way to where hordes of other passengers waited to board the tram that would whisk us to the other end of the airport. Atlanta's airport was several times the size of the one at Mexico City, and Cancun's airport could fit inside one concourse. I shifted Macy to my other hip before a man offered me his seat on the speeding, underground tram, which I accepted with a smile and a "thanks." I loved the South where consideration and good manners were an integral part of our upbringing. As we reached the baggage claim area, I handed Macy over to her mama and waited for the carousel to return my oversized suitcase. Luggage in hand, we walked out of the airport's air conditioning into a sultry August afternoon. Beads of perspiration dripped from my forehead as we located Kim's car in the adjacent parking deck, and I dug a scrunchie out of my purse and pulled my hair in a ponytail. Summertime in Georgia was hot and humid.

Kim fastened Macy in her car seat, and I shoved my luggage in the back of her SUV before settling in the passenger seat and buckling up. I was briefly confused when Kim eased onto the right side of the road in bumper-to-bumper Camp Creek traffic where we followed the flow to the I-285 junction. I was going to have to get adjusted to driving again. Everybody was in a hurry to get to wherever they were going, and I couldn't help but miss the slower, laid back pace I'd left behind.

My chauffeur merged onto Atlanta's bypass where the traffic swam upstream like salmon. "By the way, did you meet any men in Mexico?"

"What?" I couldn't believe my nosy niece was asking me that. Actually, I could. "No, I didn't meet any men, which was not the purpose of the trip." I decided not to elaborate on Marta's misguided matchmaking attempt or my tenacious dance partner at the Crystal Palace or meeting Miguel at the Lazy Lizard. She would have been more annoyed than Martha if I told her I'd culled a millionaire, albeit a married millionaire. "Why is everyone so anxious for me to meet a man? Barry hasn't even been dead a year, which is irrelevant. The point is that I had a good husband who cherished me, so I know what it is to love and to be loved. And it's possible that we lucky few are blessed with one love per lifetime. Please drop the subject."

"Don't be ridiculous. If we were allotted only one love, then Bremen's answer to Elizabeth Taylor wouldn't be married to husband number five, or six. Hell, I've lost count." She glanced at my left hand and persisted. "At least you've stopped wearing your wedding rings. That's a step in the right direction. Most men won't hit on a married woman, not the decent ones anyway. Just don't rule out the chance that another man could walk into your life one day and sweep you off your feet. That's what several other widows in your age group have told me, and they're happily remarried."

I wasn't interested in being "hit on," and I ignored her comment about another man breezing into my life. I circled back to the wedding rings. "I'm eager to see Mitch at the jewelry store tomorrow. He promised to have my ring ready by the time I returned."

She got the hint and followed my conversation. "You don't have to worry about whether or not you'll like the ring. He's got a very good reputation for creating one-of-a kind designs that suit the person. I know it will be beautiful, something you'll treasure." She flipped on the turn signal and took the mall exit. Fortunately, she found a parking place near the entrance of the large department store. "I'll get Macy if you'll get her diaper bag. I'm sure she needs changing, but we're working on potty training." She popped her two-year-old in the stroller she retrieved from the backseat and handed her a juice cup.

"Speaking of, I need to use the potty myself. I'll change her while you exchange the shoes, and then I want to look around at sale items. I might find some deals on summer clearance." As luck had it, the clearance items had been picked over, and there was nothing left in my size. I didn't really need anything anyway, so Macy and I strolled towards the shoe department to find Kim when I noticed a stylish denim jacket displayed on a mannequin. I paused to check the price tag and couldn't believe it was almost eighty dollars.

Kim and a salesclerk approached me simultaneously, and the lady asked if she could help find my size. I asked if the jacket was on sale, and she politely replied, "No, they're not. These arrived last week and are part of our fall collection. As you can see, the jacket is versatile and the price is very reasonable for a Tommy Hilfiger."

I muttered, "Muy caro" and was about to move on. As much as I liked the jacket, I wasn't willing to pay that much. I wasn't a penniless widow, but I'd learned to be more conservative with money.

Kim reached for my arm and smiled at the saleswoman. "I'm sorry, ma'am, but could you give us a few minutes alone?" The woman left to assist another customer, and Kim turned to me. "Listen, blondie, I don't know what that 'muy caro' crap is, but you're not in Mexico anymore so if it's about the cost of the jacket, nobody's playing 'Let's Make a Deal'. Unless you're at a yard sale or a flea market or there's a sale sign hangin' over the rack, then the price you see is the price you pay. Now do you want to buy it or not?"

"Nope. I refuse to pay that amount of money for something I don't have to have—unless I can save twenty percent by using my Macy's card."

Kim took control of the stroller, tugged me towards the exit, and rolled her big, brown eyes. "You're hopeless."

Sunlight fought with closed blinds to enter my bedroom and nudge me awake, and I leisurely stretched in the comfort of my own, larger bed for the first time in several weeks. I slipped into a housecoat and wandered down the hallway. I passed the boys' empty bedrooms with wistfulness for the days when they were roused by the sound of my swishing robe as I'd hurried to the kitchen to make breakfast and get us all to school and work. I missed those mornings and those long ago Christmas mornings when two pint-sized boys clad in flannel pajamas raced to the Christmas tree. Their squeals of delight over Santa's presents woke their daddy and me before the crack of dawn. Those days had faded much too quickly, and the house was filled with silence, a silence that was a deafening reminder that I was alone.

I reflected on the unexpected detours that sidetrack our lives and put on a pot of coffee as I set about unpacking. I wanted to start the laundry before breakfast, which would be a Pop-tart until I could shop for groceries. I had a full agenda for the day and was eager to get busy. I was also ready to pick up my ring from the jeweler, which would be my first stop on the list of errands I'd compiled the night before. Kim and I hadn't gotten home until almost nine o'clock and after helping me to unload my luggage, she'd gone home to get Macy to bed and was thankful her husband had gotten their older son tucked in. She lived only a few miles down the road from my subdivision, which was convenient for both of us.

I tossed a load of clothes in the dryer and took a few minutes to call Daddy and assure him that I was safely home and then called my sons to invite them to supper. The morning was getting away from me so I hurriedly showered and dressed in the standard uniform of summer in the South: a tank top, shorts, and flip-flops. I gathered my purse, to-do list, and keys and was relieved when the Mustang cranked on the first turn of the ignition. Brad had evidently kept his promise to drive the car once a week during my absence in order to keep the battery charged. I dropped the ragtop and cranked up the radio and was thankful he'd thoughtfully filled the tank. I glanced at the dashboard clock and realized I would have just enough time to pick up the ring before meeting Pat for lunch, a luncheon I couldn't postpone. She had to see for herself that I was all right.

I parked the convertible in front of the jewelry store and noticed how the midday sun was reflected in the car's red exterior and felt the heat wave from the asphalt. Maybe I should have left the top up and ran the air conditioning, but I loved the sun and wind in my face. I entered the jewelry store and was greeted warmly by the owner. "Well, hello, Sheila. How was your trip?"

"It was a wonderful experience, but I missed my family and friends. Of course, I'll have to readjust to having a whole house all to myself. I spent a good part of the morning sorting through mail and paying bills, a chore I haven't missed."

He laughed and answered, "None of us like paying bills. But enough small talk. You are undoubtedly here to pick up the ring which, as promised, is ready." He turned to a locked filing cabinet, flipped the key, and searched alphabetically until he found a small, manila envelope that carried my name. Mitch carefully shook the ring into my palm. "I hope you're happy with the design I came up with following your basic guidelines."

A small gasp of delight escaped as I held the heart-shaped ring. The larger diamond, which was from the long-overdue "engagement" ring Barry had surprised me with one Christmas, years after our elopement, rested at the base of the heart. The smaller diamonds from the eternity ring my husband gave me as a twenty-fifth anniversary present filled the remaining opening. White gold circles held the diamonds in place, and the ring sparkled under the fluorescent lights. The setting rested on a solid band inscribed with the words, "Love is Forever," the same inscription I had engraved on the double headstone Barry and I would share.

I truly appreciated what was clearly a labor of love as Mitch elaborated on the components of the ring. "Except for the filigree posts used to mount the setting onto the band, the entire ring is made from the two rings you left with me. The larger diamond fit perfectly in the point, and then it was easy to align the smaller diamonds to complete the interior. Are you pleased?"

I wiped away a stray tear. "You don't need to ask. It's absolutely gorgeous—and perfect. It's as if you knew my heart and created a symbol of love that I couldn't define." I slipped the heart on the ring finger of my left hand, but it looked out of place, as if it represented something lost, something irreplaceable. I removed it and placed it on the ring finger of my right hand and pledged to wear it always as a reminder that true love is a forever love. Mitch handed me the invoice, and I thanked him as I paid for a ring that was, to me, priceless.

I walked out of the store and was slapped in the face by the harsh August heat as I hurried to Bilbo's to meet Pat for lunch. I entered the local eatery and let my eyes adjust from the sunlight before I spotted Pat in a back booth. I gave the waitress my drink order for sweet tea, something I'd missed in Mexico, and made my way through familiar faces at the barbeque restaurant.

Pat stood to wrap her arms around me. "Okay, wild child, now that you're back, you can't leave for that long again. A month of worrying about you is more than I can handle." She held me at arm's length and continued, "I'm so damn relieved you're finally home."

"Pat, are you crying?"

"No. Well, maybe a tear or two. Sit down and let's order before we catch up, or as much as we can during my lunch break. What we don't have time to talk about here, we can finish at supper tonight at my house. I know you've missed good old home cooking. We eat at six, so don't be late."

And people thought I was the bossy one. "I appreciate the offer, but you don't have to cook for me after working all day. Besides, my sons accepted my invitation that they all eat supper at my house tonight. Maybe another night?"

"Okay, we'll make it one night next week." The waitress took our order and disappeared. Pat seemed to have something on her mind, but it wasn't like her to mince words. After a brief hesitation she leaned over the table to make sure I was listening—and that no one else was. "Speaking of the boys, there's a good chance Chuck may be in trouble with the business, not that it's any of mine, but I thought you could discuss the situation with him over supper."

With a sinking sensation I asked, "What kind of trouble?"

"Nothing specific, but I've noticed he's not opening until well after nine o'clock, and I've heard that some of the customers are taking advantage of Chuck by charging tires, batteries, tanks of gas, and other purchases or services they haven't paid for yet. I'm worried they have no intention of paying what they owe or of picking up bounced checks. You need to talk to the accountant to get the details because my information is from the grapevine, which could be nothing more than rumors. I wanted to give you a heads up, but I'm sorry to be the bearer of bad news on your first day back in town."

I sat silenced but not surprised. My gut instinct had told me that Chuck was much too young and inexperienced takes the reins after his older brother walked away and found another job. Although it was their daddy's decision to leave an established business to our sons, a business that had taken him twenty years to build, I didn't think it was what either of them wanted. Even so, it's hard to argue with a man on his death bed, so I'd agreed. In hindsight, I should have sold the business or liquidated the assets and divided the money equally between Brad and Chuck. Regrettably, I'd been caught in the grip of unrelenting grief and was in no condition to make sound financial decisions.

I noticed the concern covering Pat's face and realized she needed me to say something. I reached across the table and touched her hand. "Hey, it's okay that you let me know what's going on, or what's most likely going on. The rumor mill is rarely wrong, and I'd much rather hear the news from you than some busybody I might run into somewhere. You know how people in this town love dirty laundry."

"By damn, they better not let me overhear them gossiping about you or the boys. It wouldn't take me a New York minute to put them in their places. I've lived in this town all of my life, and I have a *very* long memory. Those pots calling the kettle black don't want to get me started."

My family and I were good people until someone pissed us, or one of us, off and then we would turn on them like a pack of wolves. "Thanks, sister, for always having my back. I've got a few more errands to run before going home to start supper, but I'll call Sherry and ask her for an update on the current financial circumstances. Now let's change the subject." I extended my right hand. "Look at my new ring. Didn't the jeweler do a remarkable job?"

Pat took my hand to get a better look at Mitch's handiwork. "Oh, Sheila, it really is gorgeous. I don't think anyone could have done a better job." She glimpsed at her watch and pulled her wallet from her purse. "I can't believe my lunch hour is over already, but I've got to get back to the office. Call me tomorrow and fill me in on Chuck's predicament." She snatched up both tickets and scooted across the booth. "Lunch is on me today, and I'll expect you for supper whenever you can make it."

"Sounds good. I'll call you as soon as I know more, and I'm looking forward to supper at your house. You're a much better cook than I am."

She didn't disagree. "Only because I'm older and had more responsibility than the spoiled baby of the family. Mama expected me to learn how to cook so I could help out while she worked." She laughed, hugged me again, and lit up a cigarette as she hurried across the sweltering parking lot. In the South, the summer strategy was to run from air conditioned homes to air conditioned cars to air conditioned jobs, if we were lucky. I don't know how people endured summertime without air conditioning, but we'd all made it through years of childhood summers with only fans to stir the humidity.

I left Bilbo's and headed to the drugstore to leave three rolls of film to be sent off for developing. It would take a few days before the prints were back, and I needed to pick up a photo album to accommodate pictures from my adventure in Mexico. The next stop was Ingle's, where you could find the best cubed steak in town and where I used my list to complete the grocery shopping in record time. I tossed a carton of Little Debbie Swiss cake rolls into the buggy and smiled because I wouldn't have to hide them in the dryer, which had proved to be safer than Fort Knox. It might not have been fair to stash snacks but when teenage boys came between a PMS Mama and her chocolate, it was Katie bar the door. I put the groceries in the trunk and was motivated to get home and start supper for my family. On the other hand, I was not looking forward to a confrontation with Chuck about the problems he was dealing with at work.

After discussing the matter with the accountant, I realized the situation was much direr than Pat had led me to believe. Cooking was a mild distraction, and as I kneaded the buttermilk biscuit dough, I composed my thoughts on how to best broach the subject. Patience was never my strong suit, but I would have to muster up what I could find before having a dreaded, but necessary, conversation with my grown son. Especially since the horse was already out of the barn.

Brad and Valerie arrived first, and I greeted the newlyweds with hugs. "It's so good to see you both. From your happy faces, it looks like matrimony is agreeing with you." I turned to Valerie and asked, "How are you coping with Brad's flaws now that you're married?"

Valerie put her arm around Brad's waist and smiled up at him. "Oh, yes, we're very happy. Brad doesn't have any flaws. He's perfect."

Bless her heart for loving my son and wearing blinders. He was a good man, but we all have our shortcomings. I jumped right in the middle of a sore subject. "Brad, do you have any idea what's going on at the shop? I'd like to get your opinion before Chuck and Leslie get here."

Brad didn't answer for a few minutes but finally replied, "I know he's not running the business the way it should be managed. His hours are random, and he's letting customers charge parts and labor when he needs the cash. I know for a fact that some of those people are never going to pay what they owe." He hesitated again, as if he hated to be a tattletale. "Leslie is driving an almost new Mustang convertible, and I'm guessing the down payment was taken out of the business account. But don't let Chuck know I mentioned it to you. I washed my hands of the business when I walked away from it. Whatever's going on is something you and Chuck need to work out."

A car door slammed in the driveway. "They're here. We'll keep things neutral until the two of you leave, and then I'll have a come to Jesus meeting with your brother." I opened the back door and motioned Chuck and his fiancé inside and hugged them both. "Come on in. Supper is almost on the table. As soon as the biscuits are out of the oven, we'll eat."

Valerie poured sweet tea over tall glasses of ice, and I plated country fried steak with gravy and a variety of vegetables. Right on cue the timer signaled the biscuits were ready. We congregated in the dining room where the table was set and overloaded with enough food for ten instead of five—a southern tradition of it's better to have too much than not enough. After all, if a friend or neighbor dropped by unexpectedly, it would be just plain rude not to offer them a bite to eat. I wasn't the cook Mama had been, but I could put together a meal for my family. It was impossible to raise two eating machines without knowing how to cook. Of course, Mama would have baked one of her delicious pies, but the only dessert I had time to whip up was a cool and creamy lemonade pie. It was either that or ice cream from a carton.

We gathered around the table, and I related tales of Mexico and told them about my host family. We all laughed at the adventures and mishaps, and they caught me up on what was going on in their lives. Chuck had always been a man of few words, and held his end of the discussion to a minimum. As I'd promised Brad we kept the conversation light and away from the burden that weighed heavily on my shoulders. When it was time to clear the table, Valerie pitched in to help while Leslie piled her lazy ass on the sofa and flipped through a magazine.

What in the hell was Chuck thinking? Leslie had a lousy personality, nor was she attractive. As Daddy put it, "The girl that boy of yours is planning on marrying ain't nearly as pretty as he is." Daddy was always brutally honest when it came to giving his opinion, and it never occurred to him that he might hurt anybody's feelings. Neither had he bothered to learn the names of all the grandchildren. They were labeled according to their parents' names and birth order: "that oldest girl of Pat's or that boy of Donnie's" and so on and so on.

I brushed aside thoughts of Daddy's brusqueness and served dessert in the family room. Afterwards, Brad broke up the evening by reminding me that tomorrow was a workday for them. We all agreed to get together the following week, when I would have the pictures from the trip organized in an album. Valerie gave me a goodbye hug and thanked me again for supper as she and Brad walked to the back door and left hand-in-hand. Leslie stood and yawned as if she were beyond bored and spoke to Chuck. "We better get going, too."

Chuck stood and thanked me for supper, which was more than his lovely bride-to-be had done. I snapped my fingers, a habit I'd developed when my sons were young and I needed to get their attention. "Sit down, both of you. We have some things to hash out."

Chuck looked nervously at Leslie and shrugged his shoulders before taking a seat. "I guess news travels fast. So who let the cat outta the bag?"

"That's not important. And, yes, news travels fast, and bad news travels faster. I'm surprised your trail of descent didn't make it to Mexico, except there was nothing I could have done from there. I'm not sure what to do, but we have to resolve the problems you have in running a business. I've already spoken to the bookkeeper, so I know you're going deeper in debt and that several checks have been returned, including two from the State Sales and Use Tax Division. She advised me to take care of those first because of the penalties and interest that are adding up daily." I doubted if he could answer but I asked, "What happened?"

It broke my heart to see my son dejected and hopeless, but I couldn't let him off the hook. He answered, "I don't know. I had no idea what was involved in running the shop or how much Daddy took care of to keep things going. When the bank account started getting low, I didn't even want to open the doors and face the creditors. A bad day turned into a week of bad days and then into months, and I didn't want to dump this mess in your lap. Customers I trusted stopped coming in after they racked up hundreds of dollars in charges, and I couldn't collect from them. One man, Dennis Hayes*, ordered an eight-hundred dollar set of tires. After I put the tires on his car, he told me to charge it and that he'd pay me at the end of the week. I told him I had to have the money that day, but he just laughed it off and left. I haven't seen or heard from him since."

I rested my head in my hands and fought back tears of frustration. Dennis was a scumbag who had no conscience, but by damn he was going to pay for those tires one way or another. "Ok, Chuck. I understand the hole you've dug for yourself, but sticking your head in that hole and ignoring the problems doesn't make them go away."

I noticed Leslie was biting her nails. "Leslie, have you been sending out monthly statements the way I taught you?"

She squirmed and avoided eye contact, but found the courage to answer, "I did for a while, but it was such a hassle, and nobody was paying what they owed anyway so I quit bothering."

I fumed but had another question. "How is it that y'all can afford that convertible parked in the driveway?"

Chuck cleared his throat before he half-heartedly answered, "I know I shouldn't have used money from the business account for Leslie's car, but we couldn't have bought it without a hefty down payment. The monthly payments are small enough that we can manage."

I wanted to rake him over the coals, but he was already disheartened, so I held my tongue. With all the business acumen and negotiating skills of any other twenty-one year old, there was no telling how much and at what interest rate they'd been hoodwinked into paying. I turned my attention to Leslie. "I don't know how much you're earning at your parents' convenience store, but it ought to be enough to make the car payments. Thank goodness Chuck has a truck that's paid for and in pretty good condition."

She squirmed like a worm in hot ashes. "You might as well know that I quit my job. Now that Chuck and I are living together and will be married in a couple of weeks, I don't need to work. It's the husband's job to provide for his wife."

My palm itched to slap her stupid, but it was crystal clear that someone had beaten me to the punch. I paced in an effort to calm down and figure out the best way to resolve the mess my younger offspring had made. I couldn't blame him entirely. I'd realized after the fact that he was too young and inexperienced to manage a business. Added to those facts, Leslie was an albatross pulling him down an abyss of debt and had no intention of being a helpmate.

I sat down next to Chuck and offered what advice I could. "We can't do anything tonight, but somehow we'll find a solution. Your wedding is set for Saturday week, and you've already paid for the honeymoon cruise. Did the business pay for that, too? Never mind, I don't want to know. In the meantime, you will get your ass to work on time and do all you can to bring in money. I want you to put a large 'CASH ONLY' sign in the window. Before you leave town, I'll find someone to fill in for you, maybe Jimmy. He was good to help out during your dad's illness and won't be taken advantage of. I'll also pick up the charge slips and send statements to every person in town who owes us money. If they don't pay willingly, I'll haul them to court and have their wages garnisheed to collect, especially that snake in the grass Dennis Hayes. Hopefully, the majority of them will pay what—"

Chuck cleared his throat nervously and interrupted my plans. "A few people have suggested that I file for bankruptcy. That's how a lot of businesses get out of paying what they owe—"

It was my turn to interrupt. "No, and that's the end of the discussion. You're daddy built his business on his reputation, and we're not about to tarnish his good name by defaulting on bills we owe. You've bought gas from our supplier, parts from the local auto stores, and tires and batteries from salesmen who work on commission—all on credit. They extended credit to you in good faith, and now we have to pay them in full before we close the doors."

"What? You're selling the business and running me out of a job?"

I almost laughed. "Business? What business? You can't sell a business operating in the red and in debt to the ceiling. We don't own the property, but we can sell the equipment and stock. There's a chance we can make enough to pay off some of what's owed. As for a job, you start searching the want ads and applying at as many places as you can. And I don't give a damn if you have ask, 'Would you like fries with that'? A job is a job, and you don't have the luxury of being picky when you're desperate for a paycheck, given that your fiancé has opted out of being a full partner who's willing to pull her own weight."

They said nothing as I walked towards the door, and they followed like children who'd been caught with their hands in the cookie jar. "Go home and get some rest. I expect you to have the doors open bright and early in the morning."

The two of them left and no doubt Leslie gave Chuck an earful of what she thought of his mama. However, I didn't give two hoots in hell what her opinion of me was because that was the least of my concerns. I walked through the den and retreated to the screened porch—my reading, napping, crying, thinking, praying haven that was bathed in moonlight. Bright red geraniums filled a barrel, multi-colored petunias sat in assorted planters, and hanging baskets overflowed with Boston ferns that swayed in the murmur of a warm breeze. I would have to thank my neighbor Jan for watering the porch plants during my extended absence.

I tried to relax in the calming surroundings, but the symphony of a summer night where katydids and crickets vied for the lead in an orchestra of discordance disturbed the mood. The occasional song of a robin in search of a nighttime snack conspired with the colorful plants to mock my gloomy mood. I longed for my husband, but my knight in shining armor was not there to rescue me.

Conversely, if he'd been there then there wouldn't have been a crisis to resolve. Irony aside, it was up to me to find a way out of a financial fiasco, and I racked my brain. I'd already sold Barry's Harley motorcycle, as well as the second car I no longer needed, and paid off those loans. Our savings account was all but empty, and I'd invested what was left of the life insurance money in a Roth IRA and couldn't make a withdrawal without paying stiff penalties. My mind raced like a caged hamster on a wheel.

As close as we were I refused to even consider turning to family members for money. While Jerry had done very well for himself as a salesman for one of the local clothing manufacturing companies, I couldn't ask my brother for money. Even if he could easily afford to pay my debts, it wasn't his place to bail Chuck and me out. I was out of options. I wearily leaned back in the chaise, swept away tears, and prayed for guidance. Eventually the summer night, heavy with the day's lingering heat, drove me inside to air conditioning.

Insomnia was my companion during a long, restless night, but sunrise brought its customary chorus of chirping birds, the dawn of a new day, and an answer. I ate a quick breakfast and hopped in the shower before going to the station to make sure Chuck was opened for business and to pick up the charge slips, which was a much bigger stack than I'd expected. With that kind of cash flow problem it was apparent the business couldn't support itself, let alone provide for Chuck and his indolent wife.

Nonetheless, what was done was done, and since God hadn't provided a path to the past, we had to move forward. I talked over my plan with Chuck, and despite that remorse was written all over his face he agreed that an equity line of credit on my home was our only choice. The realization was that he lacked the maturity and experience to fill Barry's shoes, and we couldn't afford to keep throwing good money after bad. I'd evidently inherited Mama's pragmatic attitude.

My next stop was at the bank to complete the credit application, a requirement the loan officer stressed was a formality. I dreaded relinquishing the deed to my home, but it was necessary in order not to file for bankruptcy, which may have been the easiest way out but was not an option. I left the bank and reminded myself that money comes and goes, and in the great big scheme of things, it wasn't important. My salary would suffice and even though I hadn't planned on a mortgage payment, I would be able to support myself.

I pushed those problems aside and bought lunch for Daddy and me at Arby's drive-thru. My sisters and I took care of him as much as possible so he could stay in his home, and they had picked up the slack for the past month. I promised Pat that I would stop by and throw in a load of laundry, clean the kitchen and bathroom, and run the vacuum. Pat and I both had fulltime jobs, so Joyce, our middle sister, usually did light housekeeping several days a week. Given that I was back in town, I volunteered to fill in since I would be back at work next week.

Daddy was on the front porch, resting in a cushioned rocker, reading the latest, large-print edition of *Reader's Digest*. I ambled along the walkway and up the steps, where I propped against the porch post. "Hi, Daddy. How are you?"

"Oh, I'm as well as any man my age could be. It's good to have you home, kitten?"

He hadn't used that term of endearment since my childhood. "I'm all right, Daddy. Happy to be home. Do you need anything from the grocery store? I can go after I finish the housework."

"No, I've got everything I need, sugar." He didn't beat around the bush—he never did. "Nobody's said anything to me, but I believe your youngest boy may be losing his hide."

Nobody had to say anything to Daddy for him to know what was going on. Even though he was eighty-seven, he was sharp as a tack and not much got past him when it came to family. "I really don't want to talk about it,

Daddy. We've worked things out and will be collecting what's owed and selling what we can before we close up shop. I'll come up with the rest of the money we need to pay the off what we owe. Chuck will find a job, and now that I'm finally a college graduate, I plan to look for another job that pays more. We'll get through this setback."

He sat staring into space, gathering his thoughts before he said anything. "You know, collecting those debts may be like getting' blood out of a turnip. Most of 'em have no intention of settlin' up, or the dirty crooks would have already paid their bills." He cleared his throat and continued, "If I had the money, I would gladly give it to you."

A few months after Mama died there was a mutual agreement to transfer Daddy's assets to ourselves, the six siblings, to be used for his living expenses and home maintenance. "I know you would but don't worry about me. I've got things under control, and I'm fully prepared to meet with my lawyer and file for wage garnishment in order to collect from those in arrears. Like I said, Daddy, I don't want to discuss the matter anymore."

He shrugged and kept rocking. "Suit yourself."

I changed the subject. "I brought you a roast beef sandwich and a chocolate milkshake." I kissed his forehead, unpacked our lunch, and folded myself in a rocker next to him. "Let's eat before I start the chores. I hope the bathroom is not in its usual state. I don't know how a man who lives alone can make such a mess in the bathroom. Thank goodness you don't use the guest bathroom, or it would have to be cleaned, too."

He dismissed my complaint with a wave of his hand. "Aww, don't worry about the bathroom. One of 'em girls will clean it."

A yellow butterfly hovered over Mama's fragrant pink rosebushes. "Daddy, I'm one of 'em girls."

When I got home there were three messages from Kim on the answering machine, and I returned her calls. "Hi, Kim. What's so urgent that you need to find me?"

"Nothing serious. You graduate on Sunday morning, isn't that right?"

"Yes, finally, after years of holding down a fulltime job, finishing raising two sons, juggling classes, and losing my husband to cancer. I almost elected to have my diploma mailed, but at the last minute I signed up to participate in the ceremony for my hard-earned diploma."

"You can bet your ass that's what I would have done. You deserve to be recognized for your hard work, which brings me to the point. Cindy and I want to take you out to dinner on Friday night to celebrate. We can drive to Atlanta or eat at the Mansion in Carrollton, wherever you want to go is good with us."

The "Mansion" was the Maple Street Mansion and was originally the home of L.C. Mandeville. He was born to a family of privilege but didn't need his father's wealth because he opened a textile mill in the late eighteen hundreds and made his own fortune. Although his father had given his son, the seventh of ten children, the land, L.C. built the three-story home in eighteen-ninety. It was a beautiful example of Victorian architecture—complete with a turret and characteristic gingerbread trim. Rumors abounded that the popular eatery was haunted, most notably by a young woman who'd committed suicide there decades earlier. The possibility of ghosts at one's dinner table only added to the distinctive ambience of the restaurant. The location had served as the perfect venue for Brad and Valerie's rehearsal dinner.

I objected, "Kim, that's really not necessary. Actually, I've already planned to crash and watch an old movie. But I'll think about it, and if I agree we can go to Carrollton instead of driving to Atlanta when the rush-hour traffic will be a headache from hell. I plan to spend a few hours in my office over the next couple of days to review student schedules and class sizes. Technically, I'm not on the clock until Monday, but I don't want to leave too much unfinished before registration day. It's going to be good for me to get back to my routine."

"Do whatever you want tomorrow, but on Friday night we're going out to celebrate your success. Don't even try to argue with me. I'll pick you up around six o'clock. And for goodness sakes wear something besides jeans and a t-shirt. You should look nice for your celebration dinner, and the bar is for casual dress. Since it's always packed on weekends we'll probably be seated in one of the dining rooms." Another phone line on her desk demanded her attention. "No more discussion. I'll see you Friday."

Her click ended the conversation. Maybe it would be fun to go out with my nieces and take a break from worrying over the business and Chuck's future. I perused my closet and began sorting through clothes and decided I should make a run to Sweet Pea's Boutique before I remembered that I'd inherited money problems. After a critical scrutiny of my closet, I realized I didn't need anything new. I retrieved a sleeveless, beige dress and found a pair of low-heeled strappy, taupe sandals that would suffice. I selected a necklace and earrings that would add polish to the outfit. I hung the ensemble on the closet door so that I wouldn't have to think about what to wear and found myself looking forward to celebrating graduation with Cindy and Kim.

I finalized the arrangements for Chuck and Leslie's rehearsal dinner the following week, but my heart wasn't in planning a party. It wasn't a secret that my son's marriage to an immature, spoiled, and selfish woman was certainly not my dream for him. I had a nagging sense that Chuck had gotten himself in a situation he didn't know how to get out of and that Leslie and her mama had hoodwinked him into proposing. Instead of rocking the boat I suspected he'd resigned himself to a marriage he didn't want any more than I did. I revised my prediction of the marriage lasting a year to a mere six months. Despite my misgivings, I wanted to be fair to the young couple and to do my best to make the dinner a festive event.

I made an effort to put those worries in the "later" file as I dressed for my celebratory dinner. True to her word, Kim was at my door promptly at six wearing dress pants and lacy top. She greeted me with an inspection. "You clean up very well. That dress is flattering, and it looks like you took time with your hair and makeup."

I stowed the house keys in my small handbag and smiled. "Thank you, but I really don't know why I couldn't have just worn cropped jeans and a blouse. Despite your not-so-subtle suggestions about dating, I'm not in any way on the prowl."

"It doesn't hurt to get dressed up once in a while. Cindy called to tell me she had a late afternoon dentist appointment in Carrollton. She's meeting us at the Mansion."

We made small talk during the short drive and pulled into a crowded parking lot but found an empty spot in a matter of minutes. Kim led me directly to the large dining room where I was greeted with shouts of "Surprise!"

Surprise, indeed. I was overcome with awe to see the room packed with friends and family. I didn't know how Kim had managed to keep a secret. I mingled among the guests, many of whom had brought cards and gifts, and thanked each of them for coming. We all appreciated an array of appetizers and drinks before a huge cake, decorated with a graduation cap with a gold tassel and a scroll with the word "diploma" etched in blue icing, was served. Before the crowd dispersed, I wanted to express my gratitude. Public speaking, even in front of familiar faces, was not my forte; nonetheless, I made my way to the front of the room.

A hush fell over the crowd as I cleared my throat and began to speak. "I had no idea how many friends I have, and I'm very grateful that all of you made time to celebrate this milestone in my life." Tears blurred my vision, and I inhaled deeply before I continued, "My heart is heavy with disappointment that Barry is not here to share this moment with me. On those discouraging days when I'd wanted to give up, he believed in me and in my endeavor to earn a college degree. But he is here in spirit and in my heart." Pat handed me a tissue to wipe away contradictory tears of regret and happiness. "I want to thank each of you for your presence in my life."

Hugs followed my brief address as people moved towards the exit. When the room finally cleared, I embraced my sister and her daughters and thanked them for the time, effort, and money it took to host a party for me. Cindy was boxing up leftover cake. "We were happy to do it for you. It's what family is for, Sheila."

The rehearsal dinner was behind me, and as I dressed for the wedding I thought about the differences in backgrounds between Leslie's mama and myself. Eileen was a divorcee who'd supported herself and both of her children by working two, sometimes three jobs. Her education was limited, and she had no marketable skills so she'd mostly waited tables or cleaned other women's homes. She'd shared with me that after several bad relationships, she was lucky to have met a good man years ago. They married and had a child together. Eileen continued to work at the convenience store her husband brought to the marriage. She seemed happy with her lot in life and based upon appearances, accepted what was and carried no remorse.

I, on the other hand, had had one very good relationship and had stayed home with my children until my younger son began Pre-K. I gave up being a full-time housewife for a job with the school system, with a schedule that matched that of my boys. I took computer classes to improve my chances of promotion and accepted every opportunity for advancement. I didn't carry baggage, but unlike Eileen I allowed a few random regrets to occasionally plague me, and one of those in particular triggered turmoil. Why hadn't I recognized that Barry was sick? What if I'd insisted he see a doctor months before his diagnosis? Could I have done anything to alter the outcome? I put those regrets on a shelf because they led to a hurtful, dead-end road.

It was also a waste of time to dwell on life's what-ifs, especially when I had a wedding to attend. With a touch of lipstick, a few drops of perfume, and a comb through my hair, I was as ready as I ever would be. Once at the church, I was escorted down the aisle by one of the groomsmen, an old friend of Chuck's. I was seated on the pew reserved for the groom's parents, where I sat alone and concentrated on making it through the ceremony.

When the preacher said, "If anyone here objects to the union of these two people, let him speak now or forever hold his peace" I wanted nothing more than to snatch my six-four "baby" from the altar, and Leslie's clutch, and run like a bat outta hell. Beyond those musings, I had no plans. In a matter of minutes, for better or worse, Chuck and Leslie were pronounced man and wife. The die may have been cast, but the writing was on the wall.

*Name changed

Chapter Eight

There's Life out There

Cyndie and I fell back into the comfortable camaraderie that had developed over years of working together, with the added bonus of friendship. We no longer shared an office suite as she'd accepted the position of full-time counselor at the middle school a couple of years earlier. The middle school classes were located on the same campus as the high school, but out of necessity Cyndie relocated to the first floor. As registrar my job description encompassed grades six through twelve in our small school system. Cyndie and I were in regular contact, and I'd adapted to working with the new high school counselor Janis, another alumna.

I was appreciative of the fact that I had a job with an extended "family." My work was varied, allowed for plenty of interaction between students and faculty, and, most importantly, filled my days. Although I wasn't struggling financially, I was ready to pay off the home equity loan and rebuild a nest egg. Therefore, I submitted applications for various vacancies and interviewed for several positions, but none were particularly promising. One of the jobs I was offered involved a great deal of travel, and I'd become accustomed to only a two mile drive from home to office. Additionally, none of the handful of jobs "felt" right, as if my gut instinct was telling me to stay put and bide my time. While the days passed quickly, the evenings were endless. My workday was over at four o'clock, but I often stayed later to postpone the inevitable: going home to an empty house that screamed of loneliness. Walking through the back door was as painful as a slap in the face.

I did what I could to fill the emptiness. I walked three miles, weather permitting, each afternoon, and I accepted invites from friends and family to go out to eat or see a movie or shopping. But I needed something more to occupy my free time, something that would keep me from slipping into the void of depression. Patti, my grief counselor whom I continued to see on a monthly basis, suggested I step out of my misery and find something that interested me where I could volunteer. So when Betty Jean, one of our English teachers, approached me about volunteering for the county's literacy program, I jumped at the offer. She was chairperson of the continuing education program, and there was a need for tutors to help high school dropouts earn their GED certificates. On Tuesday and Thursday nights I would work one-on-one with adults who wanted nothing more than to improve their lives, but doors were closed to those who, for whatever reasons, hadn't been able to graduate high school. A high school equivalency diploma was the first necessary step to getting off the treadmill of poverty. Betty Jean warned that it was a daunting task, but armed with a college degree, I was confident I could meet the challenge.

Five minutes after meeting Wanda* I realized I didn't need a college degree to tutor my charge. She was a shy black woman, approximately ten years older than I, who was having trouble passing the math portion of the exam. Math was not my strength, but Wanda lacked the most basic skills. She could barely add and subtract; multiplication was Greek to her, as were fractions and decimals. She didn't even know how to make change. I was stunned until I realized that when she was a student in the fifties, despite the Supreme Court's 1954 landmark decision to desegregate public schools in Brown v. Brown, the disparity in the quality of education between blacks and whites was a chasm. There was a school for "blacks only" across town from where I attended school; many parents refused to send their children to an all-white school in an environment of racism. Not until after the Civil Rights Act of 1964 did a few stray students venture outside their comfort zone and cross the threshold of my middle school classroom.

I decided the best approach was to put Wanda at ease by becoming acquainted and to use caution so as not to intimidate her. She wore her insecurities as a shield. She'd dropped out of school in the eighth grade to help her mama clean houses for wealthy white women. Eventually, she was able to secure a position cleaning for several offices in town. I hoped she wanted more and asked her why she wanted to earn her GED.

Her answer was simple: "Because it's something I need to do, for me, for my children. They need to know their mama ain't stupid. I mean, isn't stupid." She dropped her head to hide her shame. My heart broke for a woman who'd had a life I couldn't begin to conceive, even knowing that Mama's life hadn't been a bed of roses. Much of her road had been paved with poverty, but she had the benefit of being white in an era of racial prejudices that would continue for decades.

Wanda and I became friends and as she learned to trust me, teaching her became less stressful because she relaxed and didn't worry about giving the wrong answer. We used the worksheets provided, which were a review for me but opened a world of knowledge for Wanda. She was most excited about learning how much change she should be given after making a purchase and I wondered how many times some unscrupulous cashier had taken advantage of her. She would also be tested on what she knew about Algebra, something that terrified her. I reminded her of all she'd learned and that those abilities would help her to solve algebraic formulas. With coaxing and patience Wanda could solve most of the problems on the worksheets, enough to pass the final exam and achieve her goal. Although I tutored a few others, Wanda's unbridled pride was a poignant reminder of my advantages.

I was disappointed when state funding for the program was cut shortly thereafter. Other volunteer opportunities in my community conflicted with working hours. I found myself seeking alternate activities to fill my spare time, especially on the long weekends. Living alone required minimal housekeeping, laundry, and grocery shopping. I didn't appreciate, until it was over, that one day I would miss the hectic demands of both time and energy it took to take care of a family and home. The problem of not having enough hours in the day had transitioned to having too many hours, empty hours.

It was my friend Carla who recognized my lonesomeness and suggested I go out with her on Saturday night to a bar in Carrollton where her husband was playing in a band. "It's almost a year since you lost Barry, and Skip and I think it will be good for you to get out of the house and mingle. And you don't have to worry about fitting in because there's a group that will welcome you with open arms. I rarely go out anymore to hear the band but please think about it, and we can ride together. I'll introduce you to everybody."

Skip, her husband, was one of the members of Backstreet, and Carla caught me up regarding the band members. It was comprised of guys I'd known most of my life who'd recently reconnected after putting their musical interests on hold while their children were young. Twenty years later they found themselves together again, playing oldies from our collective youth. Three of the bandmates had been classmates, sort of. Richard was a few years older, Skip was a year older, and Willi a year younger, but I remembered them all from high school. Victor was the senior member of the band and hadn't gone to school in Bremen. His older son and my younger son had been friends growing up, so he and I were passing acquaintances. I had the opportunity to meet Victor when his son had "borrowed" his dad's new, expensive sleeping bag for a campout with Chuck beside a creek near both subdivisions. The twelve-year old boys built a campfire, which they left unattended while they fished downstream. The sleeping bag caught fire and burned to a crisp before either boy noticed the rising smoke and raced back to the campsite. That was the boys' last camping trip for several months.

My thoughts had wandered while I was filing student records and debating about Carla's invitation when she stuck her head in my office on Friday afternoon. "Got a minute?"

"You must be clairvoyant. I was just thinking about you."

"Please tell me you've decided to go out with me tomorrow night. There's no reason for you to stay home by yourself when you have friends who love you and enjoy your company."

I hadn't made up my mind yet, but figured going out with a friend would be better than another Saturday night channel surfing or renting a movie at Blockbuster. "Ok. I'll go, but if I'm a misfit and want to leave early, promise me that you'll take me home. By the way, what's the dress code at a place like TC Rose?"

"Casual, definitely casual. The bar is kind of a dive, and I wouldn't recommend you go alone, but with a group it's a good place to have a drink, dance, meet people. They serve food, but the menu is limited. We can eat out before we go, or eat at home. Either way, we have plenty of time. The band doesn't start until nine."

Nine o'clock? By that time I was in my pajamas, watching a movie with a bowl of popcorn for company. "I usually eat an early supper, so why don't we pass on a restaurant? What time should I be ready?"

She showed off her gorgeous smile. "I'll be at your house around eight-thirty. I'm so glad you'll be joining us. Skip will be pleased, too."

Carla may have been delighted that I was going out, but as I tried on clothes in front of my bedroom mirror, I regretted agreeing to go to a bar. Barry and I had never been a couple to go to clubs and chose instead to spend time together as a family. When the kids outgrew us, we continued hiking without the boys. We enjoyed eating out and seeing a movie or pilfering around junk stores or spending Saturdays riding the motorcycle. But that was then.

I touched up my makeup and realized the afternoon walks had extended my summer tan into late September. I pulled hot rollers out of my hair and fluffed it into an unconcerned mess before I slipped on a pair of well-worn Levi's and a white shirt. Silver hoop earrings and watch were added to the laid-back outfit. Before cancelling on Carla, I convinced myself that going out with friends was no different than it had been in Mexico, and the rule June and I'd had about arriving and leaving together would also apply at home.

I was changing sandals for a more practical pair of ballerina flats when I heard the toot of a car horn. I set the security system and flipped on the porch light, closed the locked door behind me, and hopped into the passenger side of Carla's SUV. As always, she looked beautiful and greeted me warmly. "You look great. I told the gang you were coming with me, and they're all excited to meet you. I think you've already met Debbie, maybe through her kids. They're younger than your boys, but I'm sure her son and daughter have been in your office for some reason or another. She's sweet as sugar, not a mean bone in her body. You probably already know Kathy, too."

Carla was right in that I knew both Debbie and Kathy. Debbie lived in my neighborhood, and I'd gone to school with Kathy's ex-husband. When we got to the bar Carla led the way to a large table near the back where several people were laughing; we interrupted the merry group with introductions. Debbie gave me a warm hug and welcomed me to join them. She introduced me to her husband, Roger. Kathy also greeted me with a hug and a smile, and neither of us could remember the last time we'd seen each other. I'd never met Stanley and Jane, who lived in a nearby town. Jane was tall, blonde, stacked, and carried a friendly smile that put me at ease. Stanley was tall and slender, with blues eyes that twinkled with mischief. He pointed out Jonathan on stage, the youngest member of the band.

There was also a woman, very petite, who shared my name. We all gathered around the table reserved for the band and spent the next hour becoming better acquainted. Stanley was the band's designated driver so the others could have a drink without worrying about driving under the influence. We laughed about the fact that back in their younger days, the designated driver was the one who could find the car. We all agreed that with age came wisdom and responsibility.

We danced mostly as a group, but I danced a few times with the guys at the table and with the band members when they were on break and Jerry, the sound man, put on a soundtrack of popular music. We all hit the floor when the "Electric Slide" blasted the bar and returned to our table when a slow song serenaded couples. I had to admit I was having a good time but was caught off guard when a stranger approached and asked me to dance. He was tall and reasonably handsome, brown hair and hazel eyes, dressed in jeans, a blue plaid, button-up shirt with the sleeves rolled up, and battered cowboy boots. There was no South in his mouth, which was a dead giveaway that he hadn't grown up in this neck of the woods. I politely declined his invitation to dance, and he looked disappointed.

Carla reached across me to drag out a chair and asked the stranger to join us. I shouted above the noise, "What are you doing?'

She leaned over and whispered in my ear. "You're here to meet people, remember? Don't worry, Sheila. The man asked you to dance, not to go home with him."

I shrugged off my rejection of the man who introduced himself as Steve, from Arizona. He happily seated himself in the empty chair next to me and offered to buy me a drink, which I also refused. During the course of the conversation, he told me he was in Georgia for work, a big construction project at the university. He was an electrician who'd lived in the Phoenix area all of his life, where he'd married—and divorced—his wife. He had two grown daughters and one granddaughter, a one-year-old named Rosemary, after his mother, who was the light of his life. "Missing her is the only downside to working out of town, but I like my job and traveling, meeting people, and the money is good." He finished his beer. "Hey, I've been rambling on for half an hour and other than your name, I don't know anything about you, Sheila. Let's change the subject and talk about you."

I didn't particularly want to share my life's story with a man whom I'd just met, so I followed his lead and kept things neutral. I told him that I had two sons, both recently married, and that I lived in Bremen, a few miles north of Carrollton. I pushed my hair away from my face, and he noticed the ring on my right hand and took note of my bare left hand.

"Well, it doesn't appear that you're a married woman, and I already know you're not here on a date because he would be crazy to leave you alone in a bar. Are you also divorced?"

The moment I'd dreaded arrived. "No, I'm a widow, for almost a year." There, I'd said it, the cards were on the table and I felt nauseous. The anniversary of losing Barry was less than two weeks away, and the first year, which several other widows declared to be the hardest, would be behind me.

Debbie noticed my discomfort and suggested we all dance to ZZ Tops' "Hot Legs." I sighed with relief and gave her a grateful glance. Steve pulled out my chair and led me onto the jam-packed dance floor where, thankfully, the loud music made conversation impossible. We danced to several more old hits and a few new ones before I excused myself to go to the ladies' room. Steve parked himself at the door and waited like a loyal Labrador.

When I exited he said, "I don't know about you, but I've had enough dancing for one night. Would you like to go somewhere and have a cup of coffee and a meal? I'm starving."

Before I could refuse, Carla was at my side and answered, "We'd both love to meet you for a bite to eat. Are you hungry, Sheila?"

Surprisingly, I was. Between eating early and all the dancing, I'd worked up an appetite. I checked the time on the luminous clock behind the bar, a reminder of "last call" and faced Steve. "As it's after midnight the only thing open is the Waffle House."

"Waffle House sounds great. We don't have those restaurants in Arizona, so it's a novelty for me to eat there whenever I'm in one of the southern states."

I laughed out loud. "A novelty? The Waffle House? The high school kids refer to it as the 'Awful House' but meet there every Friday night after home football games."

Carla told the others we were leaving and waved goodbye to Skip as the three of us walked out to the parking lot. She told Steve know we would meet him at the Waffle House in Bremen, located adjacent to I-20. "Sheila rode down with me and will be leaving with me."

He held the door for us and replied, "That's perfect. I'm staying at the Hampton Inn at the Bremen exit, across the street from that Waffle House."

Before I could respond Carla let him know that it didn't matter where his hotel was because she would be delivering me to my door. He thanked her for watching out for me and told me I was lucky to have such a good friend. Steve was also quick to clear up any confusion. "I'm not looking for a one-night stand, Carla. It's just nice to meet people for companionship. I really enjoyed the company of all of you tonight. See you two at the Waffle House."

We all arrived at the Waffle House fifteen minutes later and walked in together where we found an empty booth I looked around the small eatery and was surprised the place was crowded at such a late hour. I noticed a few people who looked vaguely familiar. "Carla, do we know any of these people? I recognize some of them but for the life of me, I can't place them."

She glanced over her shoulder and surveyed the gathering of customers before she clarified my confusion. "Most of them were at TC Rose, apparently here for the same reason we are."

I took another look around at the motley crew before I replied, "They look a helluva lot better in the dark—and after I've had my two wine cooler limit."

Steve and Carla laughed, and a tired-ass waitress showed up to take our order. I decided on a waffle and hot chocolate, and Carla ordered a Coke with a bacon, egg, and cheese sandwich. To my surprise Steve ordered coffee only. "I thought you were starving, Steve. There was no need to meet us here if you're not even hungry."

He smiled and placed his hand over mine. "I didn't come here to eat. I came because I wanted to delay the evening's ending. I want to spend as much time with you as possible before we say our goodnights." He tipped his coffee cup in Carla's direction in a mock salute. "And it goes without saying, time with you, too, Carla."

Carla laughed at his bullshit, and I blushed and pulled my hand away. "It was nice meeting you, but we both know the night has to end."

The waitress brought our order, and Steve waited for her to leave before he said, "I want to see you again, Sheila. I'll be here for the next two or three weeks. Do you have plans tomorrow? My crew works until four tomorrow, due to a looming deadline, but maybe we can go out to dinner. Please think about it before you turn me down flat."

I hesitated and stirred my hot chocolate before I answered, "It sounds like you're asking me for a date, and I'm not ready to date. Thanks anyway."

Steve persisted, but Carla interrupted. "You seem to be a nice enough guy, but my friend isn't ready to date. Why don't you give her your cell number? If she has a change of heart, she'll give you a call, which puts the ball in her court." She nudged me. "Is that fair enough, Sheila?"

I shrugged and stammered, "Um, yes that seems fair."

We finished our meals, and Steve walked us to where Carla had parked. She unlocked the doors and waited in the driver's seat. I reached for the door handle, and Steve leaned in for what I feared was a kiss. I turned my face away so that his kiss landed on my cheek. He opened the car door and said, "I'll be waiting to hear from you, since I have no way to get in touch with you. Goodnight, Sheila."

On the short ride home, Carla encouraged me to think about putting myself out there but only if I was okay with it. It was the same advice other friends and several family members had given me: time to move on, you're too young to be alone, you have to let go of the past, etc. In the end, according to Patti, I was the only one who could give myself permission to date, to leave the past in the past. Having married my high school sweetheart, I hadn't dated in almost thirty years and had no idea how to begin. I was a misfit in that I wasn't a young single woman expecting to marry and raise a family. Nor was I an elderly widow who'd readily made a new life filled with friends and grandchildren, with no contemplations of romance. I was agitated when I got in bed, and despite being exhausted I couldn't sleep.

Eventually those tiresome thoughts lulled me to sleep, but I awoke to the first fingers of sunrise that shed a rosy glow over the bedroom. I pulled the covers over my head and slept for another two hours to avoid facing the day of decision. I didn't have to do anything. Steve didn't have my phone number and didn't even know my last name, so he couldn't find me in the phone book. I played devil's advocate and reasoned that it wouldn't hurt to have supper with Steve, given that we both had to eat. And nothing would come of the date because we were separated by almost two thousand miles, making a relationship geographically impractical and undesirable. If the date went badly, I wouldn't have to worry about our paths crossing, which was the determining factor in my decision to call him.

Before I committed to anything I went to Daddy's house. It was my day to check on him, pick up his lunch, and clean or laundry whatever he'd managed to mess up since the day before when Pat was there. I went about washing the breakfast dishes, sweeping the floors, and folding a load of towels Pat had tossed in the dryer. I was engrossed with thoughts of a perspective date when Daddy interrupted those thoughts. "Sheila, did you hear me?"

"No, sorry, Daddy. What did you say?"

He handed me a short list of items he needed from the grocery store. "I forgot a few things when Joyce went to the store on Friday and need you to pick them up for me when you have time. I don't know how I forgot to tell her I'm out of corn flakes and milk."

I didn't point out that he wasn't getting any younger and that memory lapses were to be expected. Daddy had a car and could drive to the grocery store, but we did our best to limit his driving without taking away his car, his last symbol of independence. I took the list from his aging, withered hand and stuffed it in my pocket. "It's okay, Daddy. I have to get your lunch from Arby's or Wendy's, whichever you'd rather have, and I can stop by the store while I'm out."

I stacked the clean towels on the bathroom shelf and found Daddy in his usual spot, in one of the rockers on the front porch, taking pleasure in the warmth of sunshine that painted the porch. I sat on the stoop, and he asked, "What've you been studying on so hard this morning?"

No, Daddy didn't miss much, and there was no reason to lie. "I've been preoccupied with thinking about accepting a date with a man I met last night." I deliberately didn't mention where I'd met Steve because Daddy would disapprove. Omission was not a lie.

He rocked for a few minutes, and the sound of wood on wood creaked between us. "Pat said you went out with some friends last night, to a honky-tonk. Is that where you met the man who's asked' you out?"

I would have to thank my big sister. "Yes, Daddy, I met him last night at a bar in Carrollton. There's nothing wrong with going out with friends to have a drink and a few dances, and I've known the band members and their wives for years, went to school with most of 'em.'" As I justified my actions, I couldn't comprehend a parent's ability to make us feel like children again.

"No, there's nothing wrong with goin' out and having a good time, as long as you keep company with folks you know and don't trust the ones you don't. Who is this fella? Is he from around here? Does he have a name?"

"His name is Steve, and he's from Arizona. I don't know much about him except that he's divorced and has two daughters and a grandchild. He's in Georgia working on a construction expansion at the university." Sunlight washed over me as I propped on the porch post. "I'm considering going out to supper with him. In any case it'll give the old men in town something new to talk about. I've heard rumors they're worried I'm too picky and may never date anybody. Those bored, retired, barber shop buzzards evidently have nothing better to talk about than me and my dating life, or lack of. They really need to mind their own business."

Daddy continued to rock and laid the Sunday paper aside. "'I agree 'em old goats ought not to be meddlesome, but don't give 'em fodder for gossip. In the end all a body's left with is his reputation. That, and his regrets."

"Daddy, I won't forget how I was raised, and I'm not going to do anything to embarrass my family or myself."

I'm not sure he heard me, but he appeared to be weighing his words. "You're a grown woman, a stubborn woman, with a mind of your own. No need in me buttin' in, but this man's a drifter who *said* he's divorced." He was woolgathering before he finished his piece. "Me and your mama had sixty years together before God called her home, but it wasn't nearly enough time. I'm an old man whose days are filled with waiting—waiting for my day to die. But you're young, with years of life ahead of you. Whether you believe it or not, 'em years will stretch into loneliness. Its best if you go out now and again, meet a few men. Just trust that the Lord is preparing the right man to send to you in His own time."

I'd never known Daddy to discuss matters of the heart. Tears I hadn't anticipated stung my eyes, and I dusted them away with the back of my hand. I walked over to the rocker and took Daddy's hand in mine. "I'm sorry Mama is gone and that your days are long and lonesome without her." He didn't respond; the window to his soul was closed. I sighed and continued, "I'll head to the grocery store and then get your lunch. What would you like to eat?"

"Seeing how you gotta go out towards the interstate anyway, I'd like to have a Big Mac meal from McDonald's and throw in a cherry pie."

"Okay. I'll be back in about an hour."

Steve was thrilled to hear my voice. "I'm glad you called! I have to jump in the shower but can pick you up at six. It doesn't matter where we eat, any place you like is fine with me. Oh, I need directions to your house."

I thought about Carla's analogy of having the ball in my court, and I wanted the advantage in my favor. Besides, I wasn't ready to provide directions to a man who was pretty much a stranger and who may or may not have been a serial killer, which I seriously doubted. "I'll pick you up in a red Mustang convertible at your motel. It's the Hampton Inn, right?"

Steve sounded as if I'd rejected him but agreed. "Yes, that's fine. I'll be waiting for you out front. Thanks, Sheila, for allowing me to be your first date."

I was about to repeat "first date," but the words stuck in my throat like sawdust. Maybe I'd made the wrong decision. But maybe I was overthinking the circumstances. It was only dinner, but I didn't remember dating being such a dilemma.

Steve sensed my indecisiveness and reassured me. "It's really okay for you to go out with me. I'm looking forward to seeing you again."

"Yes, me too. I mean, I'm looking forward to seeing you again, too." I returned the phone to its cradle and began rummaging through my closet. I decided that khakis, a pink t-shirt, and sandals would keep things casual. I was putting the finishing touches to hair and makeup when the phone rang.

Kim's voice zipped through the line. "Hey, what are you doing? We're taking the kids over to Chuck E. Cheese, better known as the parent trap. You're welcome to join us, so get yourself ready, and we'll be there in half an hour. You can catch me up on how your Saturday night out with Carla and the band went. Did you have fun? Did you dance with anybody?"

Carla had suggested that if I changed my mind about going out with Steve, then I should let her or someone know when and where I would be going as a precaution. If Steve had been from around Bremen, I could have made a few calls and gotten a full background check, including his family and how long they'd lived here and whether or not the man had ever been arrested. Unfortunately, none of us had any contacts out in Arizona, so I nonchalantly apprised Kim of my plans. "Yes, I had a good time, and I have a date tonight but thanks for thinking of me. Maybe we can get together one night next week. Gotta run."

I heard the phone clatter onto the countertop and her rescue of the receiver. "'Gotta run' my ass. Who do you think you're talkin' to? Who are you going out with tonight? Did you meet him last night? Is he single, divorced, widowed? How old is he? Does he have kids? How old are they? Where does he—"

I interrupted her barrage of questions. "Slow down, Nosy Rosy. His name is Steve. I met him last night. He's divorced and has two daughters. I don't know how old they are, don't even know how old he is but I'd guess mid to late forties. He's from Arizona, here for a few weeks working construction. Are you satisfied? I really have to go. I'm picking him up at his motel at six. Goodbye, Kim."

She screeched, "Don't you dare hang up this phone, or I'll drive straight to your house before you can get outta the driveway." She called out to her husband, "Bob, Bob! Our plans have changed. Tell the kids they can play outside a while longer. We're cooking out for supper and we'll take them to the pizza place next Saturday. Sheila is bringing her date to meet me, some guy she met last night. He's a stranger, and she thinks she's going out with him without any of us knowing who the hell he is." She turned her directives to me. "It's settled. Pick him up and come by the house before your date. We can throw extra steaks on the grill if you want to eat here with us. It's almost six, and if you're not here in twenty minutes, I'll call the police and report a kidnapping."

"No, don't bother with supper for us. We're going to Longhorn's." Without another word the phone call was over. I listened to the dull hum of the disconnected call and knew Kim was serious about calling the police with a fabricated tale of kidnapping. I glimpsed in the hall tree mirror on my way out the back door and saw a fully grown woman, one surely capable of making her own decisions. Apparently I wasn't that woman, and I smiled as I dropped the ragtop on the Mustang. It was good to have a caring family to worry over me, though trying at times. Steve was standing at the entrance to the Hampton Inn when I wheeled into the parking lot. He was more handsome than I remembered, with touches of gray hair and eyes that weren't hazel but more of a blue-gray, the color of a slightly overcast sky.

He flashed a friendly smile and settled in the passenger seat. "There's nothing like a good-lookin' blonde in a red convertible to put a spring in a man's step. Fall weather in Georgia is remarkable, even if the leaves haven't started to turn yet."

"This is actually Indian summer, perfect convertible weather, although we may have to put the top up against the night chill on the drive back. It's too early for fall foliage. Mid-October is peak in the North Georgia Mountains, and the leaves here change color shortly thereafter." I adjusted the volume on the radio so we could continue our conversation. "I hope you don't mind, but we have to make a pit stop on our way to the restaurant. My niece, Kim, is anxious to meet the man who convinced me it's time to start dating. We'll stay for only a few minutes, but be prepared for the third degree."

He hooted a hearty laugh and shook his head. "You really are a babe in the woods. Is your niece going on the date to chaperone? What if I don't measure up to her standards? Does that mean the date is off?"

Steve's teasing was good-natured, and I responded jokingly, "You never know. I could be delivering you to the Southern Mafia. Or Kim and I could be planning to hold you hostage for ransom. Does anyone know who

I am? Did you tell anyone you were going out tonight?" I laughed as dire possibilities sat uneasily upon his face.

He laughed again, a bit nervously, as I parked in Kim's driveway. She and her husband had built a beautiful two-story home less than two miles from my neighborhood, but I didn't point out that fact to Steve. The aroma of steaks on the grill glided around the house to greet us, and I heard Kim tell the kids to stay away from the pool, which had been treated and closed for the season. She must've heard the slam of car doors because she came out to introduce herself to Steve. "So you're Sheila's date. Actually, that remains to be seen. Come on in. Would you like a beer or a drink?"

We climbed the porch steps, and Steve held the door for us. I didn't know if he was going to follow us inside or run. Evidently, neither Kim nor I had put him off. He made himself comfortable on one of the kitchen bar stools and accepted the beer Kim handed him. Bob came inside to meet the mystery man, and the four of us chatted until Bob excused himself to take food off the grill. Kim set out dishes, napkins, and condiments as she continued to play twenty questions with Steve until I declared that it was time to go, and Steve joined me at the back door.

Kim held up her hand. "Since Sheila is driving I'm sure you won't have any problem leaving your driver's license with me. It'll make it easier for the FBI to find you should my aunt come up missing. You can swing by and pick it up before Sheila takes you back to the Hampton, and I know she's safe."

Steve thought she was kidding, but she was not—which is exactly why I didn't want to tell her that I had a date. He retrieved his license from his wallet and willingly handed the card over to Kim. Satisfied that all was well, he and I made our escape to the popular steakhouse where we enjoyed a leisurely dinner. Steve did most of the talking and kept things impersonal, which I appreciated. I tried to stay focused and keep up my end of the conversation, but I kept looking around the restaurant to see if I recognized any of the other patrons.

Steve noticed my inattentiveness and asked, "Am I boring you, or are you expecting someone to meet us here?" He scanned the restaurant. "Maybe Kim followed us."

"Now you're being plain mean. I'm sorry if I seem distracted, but this feels wrong, like I'm doing something I shouldn't be."

"What are you talking about? You've done nothing wrong, and I certainly don't expect anything of you at the end of the evening."

I blushed at the very idea of him "expecting" something when I returned him to the motel. I had no intention of even getting out of the car. "It's not that. You've treated me with the utmost respect. But I have the sense that I'm cheating on my husband and that I'm going to be caught for betraying my marriage vows. Does that make any sense?"

"You're not cheating on your husband, but whatever you're feeling doesn't have to make sense to me. I'll ask for the check so we can leave."

When the waitress brought the check I pulled my wallet from my purse. Steve picked up the tab and said, "You don't need money. I've got this."

I thanked him and put my wallet away. "It's been awhile since I've been on a date, and I thought maybe going Dutch was the new thing."

He shook his head and smiled at me. "No, it's not the 'new thing' and don't forget that on your next date, which I hope will be with me."

It wasn't. We reclaimed his driver's license, and I drove back to the Hampton Inn. We sat in the parking lot and talked for a few minutes before Steve leaned over and kissed me. It was a deep, passionate kiss, and I abruptly pulled away. Steve was noticeably disappointed at my response, but there was no chance for a relationship to develop as neither of us was willing to relocate, even if we hadn't met until a year down the road. Besides, if I were interested in nothing more than a meaningless affair, I could have had that in Mexico with a very handsome, very rich man. Steve didn't kiss me again but asked for my phone number, which I relinquished on the condition that he not call me. He promised, but the phone was ringing when I unlocked the back door.

It was Steve calling to make sure I'd gotten home okay and to thank me again for going to dinner with him. "I won't call you again, until I'm working in the area some other time. My company bid on a project in Atlanta, and there's a good chance we'll get the job. If so, that means I'll be working there sometime next year. If it's okay, I'd like to call you again and see if you're ready to date."

Daddy had hit the nail on the head: Steve was a drifter, a man who drifted into—and out of—my life. "Goodnight, Steve. Take care of yourself."

I visited the cemetery on a regular basis to take flowers and to insure the gravesites in my family's plot were maintained, but I rarely ever stayed to chat. However, my visit on the first anniversary of Barry's death was as cliché and predictable as a Hallmark Channel movie. I placed the floral saddle of cattails and silk mums in yellow, red, and bronze over the headstone and tossed a blanket down next to his grave where I sat and caught him up on my life. I told him all about Mexico and the friends and good times I'd had there. I discussed the ring Mitch designed for me using the diamonds he'd given me and that I would wear it always. I shared with him the surprise party that was thrown for me when I graduated. I explained that his business hadn't made it, which was water under the bridge. I let Barry know how much I missed him and loved him, but that I was slowly adjusting to a different life.

A few fallen leaves rustled in the wind, and gray clouds glided in front of the sun. A chill filled the October afternoon, and the ground was noticeably colder. I confessed to my late husband that I had a first date with a man I met in a bar, which sounded worse than it actually was. I reminded him that a piece of my heart would be his forever and that I didn't plan to ever remarry. I laughed as I explained that he would be a tough act to follow and that living with "Lucy" wasn't a cakewalk. But I needed for him to understand that I was lonely and couldn't live in the past forever, even though he was the one who'd encouraged me to meet someone else. What he hadn't told me was how to find my way without him.

I sat in the isolated cemetery surrounded by silence and waited—waited for an answer to a prayer for guidance. Waited for Barry to somehow let me know it was okay that I'd gone out to supper with a man.

Minutes turned into hours, and the sun hung low over the secluded land-scape. I pulled my jacket closer against a dampness that announced rain was not far away. Dusk was descending over the muted sunset, and the only sound I heard was the squawk of geese that flew overhead in an offset vee. It was sprinkling when I gathered the blanket and whispered goodbye to my love.

Saturday afternoon stretched emptily before me, so I tackled the basement and discarded some of the junk while organizing the rest. I dusted off a backpack and remembered how my family and I used to enjoy camping and hiking trips. Chuck had always packed his backpack as if we were going to spend weeks in the wilderness and was exhausted by the time we'd finished the hike. Hiking was something Barry and I had enjoyed and continued after the boys outgrew the pastime. I saw no reason for me not to recommence those hiking trips to fill my Saturdays. North Georgia was a wealth of state parks and hiking trails and was a day trip, easily accessible via Interstate 400, north of Atlanta.

I was packing a backpack and cleaning my hiking boots when Brad stopped by to change the HVAC filters. When he asked why I'd dragged out my hiking gear, I told him I planned to go to Helen one Saturday and get back in shape for the strenuous trails that led to waterfalls and stunning, panoramic views. The leaves had just begun to change into their red, yel-low, and orange fall wardrobes.

I was surprised at his objection. "Are you crazy? You can't take off on those remote trails alone. What if you fall and break an ankle or take a wrong turn and lose your way?"

"I appreciate that you're worried about me, but I'll be fine. The trails are marked, and I'll leave the mountains well before dark. It's not like I'm too old and decrepit to maneuver a hiking trail. Besides, I'm sure I won't be the only person enjoying the fall weather, even though the leaves aren't predicted to peak for another week or two. Nevertheless, the leaves will be pretty, especially in the higher elevations, and the fresh air and exercise are a bonus."

"You're right about not being the only person on the trails. Suppose you come across a man who isn't hiking for his health or the scenery? He could rape you, strangle you, and throw your body over a cliff or bury you far from the main trail." Brad was more than agitated. "Promise me that you won't venture out on your own when it comes to hiking, at least not any further than Sweetwater Creek. That park is a thirty minute drive and is always crowded on the weekends and not nearly as widespread as the North Georgia trails. All you'll have to do is stay on the loop trail or hike beyond the factory ruins to the creek, turn around, and follow the trail to the parking lot."

I'd lived a sheltered life, and I considered my son's concerned advice to be cautious. The tables had turned, and the child had become the parent. For the second time in a month, I was made to feel like a child. Although I was disappointed he was right in that anything could happen to me alone on an isolated trail, so I agreed to a compromise. "Ok, I'll put plans on hold for now, but I'm going to ask around and find someone who enjoys hiking and has the time to go with me."

Luckily for me on one of the afternoons when I stayed afterhours at the office, I surfed the web for hiking groups in the area and a few clicks led me to the Atlanta Single Hikers. The website boasted fifteen members, both male and female, and the only requirement given was being single. I picked up the phone and dialed the number listed, which took me to an answering machine. I left a message with the coordinator, David, regarding the upcoming hiking trip to Tallulah Falls, along with my name and contact number.

I locked up the office and had been home about twenty minutes when my call was returned. "Hi, this is David. Is this Sheila?"

"Yes, this is she."

"I got your message, and you're welcome to join us on Saturday for the Tallulah Falls hike. We meet at the Park 'N Ride off Georgia 400, the Mansell Road exit, and there are seven of us signed up to participate. If you're interested in going, we leave at nine o'clock and carpool to the park."

"Sounds good, but I drive a Mustang that's not very practical for carpooling. I'll be happy to chip in for gas. Are there any dues for joining?"

"No, no dues. I drive a blue seven passenger van, and one of the other guys has an SUV that holds five people. You can hitch a ride with one of us. Thanks for offering to help out with gas but it's not necessary. You're responsible for water, snacks, lunch, and be sure to pack a rain jacket or poncho. So should I add your name to the list?'

I readily agreed. "Yes, please. I'll be at the designated meeting place on Saturday morning, and I look forward to meeting you, David."

"I'll add your name to the roster. I look forward to meeting you as well."

I hung up the phone and concluded that I was a trusting soul to meet up with a group of strangers, climb into the back of a van, and tramp through secluded mountain trails. I shrugged off those insignificant concerns because, after all, what could possibly happen? I left the office with a sense of excitement about getting back into a hobby I enjoyed.

Pat, on the other hand, had a very different opinion. She, Cindy, and I were leaving Juanito's where we met for our standing Friday lunch date when I remarked that I was going hiking on Saturday with a group of like-minded single people I found on the Internet. Cindy told me to have a good time and be careful before she hurried on her way.

Pat was in no hurry and lit a cigarette while she parked herself on a bench. She took a long drag and exhaled slowly. "Let me see if I understand what you're tellin' me. You hooked up with strangers online who like hiking, people you've never met and don't know anything about. You plan to meet those people on the other side of Atlanta, load up with them in a car without a description, and go to a state park somewhere in North Georgia where you'll spend the day traipsing through the woods." She inhaled another drag of her cigarette before she said, "Have you lost your damn mind? You haven't thought this thing through."

"Of course I have." I hugged her and assured her that I hadn't lost my mind. "I know you worry about me, it's what you do, but I'll be fine. I promise to be careful and to call you the minute I get home, so please stop thinking you have to be responsible for me. And, by the way, thanks for letting Daddy know I went out to hear a band with friends, which was none of his business. So spare him the worry of knowing that I'm going off with a group of, shall we say, new friends to spend the day in the mountains. Neither of you has to trouble yourself taking care of me. I did, after all, manage to spend a month in Mexico without either of you watching me like a hawk." Pat didn't like it but resigned herself to the fact that I wasn't going to change my plans out of fear.

Saturday's alarm woke me at six a.m., and I put on the coffee and hoped in the shower. After a breakfast of bacon, eggs, and oatmeal, I dressed in hiking pants and layered a sweatshirt over a long-sleeved t-shirt. Wool socks and Timberland boots completed the outfit. I tossed several granola bars, peanut butter crackers, an apple, and two large bottles of water into my backpack, along with a few other items, and made my way to I-20, eastbound. Traffic was light early on Saturday morning, and I reached the exit I needed in just over an hour. I pulled into the almost empty lot where I spotted a blue van. I eased into a space next to the van, and the driver and I lowered our car windows.

A man who appeared to be in his early thirties greeted me with a brief wave of his hand and a smile. "Good morning, I'm David. I'm guessing you're Sheila since you're driving a Mustang."

"Good morning. Yes, I'm Sheila, and it's nice to meet you. Are we the first to arrive?"

"Yes, but it's not yet nine o'clock. With the exception of one, the others are pretty dependable and should be here soon."

I got out of my car, backpack in tow, and chitchatted with David. Our discussion was interrupted when a Toyota pulled up next to us, and two women climbed out. They acknowledged David and me with a friendly smile as they unloaded their gear from the trunk. The taller of the two halted her unpacking and addressed David, "Do we need to drive this time?"

"No, if more than seven show up, John said he would drive."

The other woman extended her hand to me. "Good morning. I don't believe we've met. Is this your first time hiking with us?"

"Yes, and I'm looking forward to the day. It's been a while since I've hiked, but I walk every day, and I'm hoping I can keep up with the rest of you."

The taller woman introduced herself as Sharon and motioned to her friend who was engrossed in conversation with David. "That's Beverly. Don't worry about keeping up. We hike for the pleasure of the outdoors. None of us is trying to run a foot race." She slammed the trunk shut and locked the car. "Welcome to the group."

"Thanks, that's good to know." I began to relax, even though I hadn't admitted to Pat or myself that I was slightly apprehensive about the whole thing.

A tan SUV pulled alongside us, and the driver stuck his head out the window and asked if we were going to need two vehicles. David told him we would wait a few more minutes, but if Melanie wasn't there by ten minutes after nine, she would be on her own. I gathered Melanie was the one exception when it came to punctuality. Two more hikers, John and Greg, climbed out of the SUV, and David opened the back of the van. We all stowed our backpacks inside and left the parking lot at ten past nine, without Melanie. Along the way we exchanged names and impersonal information and swapped stories of other hikes.

The Tallulah Falls hike had several choices, one of which was a loop trail that was less than two miles and ranked as moderate in terms of difficulty. Our group would be crossing the suspension bridge over Tallulah Gorge to the Sliding Rock Trail, which led to a beautiful waterfall deep within the gorge, the Bridal Veil Falls. The hike was approximately four miles, but the boulder-filled trail made for a very strenuous hike.

We arrived at the park and paid the entrance fee. David went to the main office to secure the permit necessary for that particular hike and to give the ranger the names of those in our party. I can't say I wasn't relived that someone would know my name and where, and with whom, I was hiking. All of us slipped our backpacks on, and I checked my boot laces to make sure they were tied snuggly. We marched onward, and I'd forgotten how exhilarating a hike through the woods in the crisp mountain air could be. Any misgivings I had about my decision evaporated under a blue sky and a canopied trail. Along the way Greg spotted a bald eagle soaring high above us, and we retrieved binoculars to get a better look at the powerful yet graceful bird. Further along the trail we interrupted several deer drinking from the refreshing stream and watched the small herd jump effortlessly over rocks and fallen trees to flee our intrusion.

Rain wasn't forecast but rain it did, and the cloudburst caught us all off guard. I hurriedly pulled my poncho from my backpack. David led us a short distance to an overhang where we huddled against the downpour. We were grateful for the protection offered by the huge, flat rock that jutted from the side of a cliff and grateful, too, that there was no thunder and lightning. Spirits dampened, we each found a spot to sit and used the break to snack and rehydrate. Everyone was quiet, seemingly self-absorbed, and I thought about the unexpected rainstorm and how the weather mirrors our lives. Most of us experienced sunny and calm days, but the occasional storm was inevitable. Some of those storms were predictable and allowed us time to prepare, to batten down the hatches. Other storms blindsided us and hit us with an unforeseen force that knocked us to our knees. The lesson to be learned was how to survive those unpredicted storms.

John disturbed our meditations. "To pass the time, let's compare what we each packed in our backpacks as sort of a personality determination. I'll go first." He retrieved his items one at a time, and beyond water and munchies he carried binoculars, a flashlight, a compass, a rope, an extra pair of socks, and a knife. Our group summed him up as being prepared for whatever might happen on the trail. John turned to me. "As the newest member, why don't you go next?"

"Okay, sure, but I won't be classified as 'prepared'." I dumped out what I'd packed to be displayed and judged by my peers. "I brought binoculars, extra water in case the hike runs longer than I anticipated, and a hairbrush, a nail file, a compact, lip gloss, sunscreen, insect repellant, and a small pouch with my wallet and car keys. Oh, and a hat."

John and Greg stared at my belongings and laughed out loud, but not in a mean sort of way. Greg said, "I can't believe you don't have the most basic of hiking gear in your bag. What if you get lost and need a compass? What if darkness catches you on the trail? What if you find it necessary to tie on to a tree to keep you secure while you slide down a slippery slope?"

I gathered the objects of their mockery and stashed them away, like a squirrel hiding nuts for the winter. "That's a lot of 'what ifs'. First of all, I don't plan on getting lost because I'm with companions, and I know enough to stay on the well-marked trail. Secondly, I plan to get my ass out of the woods way before sundown so I won't need a flashlight. As for a rope, the likelihood of tying myself to a tree is absurd." I didn't get any arguments regarding my logic, so I persisted. "On the other hand, should any of those scenarios you described come to pass and the ranger has to send out a search party, it's very likely that a news crew will be on hand to report on our rescue. Of the two of us, who do you think will be camera ready?"

It was Sharon and Beverly's turn to laugh out loud, so the subject was changed when John asked David if he still worked at the Weather Channel, and David reluctantly admitted that he did. "As an up-and-coming meteorologist I have to pay my dues before any of the bigger networks will even consider hiring me."

I couldn't believe it. "*What*? Do you mean that you admit to being a meteorologist whose job is to forecast the weather?" I waved to the dwindling rain and asked, "And you didn't predict that we'd get drenched today?" It was my chance to laugh.

"Yes, I admit to those charges, but the weather is not an exact science and can be tricky to forecast, especially in the mountains where clouds can roll in without notice."

We all had a good laugh as we gathered our backpacks and continued on our hike, using extreme caution walking over the wet, slippery boulders. We reached the falls, which made the trip worthwhile, but we didn't dally because the rain had delayed our hike, and we agreed to make our way back to the trailhead. The mood was light on the drive back to the Park 'N Ride, where David parked the van and handed out the itinerary of Saturday hikes planned up until the week of Thanksgiving. I was tired but happy and announced that I planned to make as many of the hikes as possible.

I thanked them for welcoming me to their group and was unloading my backpack when Greg came up beside me. "It was really nice to meet you, Sheila, even if you don't know how to properly pack for a hike." His teasing smile held no reprimand. "I'd like to have your phone number. I realize we've only just met, but I'd really like to ask you out sometime, you know, on a date."

I shoved the backpack into the confines of the Mustang's trunk and was cordial in my refusal. "I appreciate your asking, but I'm not interested."

He didn't seem surprised that I'd rejected him. "Not interested in me or in dating?"

The honest answer was "neither," but there was no need to hurt his feelings by pouring salt in the wound, so I smiled and answered, "Dating."

I unlocked the passenger door, waved goodbye, and promised to see them all next weekend. I merged onto the interstate, flipped the radio to an oldies station, and sang along to the tunes of my youth. When The Grass Roots, "Let's Live for Today" slid from the speakers, I couldn't help but speculate if the rock band was onto something. It could be that the secret to happiness was to surrender the past to what was, not to worry about the future, and to live only in the present. I smiled as I remembered what the kind woman who'd come to my assistance in buying an antibiotic in Mexico admonished, that we Americans are always anxious to be somewhere other than where we are. It was sage advice from a stranger that I should, perhaps, reconsider.

*Name changed

Chapter Nine

Yes...

Determined not to stagnate in the past or drown in loneliness, I accepted pretty much every invitation. Friend and coworker Vanessa invited me to Cher's "final" concert tour, which included Atlanta, and I gladly accepted. I continued to go out on a semi-regular basis to hear Backstreet on Saturday nights, mostly at the insistence of Debbie who couldn't "bear the thought" of me sitting home alone. Despite her attempts at matchmaking, she finally accepted that I wasn't interested in meeting men. While I'd grown accustomed to my own company, it was good to be among friends and to make new ones. I met another member of the group, Kim, who went out to have a few drinks, a good time, and to maybe meet a man. Kathy, on the other hand, was bold where men were concerned, and she seldom missed an opportunity to "hookup." Consequently, whenever she noticed a man checking me out, she urged me to ask him to dance.

On one such occasion she pointed out what I'd ignored. "That man at the bar has been watching you on the dance floor since the band started to play." She pushed me in his direction. "Go on over and introduce yourself. It's obvious he'd love to dance with you, probably more than dance if you catch my drift."

I caught her drift, but whether I was interested or not was irrelevant to Kathy. Her philosophy was from a seventies song by folk rocker Stephen Stills, "Love the One You're With." She enjoyed a romp in the hay and made no bones about it. Despite the differences in our lifestyle choices, I liked her because she was honest and kind and didn't bother to justify her decisions. Nevertheless, she and several of the other women I noticed were like piranhas trolling for fresh meat and even scared me. Most were divorced and may as well have had "Desperate" tattooed across their foreheads. As a widow, I didn't have anything to prove, either to myself or to an ex-husband. Therefore, it was easy for me to be nonchalant where men were concerned because I had no ulterior motive, no agenda.

"Sorry, Kathy, but if he wants to dance with me, he'll have to do the asking. Let me remind you that I'm not here looking for anything more than fun with friends."

"Well, you might change your mind because tall, dark, and handsome is walking towards our table. Maybe I should practice patience and wait for a man to come to me."

"That would be a wise strategy, for a change."

Kathy shrugged and nodded towards the edge of the dance floor where the man from the bar was standing and pointing in my direction. When I looked his way, he snapped his fingers and motioned for me to join him on the dance floor. I laughed until I snorted. The very idea of a man beckoning me like a trained dog was hilarious. Neither Kathy nor Kim understood my refusal to dance with a man who was interested in me, so I spelled things out for them. "If he's not interested enough to weave through the tables to come over and ask me like a gentleman to dance, then screw him. I'm having a great time hangin' out with y'all, and I don't need a man to make me feel better about myself. Unlike some of the women here, I won't be leaving with *any* man. I rode here with the group, and that's exactly how I'm going home."

Kim spoke up, "If you don't get off your high horse, how are you going to meet anybody? You won't consider a compromise when a man asks you to dance because you're being plain stubborn."

"No she's not," chimed Kathy. "She's smarter than the rest of us. The good-lookin' hunk is pushing aside empty chairs to make his way to our table."

The man halted in front of me, removed his cowboy hat to reveal thick, black hair, and gave me a sexy smile. "Would you like to dance? Please don't turn me down, given that you made me work for it. I usually don't have to try this hard to get a woman to share a dance...or my bed." His cobalt blue eyes crinkled with confidence. "My name is Jeff."

"I'll be damned," whispered Kathy.

I stood and accepted his hand. "Nice to meet you, Jeff. My name is Sheila. I'm happy to dance with you, but if it's sharing your bed you have in mind, then move on, cowboy."

He kissed my hand and gave me a look that made me blush. "Just a dance, for now."

The band blended oldies with country, and we danced several times. Our slow dances were easy as he effortlessly glided me around the outskirts of the dance floor. He got my message about respecting me and kept his hands off my ass. It was good to set boundaries, but it was nice to be held in his strong arms. It occurred to me that maybe the reason some women slept around had nothing to do with sex. It could have been that they were lonely and longed to be held, even if the chance meeting was as fleeting as the morning dew.

The music ended, and I disentangled myself from his hold on me. It was last call, and he suggested we cool down with a drink, but I declined. "No, thanks, but I enjoyed dancing with you. I'm going to return to my friends because the band is winding down. They're my ride home, and it would be inconsiderate to keep them waiting."

"Then let me find a pen and paper so I can get your phone number. Do you plan to be here next Saturday night? I'd like to ask you out, and we can have dinner beforehand."

My answer was indifferent. "Sorry, but I have other plans next weekend." Those plans were to go hiking with David and the others. There was an awkward pause before I continued, "I need to be honest and let you know I'm not interested in a relationship, or even dating, not right now. But we might run into each other again if you like the band and show up wherever they're playing sometime."

It was his turn to be indifferent. "No problem." He tipped his hat and walked out the door.

Kathy came out of nowhere and snatched my elbow. "What is wrong with you? Don't you want to meet a nice man? Jeff wanted your phone number, and I overheard you tell him you're not interested. How many handsome hunks do you think are going to waltz into your life?"

Debbie stood beside me and put her arm over my shoulder. "Leave her alone, Kat, she doesn't need to be pressured into dating if she's not ready. You make your decisions, and Sheila can make hers."

Kathy shook her head in disbelief at my rebuttal of a hot prospect. With the exception of her and a few others who drove their own cars, we piled in Stanley's van where laughter prevailed. I sat in the semi-darkness and dwelled on Kathy's question about what was wrong with me, a question to which I had no answer. Was Freud rightfully confounded when he contemplated, "What does a woman want?" It was the same question men had been asking themselves for centuries. If it was true that we had to name it before we could claim it, then what did I want?

Jeff was an amiable man wrapped in a gorgeous package, and I'd turned him down when he expressed an interest in seeing me again. But there was no chemistry, no burning desire that ran from head to toe. Was I expecting to be hit with a bolt of lightning, a love at first sight encounter for a second time? Did I dare even hope to fall in love again? Was Kathy right in that I was the roadblock that separated me from love?

November was upon us, and work kept me busy with second semester schedules. A student was leaving my office when Janis came in and sat in the chair across from my desk. "How's it going?"

I assumed she was there to discuss class loads, but she was also a friend who could have wanted to see how I was handling the approaching holidays. "Good, thanks. Course requests have been entered for scheduling, given there are no more changes to the master schedule. I plan to run student schedules and class rosters before we leave for Christmas break. If there are too many conflicts I can work those out during the two week holiday when there won't be any distractions. How are you?"

"Looking forward to a week off for Thanksgiving. I've bought only two gifts and plan to finish my shopping." She paused briefly. "I actually stopped by to ask if you have any plans for the second weekend in December."

I didn't need to flip through my calendar to answer her. "Nope. I rarely have anything planned that far in advance, if at all. Why do you ask?"

"Because Liz and I are going to New York City. We're leaving early on that Friday morning and flying back late Sunday afternoon. It's a group tour, one that Ann organized, and there are seventeen people going. I spoke to her last week, and she said there are three spots available and asked me to mention it to anyone I thought might be interested. I thought of you. Liz loves you, and she and I would be happy to share our hotel room. The two of us have gone several times, and we always have a great time. New York is beautiful during the holiday season." She hesitated as if not sure how to proceed. "The only downside is that the excursion has to be paid in full by the end of the month, and I understand if…"

She let her voice trail off, as if embarrassed to discuss money with me. Ann was a long-time Bremen resident and a successful travel agent. Liz was Janis' daughter, a high school student who volunteered to assist me with mundane tasks after school when she had nothing better to do. I picked up the thread of the conversation Janis had dropped. "How expensive is the trip?"

"The total cost is approximately eleven hundred dollars, which includes round-trip airfare, shuttle service, one-third of the hotel, tickets to a Broadway play, and the Rockettes at the Radio City Music Hall. The Christmas show is magnificent. If you like, we can visit a museum or the Empire State Building. One meal, a dinner, is included, but we're responsible for the remainder of the meals. I'll have to ask Ann, but on previous trips the hotel included a breakfast buffet." She waited patiently for my response.

New York for Christmas was a trip I'd always wanted to take. It would cost money I hadn't planned to spend, and property taxes were due in December because evidently Ebenezer Scrooge had been in charge of setting the date. Fortunately, the tax money was in my savings account. I carried a very low balance on my Visa card, and this trip would be worth the charge. Mama had taught us that the next best thing to cash was good credit, and I could afford the monthly payments. I smiled at my friend and said, "Yes! Thanks so much for asking me and for letting me crash with you and Liz at a fraction of the expense of another room. I'll call Ann this afternoon and add my name to the list and finalize the arrangements. I'm so excited!"

She stood and walked towards the door but came back to give me a hug. "I'm so pleased you're going, and Liz will be, too. I'll let you surprise her after school with the news."

The weeks rolled by, and Janis, Liz, and I were on our way to the airport for a whirlwind weekend. I'd never been to New York, where I quickly realized that everything was the polar opposite of Bremen. The traffic was a constant busyness that gave life to streets that never slept. Horns honked, taxis swerved, pedestrians rushed to beat the crossing light, and everyone was in a hurry. Surprisingly, we survived the ride from the airport in a van carrying tourists from all over the country. I met three sisters from Wyoming who made the trip every year. Passengers also included five women who'd been best friends since grade school, but their paths separated them by distance. Every other year they left their families and made the pilgrimage to NYC for shopping and sharing stories of their hectic lives. The rest of our entourage was scattered between two other shuttles but all three vans screeched to a halt in front of the hotel simultaneously, as if the drivers had choreographed the transport.

Ann took care of checking us all in and dispensed room keys in the lobby, based upon her carefully coordinated records. Janis, Liz, and I were anxious to squeeze as much as possible into our trip and didn't dally in finding our room, freshening up, and joining those on the crowded sidewalk. We were all hungry, and a leisurely stroll took us to the Hard

Rock Café. We waited for a table at the bar where the bartender was nothing less than amazing. She entertained her audience with her ability to mix and serve drinks in rapid succession without once serving the wrong drink to any of the customers who applauded and stuffed dollars in her tip jar.

After a delicious meal and my t-shirt purchase, we walked to Central Park where horse drawn carriages lined the curb. Janis and Liz had both experienced a ride but humored me and agreed to split the cost. We wrapped ourselves in blankets and rode through several streets where traffic grudgingly shared the right-of-way. Once in the park, I struck up a conversation with the driver, who was from Croatia and was in the country on a work visa so that he could send money home to his family. I asked him if he planned to visit his family for Christmas, but with sadness and regret he explained that it was very expensive to travel during the holidays, and he wouldn't be able to see his family. I also wanted to know if he intended to bring his family to live with him in America one day.

Again, he shook his head in sorrow and answered in a thick, unfamiliar brogue, "It is not so easy to immigrate to this country, but I am grateful to be here and to be able to provide for my family." He fell silent and shrugged in acceptance of what was. "We miss each other very much, but such is life."

I let the conversation drop and settled into the seat where I pulled the woolen blanket over me against the cold and enjoyed the company of my friends and the scenery. Once the driver returned us to the starting point, Janis suggested we go back to the hotel to shower and change before we met in the lobby for dinner and the Broadway production of *The King and I*. As we waited on the corner for the signal to cross, I noticed the sky had turned steely gray, and the wind whipped through the city with a vengeance. I wondered if snow was in the forecast. We didn't have snow in Georgia very often, and a snowfall would have been a bonus to the New York adventure. I moved closer to a woman wearing a fur coat who stood a few inches away from me and politely asked, "Excuse me, ma'am, do you think it's gonna snow?"

You would have thought I was a snake about to strike. The woman wrapped her coat tighter around her stick-thin body and clinched the handle on her purse as she tucked it firmly under her arm. Not once did she make eye contact, but I didn't want her to think I was a thief and said, "Hell, honey, I don't want your pocketbook. I just wanted to know if you thought there might be snow on the way." The light changed, and she took off in a huff.

Janis hurried me along before the light changed so I wouldn't be run over like a squirrel. Apparently, drivers didn't use their brakes unless absolutely necessary. Once safely on the sidewalk my friend smiled and reminded me that not everyone wanted to be my friend. Oh well. That fact didn't deter me from having an incredible time, nor did the fact that it didn't snow after all. The day was catching up with me, and I was tired. But not too tired to miss the Broadway play.

On Saturday we shopped, took a taxi to the Empire State Building, laughed, and ate lunch at corner cafes, none of which served sweet tea. I enjoyed the melting pot of accents as much as they enjoyed my southern drawl. Maybe everybody didn't want to be my friend, but I didn't let that stop me from becoming acquainted with strangers, especially when my curiosity got the better of me. Saturday night's performance by the Rockettes didn't disappoint as I snapped picture after picture, especially of the live nativity scene that concluded the show.

The trip was over much too soon, and we were on the flight to Atlanta. Janis read, Liz dozed, and I closed my eyes and replayed all I'd experienced. To say that Christmas was over commercialized, especially in NYC, was an understatement. In addition to the thousands of lights and decorations that decked Manhattan, there was the flawless tree meticulously selected for Rockefeller Center, the rink that held picture-perfect ice skaters dressed warmly in Christmas sweaters, and the window dressings of Fifth Avenue and Macy's that beckoned shoppers inside with their elaborate playfulness.

While in the midst of an abundance of decorations where neon lights screamed "'tis the season," I'd looked up to see one lone Christmas tree in an apartment window. It wasn't nearly as extravagant as the city below and sat without fanfare in the midst of Manhattan. The tree was draped in those old-fashioned, large, multi-colored bulbs that bordered on tacky; it wore a lopsided, gaudy golden star as a tree topper. Nothing about its simplicity shrieked for attention. Yet somehow, among the lights and noise and chaos of the Christmas that lured tourists by the thousands, that solitary tree was a reminder of the meaning of Christmas. It was a whisper that declared, "I'm here. Christmas is here." Its humble symbol touched my soul in a way the proliferation and promotion couldn't.

My family and I celebrated on Christmas Eve at Ted's Montana Grill, a new tradition we began last year, the first without Barry. We didn't need his empty chair to remind us of what we'd lost, but a year had made a huge difference in all of us. We were able to laugh again and appreciate the holidays. We reminisced over Christmases past, and I shared stories of Barry's struggle to assemble countless bikes and GI Joe planes and tanks and Star Wars spaceships. Many Christmas Eves our heads had barely hit the pillow when they were up, squealing with delight over what Santa had left under the tree. One year, after pictures, Barry and I crawled back in bed and left the boys playing Pac Man and Frogger on Atari at four in the morning. We weren't able to get the gaming system to work and thought it would have to be exchanged after Christmas. The problem was that we hadn't known how to turn it on.

We all had a good laugh over adult technical challenges, and despite Leslie's "charming" disposition I enjoyed the Christmas season. I was grateful for my blessings, even those that had seemingly slipped through my fingers. But with a will of its own time pulled me from the past and forced me into the future. It was a new year, and January loomed drearily before me. Regrettably, I had no plans for filling the empty hours away from the office.

Thankfully, Pat, who didn't know how not to be busy, stepped in with a solution when she showed up at my door on a Saturday morning with drop cloths and paint brushes. It was barely seven a.m., but you would have thought it was past noon as she snapped, "What are you doing in your pajamas? We have a lot to do so get dressed and let's run to Walmart and pick out paint for the boys' bedrooms. They moved out months ago, and it's past time to redecorate their rooms. What are you waiting for? The day is wasting while you drag your ass."

I invited her in and offered her a cup of coffee, although I suspected she'd already consumed a full pot, or two. "If I might ask, when did you get a wild hair to paint the empty bedrooms? I haven't done anything to them since the boys moved out because they took most of the furniture with them." I stretched and yawned. "I guess it's time I made a decision about redecorating and turning them into guest rooms."

"You're damn straight it is. We'll scavenge enough furniture to put together a couple of bedrooms, but you'll need to invest in new box springs and mattresses when we get to that point. You and Cindy can make a Home Depot run and choose new wallpaper for the bathroom while I paint. There's no need for it to look like a couple of boys live here anymore. Why are you still standing here? Get in the shower and get a move on."

"Cindy? Have you recruited her to help with this venture?"

"Yes. She'll be here around nine. Jerry and Jerline are going to help out next Saturday with stripping the wallpaper in the bathroom and replacing it with whatever you and Cindy choose. When the bedrooms are painted you'll have to replace the carpet. Don't worry about the cost, it won't be that expensive and will be money well spent." She clapped her hands and snapped, "What are you waiting on? Hop to it!"

When Pat got it in her head to tackle a project, there was no stopping her—or even slowing her down. She stood before me, hands on her hips, like a drill sergeant daring me to challenge her decision. I gulped down the last of my coffee and jumped in the shower. I slapped on a minimum of makeup and pulled on sweats and walking shoes for what was shaping up to be a busy day. Though I hadn't planned on doing any of the things on her list, it would be a worthwhile undertaking and a good use of my income tax refund, which also covered the balance of my NYC trip. Cindy was waiting for me, per her mama's orders, when I walked down the hall. She looked as excited as I felt. Oh well, there was no sense arguing with my bossy sister.

As requested, or commanded, my brother and his wife showed up the following Saturday at eight o'clock, almost an hour after Pat. Jerline decided that since Pat and Jerry had the wallpapering under control and given that the painting was all but finished, then she and I should drive to Carrollton to buy mattress sets. She was matter-of-fact when she said, "We'll have to make two trips because only one set will fit in the back of the El Camino. That place on the right, a few miles before you get to town, has the best prices, so we can stop there first and check quality and price. If you're not satisfied, we'll look somewhere else."

"Ok, I'll get my shoes and purse." I walked into the dressing area of the bathroom. "Hey, are you two gonna be okay without us?"

Pat answered, "Why wouldn't we be? It's not as if you actually know what you're doing anyway, and three's a crowd when hanging wallpaper. By the way, I love the soft pastel and tiny floral pattern you selected. You'll be amazed how much better it's going to look, especially after I paint the trim."

Jerry remarked, "I swear Pat had rather paint than eat. Speaking of, pick us up some lunch on your way back here." He reached into his wallet and retrieved a twenty.

I pushed the money aside. "The very least I can do is buy lunch for labor. I don't think I could have afforded all of this if I'd to hire the work done. Thanks for giving up a Saturday."

"You're welcome. Good luck shopping. It's one of Jerline's favorite pastimes."

Jerline's driving was slightly nerve wracking, but at least the roads weren't covered with snow and ice. It was a fact that southerners were as incompetent as a greased pig when it came to maneuvering on any kind of wintry mix. Whenever the weather man predicted even the slightest threat of snow or sleet or both, the warning of inclement weather sent us all to the grocery store to cart out every loaf of bread and gallon of milk on the shelves. It was on one such winter morning that a thin layer of snow-covered ice left the roads slicker than owl shit, and Jerry was stranded in Tennessee while on a business trip.

Jerline, who'd ignored the weather prediction of snow and ice in our neck of the woods, realized she needed to make a run to the grocery store. The chances were slim to none that she would find a store open and even less of a chance that they weren't sold out of basic necessities. Nonetheless, she dressed warmly, fired up the Cadillac, and slapped it in gear. As she related to my brother and the insurance investigator, she drove a safe speed and was making her way down Georgia Avenue when she reached the curve where she always braked. She braked as usual but on the slippery road, the car didn't slow down, and she lost control. That big ole Caddy took on a life of its on and was momentarily airborne as it jumped the ditch and smashed sideways into the front porch of the house that had the misfortune of sitting in the car's path. The car shimmied to a stop, but if the house hadn't stopped the car, it could have plowed through the woods for miles. Miraculously, no one in the house was harmed, and Jerline's only injuries were a broken nose and two black eyes as a result of the deployed airbags. She looked like a raccoon for weeks. Thereafter, "the house Jerry's wife slammed into" was a landmark that became a handy reference point.

I couldn't help but laugh at the thought of my sister-in-law flying across the ditch in that white Cadillac or what the homeowner must have thought when the car collided with his porch. "What's funny?" Jerline asked.

"Oh, nothing much. A laughable situation from the past." We arrived safely, and I pointed to an empty parking space near the door. "There's a spot. If we find a mattress set you'll have to pull around to the warehouse in the back, but we can park here while we look around the store."

The store was much bigger than it looked from the outside and was filled with an eclectic variety of merchandise, everything from silk flowers to paintings and bric-a-brac to ornamental water fountains to…mattresses. The owner was happy to show us to the bedding area where we found an extensive inventory of mattresses, box springs, comforters, pillow shams, and coordinating throw pillows. Jerline scanned the perimeters with the precision of a submarine's periscope. "We've hit pay dirt. We ought to be able to find everything you need to finish out the bedrooms. Are both beds the same size?"

"No, the one Cindy dragged out of storage is a queen, and the one I had in the basement is a double. Brad helped move it upstairs and set it up. It was Grandma Pearl's iron bed, and I had it sandblasted and painted a few years ago; a good dusting was all it needed. Mama told me that her mama had seen the bed in the window of the General Store and that she'd saved the four dollars to buy it out of her butter and egg money. No such thing as a Visa card in those days."

Jerline didn't hear anything beyond the sizes of the bed. She was a woman on a mission to find what we were there to buy. An hour and a half later we were standing at the register checking out, and when Jerline told the owner we were buying two mattress sets, she gave me a twenty percent discount on everything I purchased. She agreed to hold the remainder of the bedding and the second mattress set until we could make another trip and directed us to the rear of the building where a man would load the mattress and box springs.

Jerline carefully backed the El Camino up to the large opened door, and we both went in search of the workman. He was in no hurry as he straggled towards us and flipped his cigarette onto the pavement. "You ladies lookin' for me?"

I pulled the sales slip from my purse and handed it to the man. He sported a beard but not the intentional kind of beard. His scruffy facial hair crawled down his neck and served only to add to his overall unkempt appearance. He scratched his beard and reached for a rope as he read the receipt. "Good choice on the mattress. I can personally assure you that you'll find it very, ahem, sturdy." He lit another cigarette and looked us both over with a stare that made my skin crawl. The man inhaled deeply and squinted his eyes at Jerline, smiled a smile that revealed tobacco stained, crooked teeth and leered, "Either of you women ever been tied up? If not, I highly recommend it, if you know what I mean." An exaggerated wink punctuated his vulgar implication.

I was about to put the jerk in his place, but Jerline was on his ass like a chicken on a June bug. As a general rule Jerline was a church goin', God-fearin' woman who was not one to cuss unless provoked. That man had clearly provoked her because she unleashed a violent flow of venom on him like I'd never heard from her. "Listen to me, you slimy sonofabitch, ain't nobody ever tied my ass up and any man stupid enough to try will find his crotch jacked up to his damn chin. The nerve of some crude, lewd, low-life bastard like you talking to us that way is disgusting, and I ought to slap the shit out of you for your outrageous insinuations. On second thought, I ought to have your sorry ass fired."

It could be argued that Jerline wasn't exactly the epitome of a southern lady. The man backed away from her onslaught and stammered some sort of an apology as he retrieved the mattress set, heaved it onto the back of the truck, and secured it with the aforementioned rope. Jerline and I climbed in the car and left the parking lot in a tizzy. Her hands gripped the steering wheel so tightly that her knuckles were white.

I wasn't sure if it was safe to speak, but I kinda liked livin' on the edge and said, "Don't forget to swing by the drive-thru at Wendy's so we can pick up lunch."

As I made up the beds with freshly washed sheets, bedspreads and pillow shams, I had to admit that a coat of paint, new carpeting, and redecorated bathroom lifted my spirits. Not seeing the boys' empty rooms as they'd been somehow made me miss my sons a little less. The Irish saying that a son is a son until he takes a wife, but a daughter is a daughter all of her life was proving to be true. Undeniably, we women who raise boys realize we are raising our sons for another woman who will one day replace us as the only woman he'd previously loved. It wasn't that my sons no longer loved me, but they were grown and had left the nest to build lives of their own, something I was attempting to do. I wandered through the empty house and was impatient for the upcoming work week, a distraction from loneliness.

The weekend dragged by but was behind me, and on Monday morning I bumped into Megan*, a coworker, in the teachers' lounge. She was in a grumpy mood and barely spoke to me. Megan, a twenty-something single woman who needed a change of location after, as rumor had it, her breakup with a man whom she thought she'd loved and had planned to marry. Of course, gossip had to be taken with a grain of salt, especially in Bremen. Instead of inserting myself into someone else's drama, I left the lounge and focused on work, which was interrupted when Megan knocked on my door and entered my office. She'd let go of whatever had been bothering her earlier and was in a better mood when she asked, "Do you have any plans for Valentine's Day weekend?'

I hadn't yet accepted any of the requests from family and friends to fix me up with a single brother, cousin, divorced friend, or friend of a friend, so my calendar was pretty much wide open. Not knowing what hinged on my answer, I busied myself with student files for a few minutes. "Hmm, that's another two weeks away, and I don't know what will come up between now and then." I walked from the file cabinet and sat down at my desk and dived in head first. "Why do you ask?"

She plopped in a chair. "I made plans with a group of friends from my college days to spend the three-day weekend at Sugar Mountain Resort in North Carolina. I'm leaving around lunchtime on Friday to get a jump on the Atlanta traffic, and I'll be coming home on Monday, Presidents' Day. You don't have to chip in for gas because I'm making the trip anyway and would like some company on the long drive. The resort gives special package deals, and with our group rate it wouldn't cost you much. Please think about it, Sheila. I really don't want to go alone. Everyone else is going as part of a couple, but Chad and I...."

And there it was. Megan's latest relationship had fallen apart. She wanted to spend time with her old friends but didn't want to make the trip alone, even though if she showed up with me it would be apparent to all that she and her intended roommate had split the sheets. Megan and

I weren't close, but we did get along and were linked by our loneliness. I reminded myself that it would be a new adventure that would serve to fill up an otherwise long, hollow weekend. There was only one foreseeable hindrance. "You know, Megan, I would like to go on the getaway, but I don't ski."

"That won't be a problem! They have a beginner's hill and a kiddie section with tubing for all ages. We'll be staying in a gorgeous rustic lodge with a large rock fireplace where you can relax with a cup of hot chocolate and take in the mountain views. Ginny said there's a dance with a band in one of the lodge's banquet rooms on Saturday night. Please say you'll go."

I was out of excuses. "All right, I'll go. You can pick me up at home around noon, providing Mr. Rogers will let us both leave work early."

The matter was settled, and Megan left my office. I leaned back in my chair and contemplated what Megan wanted for her life. She owned a home, had a good job that provided financial independence, and was an attractive, healthy young woman. Given that I didn't even know what I wanted, I was in no position to presume to know what another woman wanted. I was, however, looking forward to a trip to somewhere I'd never been.

Two weeks later we left as planned and followed I-20 to the downtown connecter where Megan smoothly merged onto I-85 North. We chatted and laughed and scanned the radio for music we both enjoyed. The comfortable companionship helped pass the time on the seven hour drive to the Village of Sugar Mountain, which rested on the north slope of the mountain. Per Megan's previous arrangements with her friends, we met them at a 7-Eleven located approximately fifty miles from the lodge. I got out of the car to stretch and use the facilities and after happy reunion hugs, Megan introduced me to her friends. Of the three couples it was clear that Ginny was the leader of the pack as she retrieved directions for the last leg of the trip and reminded the others that she and Joel would be taking the master suite. She flashed Joel a sexy, suggestive smile, and he cradled her in his arms and nuzzled her neck. Ginny giggled, and I gagged.

Once we reached the peak I held my nose and blew hard to clear my ears that resisted the change in elevation. It was almost too dark to see much of anything but I gathered a sense of strength and beauty from the snow-capped mountains of Pisgah National Forest. Luggage was unloaded, as were the groceries we and the others had packed, and Ginny was ready to assign bedrooms in the two-story log cabin. It was logical that Megan and I take the bedroom with twin beds and a half bath, but as we each claimed a bed I asked Megan, "What if you and your fella had made this trip together. Would you two have been stuck with this room?'

"Not necessarily. Ginny made the reservations and, therefore, asserted her right to the master bedroom. The rest of us would have drawn straws to determine who would have gotten the shaft." She began to unpack and said with a shrug, "It doesn't matter now that you're my roommate instead of Chad."

I wanted to ask her what had happened between the two of them, but Megan changed the subject by suggesting we freshen up before supper. Joel and the other guys were busy firing up the grill on the patio, even though the temperature was well below freezing. Apparently, the alcohol they were consuming made them numb to the cold—that and layers of warm clothing. We "women folk" prepared the rest of the meal, and we all savored a delicious steak dinner before clearing the table and loading the dishwasher. I was exhausted and said goodnight to everyone and got ready for bed. I snuggled into the warmth of the small bed and was glad I'd packed flannel pajamas and thick socks. I drifted to sleep to the sounds of laughter among the others who'd remained downstairs to drink and play games in front of the fire. I didn't hear any of them when they made their way to bed, including Megan.

I slept like a log and awoke to the clatter of breakfast being prepared and the aroma of fresh coffee. Megan's bed was empty, and the bedcovers were straightened. I couldn't believe I was the first to go to bed and the last to rise. I wrapped a robe around me, slipped into furry bedroom shoes, and made my way downstairs. Kenny, Tiffany's boyfriend, stoked last night's fire and tossed on another log. I stood in the large den and followed the A-frame ceiling to a skylight and was delighted to see snowflakes landing on glass. Megan called everyone to the kitchen where bacon, sausage, eggs, biscuits, and hash browns lured us to heed her call. I fixed a plate, poured myself a cup of coffee, and retreated to the inviting crackle of the fire.

I'd barely taken a few bites when Ginny called out, "The snow has stopped! Time to hit the slopes." Simultaneously, everyone hurried to finish breakfast before pulling on ski apparel and gathering their gear. Ginny was definitely the commanding officer. I suspected the queen bee was also a drama queen, with a bit of a bitch thrown in for good measure.

Susie and I pitched in to clean the kitchen since we hadn't helped cook breakfast. Ian strolled in, put his arms around her, and told her to hurry up. I offered to sweep and take out the trash so she could leave with everyone else. The slopes weren't calling me.

Megan poked her head around the doorframe. "Are you going with us to the lifts?"

"I'm in no hurry. Y'all go ahead. I'm gonna have another cup of coffee before I grab a shower and then take a leisurely walk to the lodge. I read about tubing in one of the brochures and may give it a try. Or I might sit by the fire and finishing reading the novel I brought along. Go. Have fun, but don't break anything. I would hate to have to drive us back to Bremen with you in a cast."

"Your compassion is to be commended. We plan to eat at the dining room in the lodge at one o'clock. Hope to see you there." Her skis were cumbersome as she scurried along to catch up with the rest of the gang who waited impatiently for her. The cabin was silent but not lonely.

I poured another cup of coffee and walked outside to the deck. The air was frigid, and my breath was visible as I marveled at the splendor around me. The setting was one of serene solitude, and sunlight danced a ballet across snowy mountain tops that glistened under a cloudless blue sky. Thousands of miles separated these mountains from the beaches of Mexico, but I had the same sense of longing for something unnamed and searched my heart for an answer, an answer that was as elusive as snow-flakes. Resigned to waiting for guidance I decided that despite the cold, the day was much too beautiful to spend indoors reading.

I quickly showered, applied makeup with sunscreen, and dressed in layers. I unpacked the ski overalls, pulled them over my clothes, and fastened the buckles on the bib. Even though I didn't ski, I'd made the purchase of the overalls and jacket when they were on sale a few years ago. They provided extra protection when the temperature dipped into the teens and my body begged for a walk. I tugged on boots, jacket, and gloves and made my way to the lodge.

My first stop was at the information desk where I asked directions to the tubing slopes. Once there I met several others who preferred the safety of tubes that offered the thrill of flying downhill with less danger than skiing. Two hours of racing down the slope and haulin' my tube back to the top of the hill left me exhausted and famished. I returned my tube to the young man stationed at the rental booth and kicked snow off my boots before locating the dining room. Megan waved to me from across the crowded room, and I moseyed over to their table. We discussed our morning activities until a harried waitress showed up to take our order for sandwiches and hot chocolate.

Even though I was the oldest in the group, I wasn't the only one pooped and it was agreed that a nap was in order before we went out for the evening. We drudged our way along the snow covered path, hung wet outerwear in the coatroom, and disbanded. The cabin was warm and quiet when another round of snow began to drift silently across the lavender mountains. A nap was definitely the right choice.

I woke up to the silence of sleep and tiptoed downstairs to the dying embers of the fire and carefully laid a large log on the cinders. With a bit of prompting, the fire leapt to life and greedily licked the wood with its yellow and orange tongue. I relaxed in an oversized recliner and read until I heard signs of life coming from upstairs. Susie was the first to come downstairs and joined me by the hearth. She stretched and tossed her red tresses over her shoulder. "I slept like the dead. I didn't realize how tired I was until I fell into oblivion."

"I had a restful nap, too, but woke up and decided to read for a while. I hope I didn't disturb anybody."

"Not at all. I don't think an avalanche could have awakened me." She stretched again and continued, "Sheila, I don't know what happened between Megan and Chad, but I'm grateful you made the trip with her. I don't think she would have come by herself. I really wish she could meet a good man and settle down. Ian and I are so happy and plan to marry in the spring. Please don't mention that fact to Megan. I don't want to flaunt my happiness in her face."

"I want say anything, but if you intend to invite her to the wedding..."

She sat by the fire and smiled a sly grin. She momentarily resembled a jack-o-lantern. "Oh, I'll tell her later, when she's had time to recover from her latest breakup. Poor thing."

She missed the sarcasm when I replied, "You're a kind, thoughtful friend, Susie."

Unlike Susie, Ginny made no pretense about being completely self-centered. The rest of the group was rousing, and she suggested we hurry to shower and change for dinner and the dance. She called rights to the first shower, leaving the rest of us to wait our turns. Two hours later we were all ready to leave for the short hike to the lodge, which was crammed with partygoers. The band blared, beer flowed from the bar tap, and everyone was having a good time. The three couples in our group found enough room on the dance floor to move to the tempo of a slow dance, and Megan and I ordered a glass of wine at the bar and squeezed our way through the crowd in search of a seat.

My eyes adjusted to the dimmed lighting, and I noticed a tall, good-lookin' man who appeared to be about the same age as Megan. He stood and politely offered us a spot at his small table. Megan agreed, and we parked ourselves in chairs Jason, as he introduced himself, managed to rustle up for us. The two of them were noticeably attracted to each other, so I finished my wine and left them to become acquainted. I reached the dance floor just as the vocalist announced that it was Miller time and put on a mixed CD. I joined in the old Electric Slide and blended in with the rest of the disco line dancers.

A young man tapped me on the shoulder and asked me to flirt with his dad, whom he'd invited to the resort in an effort to lift his sagging spirits. I declined his invitation until he elaborated while we turned in unison to the music. His parents' divorce was final the previous week as a result of his mama's infidelity. She'd been sleeping with his daddy's best friend. Ouch.

The man, Paul, wore his broken heart on his sleeve, but I did my best to cheer him up when I bumped my hip into his. "Oops, excuse me." He was a handsome man who'd been betrayed by two people whom he trusted. I smiled and asked casually, "Are you here with anyone?"

"Only my twenty-four year old son and three of his buddies. What about you?"

The "Electric Boogie" ended and was followed by a song from the movie *Hope Floats'* soundtrack, Garth Brook's "To Make You Feel My Love." Paul twirled me around to face him, and we began to slow dance to the painfully poignant lyrics. I answered, "I'm also here with a group of young people, mostly couples."

"So what's your story? Are you divorced, too?"

"No, widowed."

He stopped dancing and pulled me closer. "I'm sorry for your loss."

We were two kindred souls who'd loved and lost love, albeit in different manners, but the grief was similar. The song was over, but he continued to hold me close until I pulled away. I don't know if it was the effect of the song or the wine or an attempt to mend Paul's wounded ego when I said, "Thanks for the dance, Paul. It could be that if we'd met at a different time and place in our lives, we would have become friends or maybe even more than friends. But I'm not there yet, and you definitely aren't. We both have to trust that perhaps love will find each of us another day."

He kissed the top of my head and was about to say something when Megan rushed up to me and grabbed my arm. "Let's go!"

"Go where?"

"Anywhere that's not here. There's a DJ in the other bar. We can go there for a while, until he leaves."

I loosened her hold on my arm. "Until who leaves? What is wrong with you? I thought you and Jason were getting along. I saw you dancing with him, and you were laughing."

"I was laughing until he told me his occupation. He drives a truck, a transfer truck! Can you believe it? He's here until the storm moves on and then he's on the road again in a 'rig'."

"I don't understand the problem. Is he smuggling drugs or promoting human trafficking?"

"Did you hear me?" She spat out his job description with the same disdain one reserved to label a child molester. "He's a *truck driver*. Had I known that I would never have accepted a seat or let him buy me a drink or danced with him. I don't dance with any man I don't think I can marry, and I won't ever marry a blue-collar worker, someone beneath me."

"Are you kidding? He's polite, handsome, and earns an honest living. And what do you mean, 'beneath me'?"

"Simply that I won't marry a man who doesn't have, at a minimum, the same level of education as me and who doesn't work in a professional field. Please c'mon before he sees us. He went to the bar to get us another drink, and I made my escape."

Escape from a man who was interested in her? I was beginning to connect the dots. I turned to wave goodbye to Paul who gave me a smile surrounded by sadness. I blew him a kiss as Megan and I made our getaway. An hour later we recovered our jackets and trudged through a heavy snowfall back to the welcoming warmth of the cabin. We noticed everybody else's gear in the coat room and realized the three couples had left the bar before us and had retired to their respective bedrooms. We did the same and as we climbed in our beds, Megan whispered in the darkness, "I want what you had, Sheila, a good man who will cherish me until death do us part."

I longed for what I'd had, too, but I doubt if she heard my whispered, "Me, too."

The metaphor that March comes in like a lion proved to be true for Chuck. The inevitable divorce followed less than a year after the wedding, and I bit back the "I told you so." My son's heart was already broken, and there was no need in pouring salt in the wound. The last thing he needed was for me to remind him that I'd tried to spare him heartache. Shortly before the marriage disintegrated, the bank foreclosed on the house they couldn't afford, and Leslie moved back home to her recently widowed mama—minus the Mustang that was repossessed.

After the business folded Chuck found a job at one of those big chain drive-in oil change places, but he couldn't make enough money to support his wife in the manner she expected. Leslie's wastefulness and laziness took its toll on the young couple, and there was nothing to be done except cut their losses and let go of what was never meant to be. It was Eileen who lit a fire under her irresponsible daughter's ass when she told Leslie that she could either find a job or live in the street. Leslie opted to work at the Dairy Queen.

Chuck's living arrangements were obvious: he would move back in with me, even though friends warned me against creating a mutual dependency that wouldn't be easy to break for either of us. I didn't think there was another option, but Pat had a more practical suggestion: that Chuck move in with Daddy for a few months. She was convinced it would be a beneficial arrangement for both of them. Daddy was afraid of being alone at night, worried about his old house catching on fire and trapping him inside. He welcomed the idea of his youngest grandchild living with him. Chuck was less than ecstatic, but he would have a rent-free roof over his head until he could get back on his feet. Living with Papa Joe might be the incentive he needed, even if eventually an old man and a young man learned to live together and to accept each other's idiosyncrasies, not necessarily because they wanted to but because they were family who needed each other.

March was a rough month for Chuck and me. Even though I didn't like Leslie, it was upsetting to see my son hurt over the end of his marriage. Thankfully, he and Papa Joe were getting along, and I was offered a break from the stress of Chuck's life. Carol, who taught s Southern History class, invited me to go as an extra chaperone to Charleston with her and her husband Mike, whom I'd known practically all my life. I was overjoyed to accompany the couple and her class on the annual trip and fell in love with the city's southern charm. I thoroughly enjoyed the tour of restored mansions, many of which had survived the Civil War. We were treated to a midnight ghost excursion, as well as tall ship sailing. The trip was over a long weekend and while brief, I very much enjoyed the sights, smells and tastes scattered along the cobbled streets.

The delicious, rich brown sugar smell of pecan pralines lured me into one of the candy shops; I relished the taste of Charleston's delicious creamy pralines. I also very much enjoyed seeing Rainbow Row with its colorful, historical houses that stood tall and proud as they faced the harbor. One of the tales surrounding that area was that the colored houses made it easier for intoxicated sailors coming in from port to locate the house where they were to bunk. Most likely the houses were painted in pastels to keep them cooler in the tropical climate. Days before I was ready to leave the beauty of Charleston behind, we rumbled back into Bremen.

But not for long. Spring break was approaching, and students and staff were making plans for vacations. My plans were to clean out the basement and ask the boys to sort through the clutter and decide if there was anything they wanted to trash, take, or continue to store in the basement. Those plans changed when an old friend called to tell me that her condo in Panama City Beach would be available the last week of March, which coincided with my vacation. Laura had rented out the three bedroom condo, but the beach-goers changed their destination and it was too late to find other tenants. My friend thought a few days at the beach would be a nice change for me and offered the accommodations free of charge. The basement could wait, but I didn't want to make the trip alone.

I sought out Cyndie to find out if she'd already made plans for spring break, which was unlikely since her husband's busy season for landscaping was cranking up. I found her in her office, and after a few minutes of chit-chat I mentioned that I had use of a complimentary, beachfront condo in PCB. I played her like a fine-tuned fiddle. "It would be a shame to waste those two extra bedrooms, but I don't have anyone to go with me."

She jumped up and hugged me. In a voice as sweet as sorghum syrup she said, "Of course you have someone to go with you! Sunny and I will be more than happy to go with you. That's what friends are for, Sheila."

Cyndie had seen right through my ploy. Sunny was her ten-year-old daughter whom I'd grown to love. Of course she was thrilled to be in-cluded in the beach getaway, despite the six hour drive. When spring break rolled around, Cyndie and I were excited about running away to the beach. Luggage was loaded into the trunk of her car, and a pillow and blanket were thrown in the backseat for Sunny. We arrived at the Redneck Riviera where blue skies and sunshine greeted us, although it was too cold for swimming—much to Sunny's disappointment.

Nonetheless, the three of us spent time walking on the sun-drenched beach, retrieving shells the sea had tossed ashore. We ate in local restaurants or cooked in the condo, and occasionally we sought out souvenir shops. One evening after supper, Sunny asked if we could go for a walk along the Strip in search of an ice cream shop, and Cyndie consented. The "Strip" was a stretch of Highway 98 that ran parallel to the beach and was packed bumper-to-bumper with spring breakers. Cyndie and I had already run into several students celebrating their first taste of freedom and warned them that news of their behavior would beat them back to Bremen.

We joined them and other spring breakers as we strolled along the road-side, waving at passersby who deemed it appropriate to toot car horns at two women in their forties. Sunny was about to give up on an ice cream shop when we found ourselves in front of a Dippin' Dots. She was enticed to try the unique ice cream, a conglomeration of flavored, frozen "dots" that could be served only in a cup. Sunny was eager to try the treat, but I assured her that I preferred my ice cream as it was intended: out of a hand-churned freezer or a scoop served in a cone. We continued to meander through a number of shops until we stumbled onto the Purple Haze, whose bright purple storefront screamed for attention and we obliged.

Cyndie parked Sunny on a bench just inside the door with instructions to sit there and finish her treat while the two of us browsed. It was not the usual run-of-the-mill souvenir shop, and I wondered if it had been named after a sixties song by Jimi Hendrix with the same title. The correlation between the two made sense given that many interpreted the song, "Purple Haze," as an implied psychedelic experience, and the store was filled with drug paraphernalia. The vendor also carried colored condoms and edible underwear. The novelty shop was noticeably geared towards a specific clientele. The scent of incense was overpowering, and I nudged Cyndie. "I don't think this place has the kind of items were looking for, and I need some fresh air. Let's take Sunny to the beach to catch sand crabs."

Before Cyndie could reply a young woman who was poured into black leather pants and a low-cut vest appeared out of nowhere. She boasted multiple tattoos and body piercings and stood tall in black stilettos. She also carried that "Do me and take me to Burger King" vibe. I don't know if I was startled by her sudden intrusion or by her fuchsia and purple hair, various shades of blue eye makeup, and black lipstick. She leaned in close, surveyed the shop, and whispered, "Are you ladies interested in the backroom?"

What flashed through my mind as I assessed the lanky woman in black was a poem written in the early 1800s by Mary Howitt in which a sly spider welcomed a fly into her "parlour." Neither Cyndie nor I had any idea what was hidden in the "backroom" and even less of an idea why the bizarre young woman thought we might be interested. We mumbled words akin to "no and hell no", snatched Sunny by the hand and left the premises before we were arrested for only God knew what. We laughed our way back to the condo, retrieved a flashlight and a sand bucket, and escaped to the beach where Sunny occupied herself chasing elusive sand crabs.

The ocean breeze brushed over the sand with a cooling hand, and I was glad we'd thought to throw on sweatshirts. Cyndie and I found a couple of empty chairs, reserved for renters during the day, and spread beach towels over the wooden slats. A luminous full moon swirled over white lacy breakers, and we sat in companionable silence, listening to the timeless rhythm of the tide.

Despite the tranquil setting melancholy found me, and I shared an inner conflict with my friend. "Cyndie, I think I could be my own worst enemy by holding on to a man who isn't coming back to me. I'm the one keeping myself from moving forward with my life and being open to possibilities. Or maybe I've run out of rainbows."

Cyndie relocated herself to sit beside me. "I agree, all of your friends agree. It's way past time for you to get on with your life. As for having no more rainbows, that is blessings, you seem to have forgotten that God gives and gives and gives."

I inhaled the salty air and exhaled slowly. "You're right. He does, and I'm tired of getting in the way of what, or who, is waiting for me."

*Name changed

Chapter Ten

Shark Tank

Beth* parked herself in a chair next to mine in the school cafeteria and offered her unsolicited opinion. "It's high time you started dating, and I have a friend who's interested. The two of you met a few weeks ago at a community gathering, and he asked me to introduce you. Do you remember?"

"Have you been talking to my family? Did Kim call and tell you to fix me up with someone? And yes, I vaguely remember the meeting. Was his name Jacob?"

"Not even close. His name is Ron*, and he's divorced, no children. He's not interested looking for anything serious, but he would like to take you out to dinner this Saturday night. I accepted the invitation for you, and it's too late to back out."

"Why would you do such a thing? And it's not too late for me to cancel, and you shouldn't made plans on my behalf." In spite of the fact that Beth had taken the liberty of accepting a date for me, she and everyone else was right that it was time to put myself out there. "Okay, Beth, I'll go. What time is he picking me up?"

She clapped her hands like a happy child. "Oh, yay. He will be there at six o'clock, and y'all will have time for supper before he takes you to a play at the Fox Theatre so dress appropriately. I didn't ask which play, but I know you'll enjoy it. I gave him your phone number so he can confirm the date. I'm really pleased you're going out on a real date. Ron is tall and handsome, and you're going to have a great time."

I certainly hoped she was right when Ron called to confirm, and I gave him directions to my home. I hadn't been to the Fox in years but recalled that people usually dressed up a bit more for a Saturday night performance. I added a pearl necklace to the sleeveless, simple black dress I was wearing. Matching earrings and a hint of lip gloss, and I was ready fifteen minutes early. Kim and Pat offered to come out to the house and meet my date, but I flat-out refused their attempts to meddle. Besides, Beth knew with whom I was going out and where.

Ron was punctual, but I jumped with apprehension at the sound of the doorbell. He was tall and handsome, more so than I remembered. I invited him in but he preferred to get on the road. I picked up my evening bag, locked the door, and was escorted to his, according to him, very expensive sports car—a fact that didn't impress me. The evening went well, and by the time we got back to Bremen, I realized that I had a good time. Dinner was delicious, conversation was light but interesting, and the play *Chicago* was a very entertaining musical. It was at the end of the date when Ron walked me to the door and welcomed himself inside that the date went downhill.

"Thank you for a wonderful evening, Ron, but it's late, and I'm tired."

He followed me inside where he tossed his jacket over the back of a chair and proceeded to loosen his tie and remove his shoes. "Mind if we have a nightcap?"

I hated to be pushy, but he'd crossed the line. "Yes, I do mind. It's time to say goodnight."

"Goodnight?" He looked genuinely confused and slightly hurt as he put his arms around me. "I thought I'd stay here tonight."

Outraged, I pushed him away from me. "*What*? ' Stay here'? Do you see a Holiday Inn sign in the front yard?"

He snapped, "What is wrong with you? Didn't you have a good time tonight? Dinner cost me close to sixty dollars, and the tickets were almost another two hundred. You sure as hell appreciated the excellent meal and seats."

The sonofabitch actually kept a tab. "Listen carefully, you arrogant asshole.

There's not a damn thing wrong with me. You, on the other hand, are crazy as hell. How dare you be so presumptuous!" I snatched open my purse and yanked out my wallet. "If you'll calculate what I owe you for my share of the evening, I'll be more than happy to reimburse you. The sooner you're out of here, the better."

He shoved his feet back into his shoes and jerked his jacket off the chair. "Don't bother paying me back, but you need to understand how dating works these days."

"Oh, I understand perfectly, but I've never been a whore in my life, and I'm sure as hell not just a piece of ass. Don't let the door hit you on the way out and don't ever dial my number again!"

"Don't worry! There's no chance of that." He stormed out of the house, and the Porsche he was so proud of roared to life as it clawed its way out of the driveway. I locked the door and set the alarm and felt tears of anger roll down my cheeks. Dating was a disaster. Surely things hadn't changed that much since my high school days. I sincerely hoped Ron was an exception, a bully who was used to having his way with women and didn't know how to handle rejection. Or were all men were jerks? Disillusioned, I climbed in bed and put what's-his-name out of my mind.

Monday morning was a hectic day, which I preferred over boredom. A respite came when Megan entered my office carrying a paperback that she waved in the air. "I talked to Beth, and she said your date with Ron didn't go as well as she thought it would have."

"That's an understatement. The snake thought he could slither his way into my bed just because he spent a few dollars on me. I don't know why he didn't hire a hooker and call it a night."

"I'm sorry things didn't work out, but don't throw out the baby with the bathwater. You haven't dated in a long time, and you married your first love. Therefore, your experience with men is, shall we say, limited. Which is where this book comes in."

She placed the book on my desk, and my curiosity got the better of me as I picked it up and read the title aloud. "*The Rules*. Rules for what?"

"For dating, for how to marry a man in the shortest possible time frame. The author, Ellen Fein, offers advice on everything from being unique to how to behave on a date to staying busy in order to seem in demand. She even stresses the importance of appearance and encourages women to join a gym and invest in a makeover."

I hated to point out the obvious to Meagan, but the author's advice didn't seem to be working out for her. Instead of bursting her bubble I said, "I have no goal of remarrying. Granted, I'm lonely, and I would be willing to date a nice man with whom I have things in common, but I don't need unsolicited advice from strangers." I wasn't about to change the woman I was in order to follow the "rules" and pushed the book towards her. "Thanks, but I have neither the time nor the inclination to play games."

"But dating is a game. The writer points out that all men are hunters who enjoy the challenge of the conquest. A woman can't ever come off as too easy or available, or he'll lose interest. You have to make a man work to attain your attention, and you have to make yourself worthy of his efforts."

Megan was genuinely convinced the book of dos and don'ts held the secret to her relationship happiness. Again, she failed to see the irony. I don't think she even heard me tell her that I was lonely but that remarriage was not a priority. I remembered when I shared my lonesomeness with Valerie and that while I didn't plan to marry again, it would be nice to meet a man with common interests. Her angered protest shocked me. She was zealous in her argument that I not reconcile myself to mediocrity when I'd experienced the happiness of true love. My daughter-in-law, who loved my son deeply, demanded to know how I could even think of accepting anything less than love. Was she right to be upset that I would consider whatever was second to love? Had she seen through my loneliness to my longing for what I'd lost?

Valerie's conviction aside, Megan ignored my indifference and persisted. "Take the book home and put it on your nightstand. It will give you something to read on those nights you can't sleep, and you may actually learn a thing or two about dating."

Odds were the book would be a dust collector, but to appease her I agreed to borrow the book. "Okay, Megan. I'll peruse the chapters, but let me assure you that pretending to be someone I'm not, including coy, is not in my repertoire. I'll return the book in a few days."

"No rush. I've read the book so many times that I have the instructions memorized. Moving on, there's a group of us getting together on Friday night for a girls' night out. Beth and Paula* are joining the two of us. We're leaving right after work to go to The Comedy Club in Roswell. We may even go to the American Pie afterwards for dancing. I've been there several times, and it's a great place to meet men. I met one of my last boyfriends there. Before you say no, what else have you got to do? We don't need to drive because Paula offered to take her car, so we can have a glass of wine or two. Please say yes."

Megan was insistent and tiresome, but she had a point in that I had no other plans. "Ok, I'll join y'all, but I don't want to stay out late. I'm meeting the single hikers' group on Saturday morning at nine."

"Don't be such a drag. By the way, have you met anybody in that outdoorsy bunch of men?"

"I've made several friends, and a guy named Alex asked me out. Instead of giving him my address, we met for dinner and a movie over on Barrett Parkway in Kennesaw. He's a nice man and not bad lookin', but beyond our shared pleasure found on hiking trails, we have nothing in common."

"Oh well, nothing ventured, nothing gained. Bring a change of clothes on Friday, and we'll transform ourselves after work. We're leaving from the back parking lot so we can beat the rush hour traffic and eat somewhere before the six o'clock show. We can be at the American Pie by eight-thirty, but things don't start hoppin' until after nine."

"Transform ourselves" into what? Satisfied that she'd convinced me to go, she breezed out of my office. The Comedy Club would be fun, but I wasn't sure about the American Pie. It sounded like a meat market for hooking up for casual sex. I didn't know why Megan was looking forward to going to a bar when she wouldn't dance with a man unless she thought he would make a suitable mate. However, given those conditions, she would be a good table holder.

Monday led to a busy week, and Friday was upon me before I had time to reconsider girls' night. I changed out of my work clothes and freshened up in the teachers' lounge restroom and was ready to meet the others promptly at four. Megan was wearing a spring sundress with a matching cardigan and sandals. She frowned when she noted that I was wearing jeans, a button-up, white collared shirt with three-quarter sleeves, and flats. We were all dressed casually, and I didn't give a damn what Megan's opinion of me was. Besides, she was the one shopping for a husband.

We agreed to eat at Red Lobster before we continued to the highlight of the evening, The Comedy Club. The comedians were hilarious, and I laughed so much that I almost peed my pants. We were still laughing when we left the club, piled in the car, and found our way to the popular hangout Megan insisted we go to before heading back to Bremen. To appease her we agreed, although Paula, who was married, was the most reluctant of the group.

It was almost eight-thirty when we arrived, and the place was already packed. A group was leaving, and Beth swooped in to nab their table. She left us to order drinks, and I scoped out the bar and knew my initial assessment had been right: the American Pie was filled with lonely people with no other goal than to get laid. Men circled the dance floor like vultures, and two headed our way. Paula and I declined offers to dance, but to my surprise Megan accepted.

Beth was pushing her way back to our table when she bumped into an old acquaintance. She carefully set the drinks she was balancing onto the table and gave her old friend a hug. "It's so good to see you! How have you been? Are you still engaged to Meredith?" Beth glanced around the bar.

"No, things didn't work out between us, and we agreed to end the relationship." Megan returned to the table with perfect timing. The young man nodded towards Megan, who was about his age. "Is this a friend of yours?"

"Yes, she is, and I have a feeling the two of you are going to get along very well. Let me introduce you, Megan, this is Jeremy, an old friend who lives in Bowdon. He's a lawyer with a firm in Carrollton. Jeremy, this is Megan, a friend and coworker. Now that you've met, go, have fun."

Pleased that she'd been able to introduce two friends who were each searching for something, Beth bubbled over with excitement. The rest of the evening was uneventful, unless I counted the man who grabbed my ass on the dance floor and whispered in my ear what he planned to do to me in his bed. I slapped his hand away and told him to go to hell. It was almost midnight when we decided it was time to leave, especially since we had an hour's drive. I was assigned the difficult task of locating Megan and draggin' her off the jam-packed dance floor where indistinguishable bodies moved eerily as one under the disco ball and strobe lights and created a curtain of dancers.

When I finally found her, we met the others at the door, but Megan was obstinate in refusing to leave. She whined, "I really like Jeremy, and I think he's interested in me, too. Please let's stay a little while longer."

Paula insisted. "It's late, and we've all been up since six a.m. I told Ron* I would be home by eleven-thirty, and he'll worry that I'm late. And let me point out that we came in my car."

A lawyer was right up Megan's alley, but I was tired and needed to get some sleep before my planned hiking trip. "C'mon Megan, can't you two exchange phone numbers and get together another time? After all, Bremen and Bowdon are separated by less than twenty miles."

Megan stubbornly refused to listen to reason in her quest for a new beau. So much for *The Rules* advice to remain aloof. Beth came up with an answer for our dilemma, one that required my participation. "Megan, what if Paula and I go home and leave you and Sheila here? I'll talk to Jeremy and make sure that he and his friends will get you safely home. They have to take the Bremen exit from I-20 anyway, and it won't be more than a few miles out of their way." She turned to me. "Sheila, you don't mind giving up your hike, do you? Doesn't the group go every Saturday?"

The truth was that I would never be able to haul my ass out of bed in time to meet the hikers' group, nor would I be able to hike to Desoto Falls with only a few hours of sleep. I didn't have to worry about letting the hikers know my plans had changed because if I didn't show up by ten minutes after nine, they wouldn't wait around for me. I halfheartedly agreed to stay but warned Megan, "Two hours longer, period. You have to make sure Jeremy will be ready to leave no later than two."

She smiled and thanked me profusely. "Thanks so very much, Sheila! I just know Jeremy and I have a real connection, and he's so handsome! I'm going to tell him that I don't have to go right now, and, yes, I'll tell him that we have to leave by two o'clock."

Beth thanked me for being bulldozed into staying at the club when I would like to have left with her and Paula. We said our goodnights, and to kill some time I walked outside and found a chair on the deck. The only view was a steady stream of traffic. I wondered where they were all going at such a late hour and why they weren't home in bed. In Bremen the sidewalks were rolled up at nine o'clock, except for the Walmart that stayed open until ten and the Waffle House that was open twenty-four/ seven. I glanced around and noticed the crowd had thinned somewhat and the pickins' were slim. I recalled a sign I'd seen at Señor Frogs in Cancun, "At two a.m. ain't nobody ugly."

The sign was evidently subjective and would depend on how much alcohol one had consumed. I could only estimate how many lonely people found a temporary companion and understood why Ron had taken for granted that he would be welcomed into my bed with open arms. Instead of drawing the line which, despite the "free love" mantra of the sixties, was what women of my generation had been taught. Apparently, women had adjusted their attitudes. Many were as loose as a goose and had absolutely no moral compass when it came to sleeping around—or, apparently, self-respect. Clearly, the rules had changed, and I was going to have to come up with a few of my own, ones I could live with.

My reverie was interrupted by a jerk lookin' to get lucky. Like a solitary shark that was sure it sniffed blood in the water, he pulled out a chair and sat down next to me. His deep voice was not as sexy as he evidently thought it was, nor was he. Nonetheless, he attempted to hit on me. "It's hard to imagine a woman as attractive as yourself sitting out here all alone. Can I buy you a drink? We may as well be sociable while we get to know each other, right?" He casually laid his hand on my thigh, and I promptly removed it.

I ignored him, but he was persistent until I gave him a scathing look and said, "I'm not interested, and I'm not in the mood for that line of shit you're shoveling."

The interloper got up so fast that he almost tripped over his own two feet. "Then I guess you should've worn your boots, your Highness. You can sit here 'til hell freezes over. No woman is worth that smartass mouth of yours." He swaggered over to the bar in search of solace for his wounded ego.

A quick glance at my watch let me know it was ten minutes after two. I stood to get a better view of the outdoor bar in case Megan had come outside, but I didn't see her anywhere. I pushed my way onto the dance floor, where I thought she might be dancing with Jeremy. No luck. I was checking the ladies' room when our paths crossed at the door. "Oh Sheila, I'm in a panic. I can't find Jeremy or the friends he came with. I've looked everywhere, and they're gone!"

"Gone? What do you mean 'gone'?" It appeared Jeremy wasn't as enchanted with Megan as she was with him. Or as the rock band Queen put it, "Another One Bites the Dust."

"I mean they aren't on the dance floor, or at either bar, or shooting pool in the game room, or on the deck outside." Tears of frustration welled up in her green eyes. "We've been abandoned and have no way to get home!"

I wanted to wring her damn neck but refrained. I was angry and worried, but it wouldn't do any good for both of us to panic. "Okay, let's think things through. This place doesn't close until four, so we won't be thrown in the street for almost two hours. Maybe we can call a taxi."

"A taxi! Are you crazy? No taxi in the city is going to take us all the way home. Even if we found a driver willing, it would cost a small fortune."

"Do you have a better idea? I should have known not to let our ride leave us here at the mercy of strangers. I thought I'd learned in Mexico to always leave the party with the person you went with to avoid this bind we're in." I wanted to shake her shoulders until her teeth rattled, but we had a problem bigger than my annoyance—and admonishing her wouldn't change our predicament. Anyway, stupid couldn't be fixed, and we were both guilty of being just that.

Megan bit her lower lip. "I used to date a guy who lived in this area. If I call and explain the jam we're in, he might agree to pick us up and take us back to Bremen. We could offer to pay for his gas"

I thought her idea was a stretch, but we were desperate. I dug a quarter from my small bag and motioned towards the lobby where I'd noticed a pay phone when we came in the club. I rested my weary bones on a cushioned bench while Megan made the call. It couldn't have been easy for her to swallow her pride and call an ex-boyfriend in the wee hours of the morning.

In a matter of minutes she joined me on the bench, bent over, and cried into her hands. I touched her trembling shoulder, and she looked at me with dejection and distress. She wiped her cheeks with the back of her hand and said, "His new girlfriend answered the phone, and I couldn't bring myself to ask her to let me speak to Tony. Oh, Sheila, I'm sorry. You're right. We should have left with Paula and Beth. I don't know what I was thinking."

Neither did I, but that was irrelevant. We went back inside and found a table. One look around what was the bottom of the barrel told me we weren't asking any of them for a ride, even if they agreed. I sure as hell wasn't going to end up on *Dateline* with the teaser, "two Georgia women missing from Atlanta nightclub, presumed murdered." The only person I could think of who might come to our rescue was Kim, even though I'd rather have eaten a bucket of dirt than to call her at three in the morning and admit what a dumbass I'd been. But we had no alternative so I asked Megan, "Do you have a quarter? I gave you my last one."

She found one in her wallet and handed it over. "There's another pay phone in the ladies' room. Who do you plan to call?"

"My niece, Kim. She'll be mad as a hornet, but I think she'll come and get us." I dropped the coin in the slot and dialed Kim's number. Several rings later I was about to give up when someone answered.

Kim mumbled groggily, "Hello."

My voice was barely audible. "Hi, Kim. I'm sorry to wake you up, but—"

She cut me off. "Who is this? Somebody better be dead if you're waking my ass up at this ungodly hour. Do you have the wrong number?"

I really, really wanted to say that I'd dialed the wrong number, but we were desperate. "No, I have the right number. It's me, Sheila. Megan and I were deserted at the American Pie over on Roswell Road and need for you to come and get us before they close, which is in an hour."

I held the receiver away from her explosion of expletives. When she finished she was wide awake and bombarded me with questions. "How the hell did you get yourself in such a mess? Who left you there? Why didn't you drive your car? Or why didn't you ride home with whoever you went with last night?"

I had no answers or defense for my actions. "I made a bad decision and trusted someone to get us home, but they left without us. Please come and get us, and I'll never ask you for another favor. In fact, I'll owe you one or two or three." My plea was met with stony silence. "Kim, are you there?"

"I'm here. I'll be there as soon as I can get dressed and find my way over to the club. Is it the Roswell exit off I-285 North?"

"Yes. It's just a little over an hour's drive, but the traffic should be light at this time of night, I mean morning. Thank you, Kim. I didn't know who else to call that would be willing to come and pick us up. Be careful." She hung up the phone with an angry click.

I looked at Megan and gave her a smile of relief. "She's not happy, but she's coming to get us." We used the facilities and went outside to wait on a bench for a woman who was no doubt barreling along I-20 to the perimeter, cussing me every mile of the way.

The bar was closed when Kim pulled in the parking lot with her friend Terri ridin' shotgun, probably because Kim didn't want to make the jaunt alone. We stood when we saw her, and she honked the horn. Like children who were caught with our hands in the cookie jar, we slinked to the car and crawled in the back seat. "Thanks, again, and thank you, Terri for coming with her. I'm really sorry about—"

Kim snapped her fingers and looked at me in the rearview mirror as she peeled from the pavement. "Don't talk. I'm too pissed off to discuss this shit with you right now."

Properly chastised, Megan and I fell silent and rested our heads on the back of our seats. I was beyond tired, but I was afraid if I dared to fall asleep after waking Kim up she would shove my ass onto the interstate. What seemed to be an interminable ride ended when Kim wheeled in the back parking lot of the high school where our cars were parked for what felt like days. Megan and I opened the car doors, and Megan stepped into the early morning dew as sunrise made its appearance.

I was about to creep out of my side of the car when Kim snapped her fingers again. "Get back in the car, blondie. Teri and I are going to the Waffle House for breakfast before we go home to our kids."

Megan mouthed "I'm sorry" and made her getaway while I closed the door, pressed my hands and nose against the window, and silently pleaded with my partner in crime, "Help me!"

But it was too late for me, and Megan knew it so she saved herself and hurried to her car. I waved a weary goodbye and struggled to keep my eyes open before grasping for a lifeline. "Kim, I'm not very hungry. All I want to do is go home and crawl in bed." I pulled a twenty from my wallet as a peace offering and leaned over the seat so she could reach the bill. "I'm more than happy to pay for breakfast for the two of you, as a thank-you."

Kim took the money. "You don't get a vote in this, but the twenty dollars should feed all of us at the Waffle House, especially since you don't have an appetite."

My fate was sealed as the automatic door locks snapped in place when Kim ripped out of the parking lot. Once we were settled and had given our order to the waitress, Kim had her say. "Have you gone bat shit crazy? You're a grown woman who ought to know better than to let yourself be left at some bar. Anything could have happened to you, or didn't you think about that when you put yourself in this situation? You've made it very clear that from now on when you want to go out with a bunch of girls, I'll have to go as your chaperone."

I had no response because she was absolutely right, and I deserved the tongue-lashing. I wasn't a child, and I should have known better than to jeopardize my safety—and Megan's. My only defense was that a couple of wine coolers and Megan's persuasiveness had clouded my judgment. I chalked the whole incidence up to a learning experience and vowed to never compromise my decisions in favor of another's. Thankfully, the matter was dropped, and we finished our breakfast in friendly conversation. Kim returned me to my car, and I made it home at last where I crashed for several hours of recuperative rest.

May was an extremely hectic time of year, and the seniors were busily and anxiously preparing for a new phase of their lives. We school employees were consumed with graduation preparations, another school year winding down. As always there were a few students, and parents, we were more than happy to see go and all but turned cartwheels at the ceremony when their diplomas were handed out. Even though I loved my position, I was thrilled when an unexpected job opportunity presented itself. It was announced months ago that our superintendent was retiring at the end of the school year, and applications were being reviewed in order to narrow perspective candidates. Not surprisingly, the superintendent's administrative assistant made the decision to change careers and had accepted a job elsewhere; she would also be leaving at the end of June.

I immediately applied to be transferred to her positon and was hired by the incoming Superintendent of Schools, Dr. McCain. I looked forward to working with him and the rest of the central office staff, with whom I was already acquainted. Dr. McCain wanted a capable assistant with a college degree and made it clear during the interview that he had neither the time nor the inclination to stand over my shoulder and review my work. That was a relief because I worked best independently and didn't expect him to supervise my every move. Also, Judy, the head bookkeeper and friend, offered to help me learn the ropes.

My new contract required a slightly longer workday and a twelve month schedule, which I welcomed. My office was still a mere two miles from home, and I was able to stay in touch with former coworkers and old friends due to the proximity of the high school campus and administrative building. Not only was I ready for new challenges and responsibilities, I received a substantial pay increase. My education and patience in waiting for the right job had paid off. I was packing up my office when Carol, a recent divorcée, stuck her head in the door to tell me I would be missed.

I thanked her and continued with the task at hand, but she didn't leave. Instead she brought up the subject of dating, specifically, her older brother. "I know you've had a date or two, and I have a brother who is perfect for you. He's a few years older, divorced, and loaded. Rick* is flying in from California next week to visit family and asked if I knew anyone who would be interested in going out to dinner on Saturday night. I immediately thought of you because neither of you is interested in other than a casual date. I'll have him call and confirm what time he will pick you up. Before you say no, please consider going out with him." She winked and said, "I can vouch for his character."

I moved an empty box onto my desk and considered her proposition. "Okay, Carol, I'll go out with your brother on one condition. Rather than have him pick me up at home, I'll meet him at a restaurant of his choosing. Past experience has taught me to be wary when inviting a man to my house."

"I understand. I'm sure he won't mind at all. I'll give him your number so he can call and set up the date. Thanks, Sheila!"

True to Carol's word, Rick called the following week, and we agreed to meet at the Outback Steakhouse in Douglasville. He'd been congenial and considerate on the phone, and as I dressed in the turquoise dress I told Rick I'd be wearing I tried to relax and told myself it was only one date. Matching sandals and silver jewelry completed the outfit. As I backed out of the driveway, I felt a tinge of regret at agreeing to a blind date but didn't want to standup a friend's brother so reluctantly preceded to I-20.

Rick was waiting at the bar, as he said he would be, and stood to greet me with a chaste kiss on the cheek. "You're even prettier than Carol described you." He pulled out a stool next to his and politely waited for me to sit before returning to his seat. "Would you like a glass of wine while we wait for our table?"

"Thank you for the compliment, but no thank you to the wine." He ordered wine, and I took a moment to scan my date for the evening. Rick was dressed in khaki pants, a striped, button-up shirt, and a navy sports jacket. He was tall but wasn't a particularly handsome man. His appearance was unimportant because he was polite, well-spoken, and had a sense of humor. To break the ice, Rick briefly discussed his adventurous life and lack of regrets before he turned his interest to me.

He posed a conversation starter. "So, Sheila, if you could do or be anything in the world, what would it be?"

I tilted my head as I considered the question, a question I hadn't given any thought since grade school when we all imagined what we would be when we grew up. I answered, "A writer. It's something I've always wanted to do but can never find the time. I guess it's a foolish dream, one no doubt shared by thousands, if not millions. I don't even know if I have the talent."

"It's not foolish at all, and you won't know if you have the ability unless you try." He retrieved a pen from his shirt pocket and a napkin from the dispenser and slid them over to me. His smile was genuine when he said, "Then write. You have absolutely nothing to lose by following your dreams. It's what I did, and my life has turned out very well. And I'm happy."

I was about to explain that becoming a writer wasn't as simple as he'd implied, or maybe it was and I'd always found excuses for fear of failure. Before I could debate the issue of unfulfilled dreams the hostess called Rick's name and seated us in a corner booth. The steaks were delicious and our banter was playful without being flirtatious. After Rick paid the check he suggested we leave my car in the restaurant's parking lot and drive over to Buckhead for entertainment at a dueling piano bar, Jellyrolls. It wasn't late, but I hesitated briefly before I agreed.

Rick escorted me to his Lexus where he held the door for me, and our amicable rendezvous continued as we cruised into the city. We enjoyed lively music from several sets of ivory keys and shared a heavenly dessert, a chocolate concoction with a hint of orange buttercream frosting. As we strolled back to the parking deck to claim his car, he noticed I shivered slightly in the night air. With the courtesy of a man raised in the South, he removed his jacket and wrapped it around my shoulders.

I smiled and expressed my gratitude, "Thank you."

"No, thank you, Sheila. I've had a delightful time and if I weren't leaving town tomorrow, I would definitely ask you for a second date."

I didn't tell him the date was one of the best I'd had in part because there were no expectations of another one. He returned me to my car and gave me a lukewarm goodnight kiss. I eased out of his arms and into my car and told him to have a safe fight. He propped on the opened door and asked if he could call me the next time he was in town, although he had no idea when that would be. I considered that none of us ever knew where our lives would take us and since his plans were vague, I consented. Especially since in all probability we would never see each other again, which would be disappointing news for Pat. My overprotective sister picked me like a vine-ripened tomato when it came to any date. She figured since I'd married for love the first time, there was no reason I shouldn't marry for money the second time. Her reasoning was that it was just as easy to love a rich man as a poor man, and Rick was noticeably a wealthy man.

I was adapting to my new job responsibilities while, out of necessity, utilizing a few hours a day to train the replacement registrar. Robyn was required to learn the duties and software associated with the job before school opened again in late August, which was just as demanding as ending the school year. As usual during summer break, construction workers feverishly went about the business of renovation within a limited timeframe.

Thankfully, we were all accustomed to the chaos and worked through the temporary inconvenience.

One afternoon amidst the hubbub, Cyndie strolled past my old office and saw me working with Robyn. She popped her head in to tell me she missed me and was about to leave when she turned and said, "I've got a brief meeting, but please stop by my office before you head back to the hill."

"The hill" was the term school employees used to refer to the superintendent's office as it was situated on a small rise in the landscape. "Okay, but I'll be here for another hour or so."

I finished up with Robyn and ambled down the hall towards Cyndie's office. She was busy but welcomed me into her homey domain. "Please sit down." She smiled and waved me towards a cozy chair. "I want to talk to you about going out with one of the guys on the construction crew. He's really interested in meeting you, and I've told him all about you. And let me add that he's very easy on the eyes."

I heard that old eighties song, "It's Raining Men" spinning in my head. "Good Lord! Between brothers, brothers-in-law, cousins, friends or friends of a friend, and, yes, even ex-husbands, and now someone you spoke with in passing, it seems men are climbing out of the woodwork. Why would you think I would want to go out with a complete stranger?"

"Why not? The two of you might hit it off, but you won't know if you don't go out with him. He stopped by the central office a few times with one excuse or another, but hasn't been able to strike up a conversation with you. So he asked me for advice, and I offered to run interference for him. As a matter of fact, he has walked past here three times, anxiously waiting to find out if I'm able to convince you to accept a date."

The man had been in the administrative building a few times on false pretenses, but it took a few minutes before I remembered a tall, tanned, blond, blue-eyed guy wearing work boots asking to use the phone or check the air conditioning unit. Using the phone was plausible, but we had a maintenance department who took care of things like heating and air. Evidently, I'd missed any hint of interest he had in me and had, consequently, ignored him. Cyndie wasn't wrong: he was definitely easy on the eyes, and I replied, "Of course you agreed to run interference. Everybody seems hell-bent on matchmaking. I'll tell you what, instead of a regular date, I'll meet him at the Pizza Hut tomorrow for lunch at twelve o'clock. If we have anything in common, and he asks me out, I'll think about it. It's a compromise, and you two coconspirators can take it or leave it."

She was delighted at her success. "Oh, we'll take it! I can't wait to tell him."

"Goodbye, Cyndie. I'll be around tomorrow afternoon and let you know if he and I hit it off."

Unfortunately, the lunch date didn't go as well as I—or Cyndie—had hoped. Nick was waiting in a booth and stood when he saw me enter the pizzeria and introduced himself. His smile revealed teeth that would have glowed in the dark. His sun-steaked blond hair was longer than average and brushed the top of his blue denim work shirt. Nick was a hunk, but his weathered face made it difficult to determine his age.

He extended his hand and offered me a seat. "I'm really glad your friend was able to get you to go out with me, even if it's only for lunch. I ordered tea for myself, but I wasn't sure what you wanted or if you drink sweet tea. A lot of women these days don't and prefer Diet Coke. I'm sorry for jabbering."

"Please don't apologize. I grew up in the South, so sweet tea is my preference."

The waitress zoomed over to take our orders, and would have almost certainly thrown herself in Nick's lap if I hadn't been sitting there. She took our order and reluctantly walked away, and Nick caught me up to date on his life. It was his stint in Afghanistan a few years earlier that captured my interest. "When exactly were you in the military?"

"In ninety-one I served in the Middle East for two years, which ended my career with the marines due to a combat injury. Nothing serious, but I'd planned on a few more years in the service." He shrugged off his disappointment. "But I'm luckier than some of my buddies."

Silence filled the gap as the perky waitress placed the pizza before us and dawdled to ogle my date. Nick was oblivious, but I gave her a glare that sent her on her way. I continued the conversation. "Thank you for your service to our country." I didn't want to ask, but as near as I could figure Nick was much, much younger than I was, and it was a question that needed an answer. "Do you mind my asking how old you are?"

He folded a triangle of the fragrant pizza and shoved it into his mouth. He chewed slowly and stared at me intently with those piercing blue eyes before he asked, "Does it matter?"

I hated to admit that it did. "Well, yes, actually it does."

"All right, I'm thirty-one. But I'm very mature for my age, and I know you have two grown sons, and I don't care how old you are. All I'm asking is that you be open-minded."

Good Lord, my date was closer to my sons' ages than he was to mine. Although I wasn't old enough to be his mama, I was, unknowingly, a cradle robber. Even if Cyndie's heart was in the right place, I planned to eat her alive for not verifying details, such as a man's age. I didn't know how to break it to the gorgeous young man who waited anxiously for me to say something, but I had to nip things in the bud. "Nick, I admire that you're a veteran and that you're a hard worker, but too many years separate us. We have absolutely nothing in common." I pushed my plate away and thanked him for lunch.

He cradled my hands in his. "Sheila, please give me a chance to prove to you that despite our age difference, I very much want to get to know you. The girls I've dated over the past few years are only interested in themselves—and sex. But I'm ready for something serious, something real. At least consider a relationship with me before you toss me aside like old news."

I couldn't very well damn those girls for being interested in climbing into Nick's bed when I had to rein in my own lustful thoughts. However, unlike Mrs. Robinson, I had no intention of taking on a "boy toy." Regardless of Nick's sex appeal I wasn't about to earn a reputation as a coyote. Or was it cougar? I stood to leave and gave him some advice. "You're a good man, and you will meet the right woman if you're patient. I, however, am not that woman. Take care, Nick."

I felt his eyes watching me as I walked away, and I was glad he didn't follow me or make a scene at the Pizza Hut. Especially since the casual dining restaurant became my regular meeting place anytime a friend or family member wanted me to go out with an available man, one who would be "perfect" for me. Lunch was a logical choice in that time was limited to less than an hour, and there would be no awkward goodnight kiss at the end of what was sometimes a long, boring evening, which I was spared as none of those meetings resulted in a date. It was actually a great plan until I realized that I was meeting a different man once or twice a week at the same location over several weeks. The wait staff had no doubt begun to think of me as a hooker who checked out prospective "Johns" before committing to having sex with them. Nothing could have been further from the truth, but in all likelihood jumping to conclusions gave them something to talk about on a slow day.

My tactic for blind dates also gave Kim something to brood over. Not surprisingly, she didn't approve of my plan to shortcut the dating circuit. When I answered a ringing phone I expected a "hello," instead of a curt, "We need to talk. Trey has baseball practice at the rec fields in half an hour. We'll swing by and pick you up on our way. You and I can push Macy in her stroller and talk about your dating situation."

"Hello to you, too, Kim. Did it occur to you that I have other plans or that I don't care to discuss my dating strategy with you?"

She laughed. "We both know you don't have other plans, and I'm not interested in discussing your multiple lunch dates at the Pizza Hut. Brush your hair and throw on some lip gloss. There are all kinds of men at the ballfield, and plenty who aren't wearing wedding rings."

Had she not hung up the phone I would have pointed out that the absence of a ring didn't necessarily mean that a man was single. In fact, I'd come across a few of them when I was at various clubs with friends. Men who would remove their rings when lookin' to get lucky, but it was hard to hide a tan line or indentation. It wasn't a mystery as to why I was becoming disillusioned with men. But I needed to walk, so I freshened up, changed into shorts and a t-shirt, and was tying my shoes when I heard an impatient car horn demanding my attention. I grabbed my purse and keys, locked the house, and hurried into the late afternoon heat. As I climbed in the passenger seat I said, "I forgot to get a bottle of water and need to run back inside." I turned and spoke to Trey and asked Kim, "Where's Macy?"

"Nope, you don't need to get out of the car. I brought a cooler with water for us and a Gatorade for Trey. Macy is with Bob, so we won't have to struggle with the stroller." She slammed the car in reverse, and ten minutes later we parked at field number four. Trey ran to meet up with the other players, and Kim and I proceeded to the street's walking trail that surrounded the fields. She cut to the chase. "So what are you thinking meeting men for lunch and then not accepting real dates from any of them? Exactly what's your end game?"

"I didn't think you were interested in my pizza dates, and there is no 'end game'. I've had more than my share of 'real dates', and more often than not, I was bored to tears. Believe me when I tell you that I'd much rather stay home, pop some popcorn, and watch a good movie than go out with any of those men a second time. Besides, I go out almost every Saturday night with the band and friends. We have a lot more fun as a group than I ever have on date where I'm expected to carry on a conversation about nothing."

"Well, it's getting around that you date a lot but won't agree to a second date with any man."

"Let me guess. I'm the topic of the week for the Nosy Rosies with empty lives."

"They're not being nosy, any more than anyone else. We're all worried about you because you're way too young to spend the rest of your life alone. Everybody is wondering how you're going to ever have a relationship with a man when you won't consider taking a chance."

"'Everybody' needs to mind their own business, and I don't want to talk about this anymore. As I told several of my coworkers, when I meet the right man, I'll know. And, once again, I'm okay if I never meet a man I can love. Now let's drop it."

Kim pouted but didn't say anything else. We were winding up our walk when we ran into an old acquaintance walking with a man that neither of us knew, which meant that he was most likely not from Bremen. Geraldine, known as Jerri, stopped under a shade tree to introduce us to her walking companion. "Sheila, this is Tom. His two boys are practicing baseball, and since we're both walkers we decided to walk together." She turned towards Tom and motioned my way. "Sheila raised two boys, so she probably knows all about camping." She pivoted back to me. "Tom was telling me he's just bought a large, three-room tent and plans to go on a camping trip this weekend over at Coleman Lake in Alabama. You really should go with them. Did I mention that he's divorced?"

I blushed at Jerri's brazen suggestion that I go camping with a man whom I met two minutes earlier. The fact that I was blushing brought a comment from Tom. "I would invite you to join us, but from your evident embarrassment I don't think you would be interested."

Jerri apologized for her blunder, but Kim was enjoying my humiliation and introduced herself. "Oh, I don't know, Tom. Sheila enjoys hiking and has been on several camping trips with her late husband and their sons who, by the way, are now grown." I shot her a go-to-hell look, and she changed the subject. "So how old are your boys?"

"They had their seventh and eighth birthdays last week. There's only a year and five days between them, and I've had full custody of them for the past two years. Their mama decided raising them cramped her lifestyle, and the man she's living with doesn't want another man's sons." He paused long enough to let that information sink in before he continued, "In addition to more responsibility in my personal life, I've been promoted to Project Superintendent at the construction firm in Atlanta where I've worked for the past twenty-plus years. I moved to Bremen last year because it's more convenient to I-20, and I wanted the boys to attend school here. I also wanted to get them involved in sports. I manage to keep up, but sometimes I'm so busy that I barely have time to sleep. And there are days when the laundry threatens to eat me alive."

While Kim was snooping into Tom's life, I took the opportunity to check out the man in front of me. He was very handsome, and I estimated his height at six feet. His black hair was sprinkled with gray, as was his neatly trimmed beard, which made it difficult to guesstimate his age—as did the smile lines that surrounded green eyes that reflected sincerity. It was the beard that took me back to Cuernavaca and to something the woman predicted when she read my tarot cards: that I would meet a new love in my *pueblo*, a man with a beard. I dismissed the soothsayer's words as nothing more than silly superstition. I wondered again how old the handsome stranger might be.

Based upon the ages of his boys, he was probably a few years younger than me and was in all likelihood dating someone. Nonetheless, I couldn't drag my eyes away from him. He carried broad shoulders and exuded confidence, but nothing about his manner was arrogant. There was something about him, his attractiveness, his air of genuine kindness, and his beautiful smile that revealed dimples that added to his boyish charm. An emotion stirred inside me, a feeling I barely recognized as desire. I had to rein in scandalous thoughts that involved tearin' off clothes and…*Stop it! Shitamighty, I just met the man.*

But there was no denying the physical attraction, and I made eye contact with him only to realize that Tom had been watching me, as if he knew exactly what I was thinking. Dark lashes fringed his sea-green eyes that saw into my soul with an unleashed passion. It was very disconcerting, and another warm blush crept over me as I turned away from his gaze.

Regardless of his sexual magnetism, he had full custody of his young sons. My own two hadn't been the little hellions they might have been, but nor had raising them been a walk in the park. Out of nowhere I heard the robot from that old sixties show *Lost in Space*, "Danger, Will Robinson! Danger!" Except the mechanical man's arms were waving a warning in my direction: "RUN!"

Kim and Jerri wrapped up their conversation, and Kim said to Tom, "If you're not involved with anyone, Sheila's number is in the book. You should give her a call sometime."

My humiliation was complete. I smiled at Tom and extended my hand. "It was very nice to meet you, Tom, and please ignore my pushy niece. You apparently have your hands full, and I will pray for you. I'll ask God to send an angel to help you."

He took my proffered hand, and his touch sent shivers down my spine in the July heat. "Thank you. Lord knows I need all the help I can get." My hand was still in his when he addressed Kim, "No, Kim, I'm not seeing anyone and haven't met a woman I'm interested enough in to get to know better." He gave me another intense look and a smile. "Until now." He hesitated before he dropped my hand. "It was nice to meet you, too, Sheila."

We said our goodbyes and headed off in opposite directions. Kim nudged me and said, "Oh, he's going to call you for sure. Aren't you glad you polished yourself up a little? Love that pink lip gloss."

I rolled my eyes at her. "Shut up."

Kim wasn't the only one amused by my encounter with Tom. When I related the chance meeting to Cyndie, she smiled. "You better be careful what you pray for, my friend. God has a sense of humor, and you may be just the angel He has in mind."

*Name changed

Chapter Eleven

Men Are from Mars

Much to Kim's disappointment and more of my own than I wanted to admit, Tom didn't call me. I decided he either wasn't interested or didn't have the time to date. Kim urged me to call him and even looked up his number, but I refused. I reminded my niece of the three rules I established to help me navigate the murky waters of dating:

1. Never, under any circumstances, become involved with a married man.
2. Don't sleep around. Period.
3. I wasn't interested in men who weren't interested in me.

Per rule number three, I wasn't the kind of woman to sit by the phone just in case a man decided to call. I pushed thoughts of the good-looking man with the two little boys to the back of my mind and accepted an invitation from Jerry and Jerline for supper at Ruby Tuesdays. As usual they were a few minutes early, but I was ready to go when I heard the horn beep. I'd barely buckled my seat belt when Jerline pounced. She twisted around in her seat and proceeded to tell me about a man who was tall and handsome and loved the outdoors, especially hiking and camping, primitive camping. His sister was their favorite waitress at the Cracker Barrel off I-20, on Hwy 92, and the waitress happened to mention that she had a brother who would like to meet a woman who also enjoyed hiking and camping.

Jerline paused to catch her breath before she continued, "So of course

I thought of you right away. Tammy, the waitress, called her brother Doug and told him about us and you. Y'all are about the same age with common interests, and he agreed to drive to Carrollton this Saturday night and meet you for dinner at O'Charley's. It's all set up. All you have to do is show up at seven. If you're nervous about it, Jerry and I will go with you for moral support. I have a good feeling about this, Sheila."

She finished her spiel, and I dove into the conversation. "Jerline, I don't even know where to begin, but let me try to clarify a few things. My understanding is that you want me to have dinner with a man neither of you has ever met, a man who for all you know could be another Ted Bundy." Jerline tried to interrupt, but I kept talking. "Don't defend a man you don't know from Adam's house cat. Even if I let you convince me to go, it's too hot for hiking, which is why the single hikers have disbanded until fall. And let me tell you another thing: my camping days are over, so there's no way I'm pitching a tent in the middle of nowhere with Grizzly Adams. Sorry, but you'll have to call Tammy and tell her the date has been cancelled."

Jerline faced the windshield and remained silent, but her body language let me know she wasn't going to give up. Agitated, she turned in her seat again and reminded me that I'd gone on blind dates that other people had set me up with and that her suggestion was no different. She harped all the way to the restaurant until Jerry and I both had enough, and I gave in to her irrational expectations regarding the date with a complete stranger. But I did solicit a promise that they would go with me, and Jerry offered to drive us since the Mustang I drove would be cramped with three adults. It never occurred to me that I would be thrown under the bus by own family.

However, that's exactly what happened two days later when I called their home several times only to be answered by a machine urging me to leave a message. The message I wanted to leave was not one they wanted to hear. At six-thirty I was dressed in a white sleeveless dress and sandals; I was scheduled to meet Doug at seven. I made several more unsuccessful attempts to get in touch with my brother or his wife. I was fuming and should have backed out of the date and blamed Jerry and Jerline, who were both in for an ass chewing.

Frustrated that I'd let myself be talked into yet another blind date, I snatched up my purse and keys and headed to O'Charley's. I entered the crowded restaurant and immediately spotted a man who stood when I entered the waiting area. With a sinking heart I knew he must be Doug. He was a mountain of a man, well over six feet, with black, scraggly hair and a wayward beard that rested on his broad chest. He was wearing Liberty overalls over a white t-shirt, and I was embarrassed that I'd been had by a waitress named Tammy. Her brother was tall, but "handsome" was without a doubt a matter of opinion.

I was about to make a run for it when a hand the size of a bear's paw rested on my shoulder. In a deep growl, the man said. "You must be Sheila. I've been looking forward to meeting you."

I don't think I'd ever wanted to *not* be Sheila as much as I did in that moment. I almost lied and said he was mistaken because my name was Ginger. Or Candy. Or Sally Sue. Anything but Sheila. My would-be lie was stopped by his hopeful smile and the kicked dog expression in his eyes. I couldn't force myself to say that it was nice to meet him, but I extended my hand, a hand that was lost in his clasp. "I'm Sheila, and you're…Doug?"

"That's me. I got here thirty minutes ago so I wouldn't be late." The hostess called his name, and led the way to our booth but not without a curious glance at the mismatched twosome.

We made small talk and placed our order as soon as the waitress came over to get our drink orders. Doug was a serious hiker who spent days on the Appalachian Trail and slept on the ground or in a tent if it was raining. Whenever he could take some time off from the wrecker service he owned, he mapped out different routes. He hoped to eventually hike the entire distance from the trailhead in Springer Mountain in North Georgia all the way to Mt. Katahdin in Maine, some twenty-two hundred miles. While I admired his goal, carrying a backpack with necessities from town to town and sleeping in the woods for weeks on end was not on my bucket list. He laughed when I explained that my idea of roughing it was when two or more people had to share one bathroom at a hotel. Thankfully, the evening passed quickly and even if Doug was a little rough around the edges, he was interesting and intelligent—and a good conversationalist, which proved true the adage not to judge a book by its cover.

Our exchange over a variety of topics was interrupted when the waitress asked if we wanted dessert, which we both declined. She left the check, and Doug retrieved his wallet. "I've very much enjoyed our date, Sheila, and grateful you actually showed up. And more grateful you didn't bolt when you saw me." He pulled out a couple of twenties and placed them, along with the check, on the plastic tray. "But don't worry. I'm not going to ask for your phone number or to see you again. You've been very attentive and polite, but I knew the minute we met this would be a one-time only date. I'm not very successful when it comes to women, which is why I've never married, and you and I are incompatible in many ways. Or didn't you notice the attention the 'odd couple' attracted?"

I noticed, and he was right in that I wasn't interested in going out with him for a second date, which didn't make him unique. Rather than mislead him, I encouraged him not to give up. While he may have known his way around hiking trails, he seemed lost when it came to women. "Don't worry, Doug. You're bound to meet the right woman one day, a woman who shares your hobbies and will love and accept you exactly as you are. We all deserve that, and I was lucky to have had a husband who let me be myself." I stood to leave and Doug offered to see me to my car, but I refused. When I reached the door, I chanced a look over my shoulder to see a disappointed man watching me walk out of his life.

After that mismatched meeting I decided it was time to take a break from dating, especially blind dates, but Lynn* had other ideas. It was the week before Labor Day, but school was already well underway when she walked over to the central office to see me. She gave me a hug and said, "Hi, Sheila. I'm happy for you and your promotion, but we all miss you. How are you adjusting to your new job?"

"I miss y'all, too, especially working with students. As for the job, there has been a lot to learn, but I enjoy working here. Until I was transferred to this position, I never realized that the administrative offices are the business side of running a school system. It's different, but everyone has been good to help me learn the ropes. I get along very well with all of the people here, including my new boss, and working through the summer was a blessing instead of a burden because it occupied my time, not to mention the extra money is nice."

"I'm glad to hear you're adapting, not that I had any doubts. I hate to change the subject but I'm on my planning period, which is almost over, so I'll get to the point. I have a friend, one of my student's dads that I'd like for you to meet. He's nice-looking, has a good job, and isn't dating anybody. Jennifer*, his daughter, is the one who asked me to introduce the two of you."

I leaned back in my chair and sighed. "I appreciate the offer, but I'm gonna hop off the meeting men merry-go-round for a while. Several dates have been good ones, but I've not been interested enough to go out on a second date. I hope both you and Jennifer understand."

"I do, sort of, but you never know which one of these fixups will lead you to another Mr. Right. His name is Adam*, and he's been divorced for several years. His ex-wife won't be in the picture because she moved to Savannah years ago, leaving Jennifer here with Adam so she can graduate with her friends next June. He was engaged a couple of years ago, but that didn't work out, and whatever her name was relocated to Tennessee, I think."

Lynn seemed to know a lot about Adam's broken relationships, and it was obvious that she and Jennifer had discussed the matter. I was hesitant in my reply, "I don't know about another blind date. How do you even know Adam wants to go out with me?"

"Oh, he does. Jennifer told him all about you, and I have an idea of how you can meet him without actually going out with him. Come by my classroom on Thursday night on some pretext or another and meet him. He scheduled his parent-teacher conference for seven o'clock, and I won't mention anything to Jennifer. If you have absolutely no interest, then I'll think of an excuse to tell his daughter. But I really think you should give him a chance. He's not a redneck, but he is a good ole country boy who really makes a pair of Levis look great, if know what I mean."

"Yes, Lynn, I get it. Okay, I'll stop by your room, and you can introduce us. If I consider going out with him, the ball will be in his court. He'll have to call and ask me out. Or not."

"That won't be a problem. Thanks, Sheila. See you Thursday night."

By the time Thursday rolled around, I'd almost forgotten my promise to an old friend but unenthusiastically changed out of my walking clothes and drove over to the high school campus. There was a man waiting in the hallway when I arrived at Lynn's classroom, and I speculated that he could be Adam because he did nicely fill a pair of jeans. He wasn't drop-dead gorgeous, but he was handsome in a rugged kinda way. The man smiled politely and asked if I was there for a conference.

I returned his smile and answered, "No, I'm here on some sort of pretense because my friend has someone she wants me to meet. I don't know why I agreed."

"Are you by any chance Sheila?"

"Yes, I am. You must be Jennifer's daddy."

"Guilty as charged. She's a handful, but overall a good kid. I just can't believe she's a senior. By the way, I think I'm the man you're supposed to check out."

Embarrassed that I'd been made, I changed the subject. "I understand about the years flying by. One day they're graduating from kindergarten, and a week later they're graduating from high school."

"Seems that way." Unexpectedly, he asked, "Would you like to go out sometime? That is, if I'm up to par. If you don't have plans for Saturday night, I'd like to take you out, to the Border if that's good with you. They make the best margaritas around."

Lynn was right in that Adam was a good ole boy coupled with a sense of humor. I doubted there would be anything serious between us but replied, "My big plans, party animal that I am, are to grab a bite to eat and go to Home Depot and look for a set of a gas logs. My sons have been good about keeping firewood stacked in the storage rack on the porch, but it's a headache to keep the fireplace clean. Last winter I used the gas starter to build a fire but forgot to check the flue, which was closed. In a matter of minutes the family room filled with smoke, and the smoke detectors were screaming like a banshee. While I was running around like a mad woman, opening doors, and reaching for the chain to open the flue, the security monitoring person called to see if she needed to alert the fire department. It was not my finest moment."

Adam laughed. "I like a woman who can laugh at herself. So about Saturday night? Is it a date?"

I accepted the date just as Lynn opened her door to allow a couple to exit. She was pleased to hear that we'd introduced ourselves and had made a date for Saturday night. Before I had time to think about the date, Saturday was upon me, and Adam was ringing my doorbell.

As we were going to the Border, a popular Mexican restaurant near the university, I'd dressed casually in jeans and a blue striped shirt. Adam had done the same and was wearing Levis and a chambray shirt. We laughed over our coordinated attire, which was merely a coincidence. The conversation was comfortable, and Adam offered to go with me to Home Depot the following afternoon to find the right gas logs.

I wavered a moment before I said, "I really appreciate that, but it's supposed to be a perfect afternoon for hiking. I'm going to ride over to Cheaha State Park and hike on one of the less isolated trails. I would love to take you up on your offer one night next week, if you have time. By the way, do you enjoy hiking?"

"Any night next week is fine. I'll call you on Monday to confirm when you want to go. Hiking? Sorry to disappoint you, but why would I drive an hour to traipse through the woods, swat mosquitoes, watch out for snakes, and wear myself out when I have a perfectly good truck? As long as it's runnin', I ain't walkin'."

"Well, when you put it that way it doesn't sound like much fun, but hiking is good exercise for body and soul. It's a hobby I enjoy." I shook my head and laughed because Adam did have a bit of redneck in him. I held up my glass in a mock toast, "Different strokes for different folks."

Twenty minutes later my glass was almost empty. I mistakenly thought I'd learned in Cancun that tequila was not my friend. I barely finished the one cocktail that was not a *muy grande* when I recognized that a second drink was not in order, despite that our food had been served. Adam, on the other hand, was stone cold sober after three rounds of the flavorful concoction and couldn't understand why I refused another drink—until he did.

"Sheila, are you drunk? Good Lord, you've only had one margarita!"

"I'm not drunk, but I do have a slight buzz, which is why another drink is out of the question." I yawned. "Excuse me. I'm not bored, but I am sleepy."

Adam leaned across the table as if he had a big secret to share. "Let me give you a piece of friendly advice: if you can't hold your liquor, tequila should not be your drink of choice. A good margarita is usually strong and if one has you high, two would knock you on your ass." He motioned our waitress for the check. "I'm going to take you home and leave you at your door, but one day you may come across a man who's not as honorable as I am. You could wake up and not have a hint in hell how it is that you're in his bed. Been there myself, in an unfamiliar room with a mop of hair attached to a woman I didn't recognize sleeping on my shoulder. I wanted to gnaw my arm off and get the hell outta Dodge."

I laughed at the image he provided. Adam was funny and caring, and I appreciated that he had no desire to take advantage of me. True to his word, he left me at my door and waited on the porch until the deadbolt slid in place and the flip of a switch left him in darkness. I washed my face and brushed my teeth and thought about my first date with Adam. He hadn't even tried to kiss me goodnight, which was fine. It would have been awkward anyway, and I wanted to part on good terms. He was a nice man who'd sounded sincere about calling on Monday and following up on the Home Depot trip.

It was after ten when I pulled back the comforter, and I was startled when the phone rang and interrupted my replay of the evening. Kim sounded like a worried parent. "I was just checking on you to make sure you made it home okay. Has what's-his-name left?"

"Yes, Adam left me at the door without so much as a kiss on the cheek. I don't think he's going to be more than a friend, and I'm sure he would agree. We enjoyed each other's company, and I hope he's a man I can call on if I need to, or one who can call me for a casual meal when he doesn't want to eat alone."

She sighed loudly and was openly frustrated but accepted that Adam had already fallen into the "friends" category. "I'm not gonna damn you for not wanting to give him a chance. Besides, every girl needs a good ole southern boy for a friend, one she can count on. Night, Sheila."

"Night, Kim."

Adam proved to be a friend and nothing more. On one of our non-dates, which were always Dutch, I ventured to ask about his ex-fiancé whose name, I learned, was Janet*. "So what happened between you two?"

He took a swig of his beer and cleared his throat. "Hell if I know. We just started fighting over little things, nothing and everything. I guess the constant bickering got to us both, so she packed her bags, requested a transfer from the company where she works, and moved to Memphis." He stared into the frosty beer mug and seemed to be debating as to whether or not to share more of their story, so I waited. "The thing is that I loved her, still do, and Janet was better to Jennifer than her own mother has ever been."

The waitress brought over another beer for Adam and asked if I'd like to order anything from the bar. I declined, and she moved on. I continued with my interrogation. "Has Janet remarried or is she dating someone else?"

He shrugged his shoulders. "Not that I know of. She stays in touch with Jennifer and has promised to attend her graduation ceremony. Jennifer, of course, sings like a canary and keeps me informed about Janet's love life."

He was lost in reflection, so I slapped my hand on the table to get his attention. "Then what is wrong with you? You just admitted that you still love Janet, and it could be that she feels the same. She and your daughter have maintained their relationship, and it's not as if Memphis is on the moon. Take my advice and call her. Better yet, drive to Tennessee and surprise her with your presence—and flowers."

Adam was taken aback by my no nonsense suggestion. "I'll be damned. If you were drinkin' I'd say it was the tequila talkin'. I don't think I've ever had one of my dates tell me to work things out with another woman."

"I haven't had any alcohol, and let me remind you that this is not a date. We're only friends, which is why I'm telling you to stop being pigheaded and letting your pride keep you and the woman you love separated. Do you know how rare it is to find true love? Don't be stupid enough to throw it away. This time next year Jennifer will be in college, and you'll be alone. Is that what you want?"

He looked uncomfortable with discussing personal matters, but he did admit that I was right. "Will it make you happy if I tell you that I've been a stubborn jackass and that I would like nothing better than to patch things up with Janet?"

"It's not me that you need to make happy. It's Janet. Tell her what you told me and ask her for a second chance. At best, she'll welcome you with open arms, and the two of you will grow old together. If, on the other hand, she tells you to go to hell, you won't be any worse off than you already are. Or do you want to spend whatever's left of your life wondering 'what if'?"

He looked at me and smiled. "You're a very convincing woman. Would you mind if we call it a night?" He polished off his beer and winked. "I've got an important phone call to make."

The members of the "Backstreet Gang," as we dubbed ourselves when Robin joined our group, were out celebrating Halloween at a costume dance when Jane cornered me in the ladies room. "A man at the bar is alone, and he's someone I want to introduce you to. I've seen him several times at Publix, but he's never with a woman. Sometimes he and his two daughters shop together, so I've decided he's an every-other-weekend dad. Lots of divorced dads shop with their kids."

I didn't want to hurt Jane's feelings, but neither did I want to meet who-ever was sitting alone at the bar. "I appreciate the offer, but I'm just here to have a good time and am really not interested. I hope you understand."

"Well, I don't. He's a nice, single, good-lookin' man who's about your age, and there's no reason in the world y'all shouldn't get to know each other. Besides, one of the times I saw him he was dressed in hiking pants and boots, and I know you like hiking, only God knows why, but you do."

She looked so hopeful and sure that he and I would be a good match that I agreed to meet him. "But if he doesn't ask for my phone number, that's the end of it. Promise? By the way, what's his name?"

"Okay, I'll let it go if he's not attracted to you, but he will be." She hemmed hawed before she stammered, "I don't actually know his name, but I know he'll recognize me. We can go over to the bar together and in-troduce ourselves."

"Jane, do you mean to tell me that you want to introduce me to a guy you don't even know? No, thank you. I've already been down that bumpy road."

"I know enough about him to know he's not an ax murderer. Now c'mon."

I glanced at myself in the mirror and wished I hadn't let Debbie con-vince me to wear a costume, especially a skimpy outfit covered in sequins. Coincidentally, Jane and I, the blondes in the group, had both shown up wearing majorette outfits, complete with white, tasseled boots and batons; we were a long way from the Barbi Twins but didn't look half bad. The two of us left the ladies room and were making our way towards the bar when the man to whom Jane had referred approached us.

He extended his hand to Jane. "Hello, again. It's nice to run into you somewhere other than the grocery store. My name is Justin*. I've been meaning to introduce myself but I noticed your wedding band and didn't want you to think I was trying to pick you up."

Jane laughed and shook his hand. "My name is Jane, and I would never have thought that about you. It's good to put a name with a face, Justin." She drew me towards them. "This is my friend Sheila."

The somewhat handsome man smiled and said, "It's nice to meet you, Sheila. I was actually headed to your table when I saw you both coming through the crowd. Your costumes made it easy to spot you."

We all laughed, and he asked if he could join us at our table in the back; Jane immediately welcomed him to our group. Justin looked at me with gray eyes the color of an approaching storm. "Your crowd seems to be having more fun than anybody here, and I'd like to join in if that's okay with you, Sheila."

I shrugged as if it didn't matter to me one way or the other because it didn't. "Sure, we'll make room for one more."

We talked and laughed and became better acquainted. The band was breaking down the set, and Justin caught me off guard with a tepid, uninspiring goodnight kiss. He scribbled his phone number on a napkin and told me to call him sometime. I left the napkin on the table. "Sorry, but I don't call men. If you're interested in calling me, my number is in the book."

He looked surprised that I was so blasé about the dating scene. Nonetheless, he called the next afternoon and asked me if I would like to meet him for a bike ride on the university's trail, and I readily agreed to the outing. Justin's older daughter had a bicycle I could use, and he attached them both to a bike rack on his car. We met at the bike trail where we spent a pleasant afternoon enjoying the fall weather on the beautiful campus. When we finished the ride Justin asked me if I'd like to have dinner somewhere, but I declined. He was not deterred and called me every night for a week before I agreed to a date. After that first date, we sort of stumbled into a relationship and agreed to exclusivity.

We did everything together—from football games to hiking to dinner and dancing. On his weekends with his kids, he would often invite me to join them for a movie or grilling out at Justin's two bedroom rental house. My family and friends readily accepted him and were relieved that I was in a seemingly serious relationship. I was happy, and Justin couldn't have been more charming, witty, and attentive. He doted on me, despite that his ex-wife, a term I came to use loosely as she apparently believed Justin to still be her husband and, therefore, at her beck and call.

To my friends I referred to her as the "Wicked Wife of the West." Cheryl* wasn't the friendly sort, but she was a master of manipulation. For example, she would often have Justin's favorite meal prepared on Sunday night when he took the girls home. Of course, there was always plenty for him to join in a family dinner. And whenever Justin and I had definite plans, Cheryl would find one excuse of another to thwart those plans. Because she used the children, Justin never told her "No." Instead, he complied with her demands and promised to make things up to me. I blamed her for the fact that Justin straddled the line between married and divorced, despite the fact that he'd been in several relationships over the years since his divorce. I was beginning to understand why none of them worked out.

On one occasion when he, his children, and I were at Baskin Robbins, his twelve-year-old daughter Ashley* informed me that I was nothing more than one of her daddy's girlfriends in a long chain of them. Justin repri-manded her for her rudeness, but I assumed she was mimicking her mama and let the comment slide. In retrospect I should have heeded the idiom, "out of the mouths of babes," but I wasn't going to let a child or her mean-spirited mama come between Justin and me. Besides, he didn't feel the way his daughter did or he wouldn't have included me in his family's holiday gatherings where I met his parents and his brother. Despite outward appear-ances and assurances from Justin, something nagged me about the relation-ship, my first in over twenty-five years.

Justin and I had been dating for three months when Kathy, curious or nosy, asked me how the sex was going. She laughed hysterically when I replied, "No idea. We haven't had sex yet."

She stopped dead in her tracks on the walking trail where we took advantage of an unusually pleasant February afternoon. "Are you kidding me? Why are you holding out, girl? It's been, what, almost three years since you've been laid. That's a record." She shook her head and laughed again. "Three months and no sex. Unbelievable."

"For your information, Kathy, I've been taking my time to get to know him before I jump in bed with him. I'm not a one-night stand kinda woman."

"Ouch." She looked hurt over my comment, but it wasn't said to intentionally hurt her.

"I'm sorry. We just have differences of opinions when it comes to men and sex."

She gave me a hug. "I know you didn't mean anything by your remark. I honestly wish I had your reputation instead of mine, but I've made too many mistakes to turn the tide. The truth is that sometimes I sleep around not for sex but because I'm lonesome and want to be held in a man's arms, even a stranger's. Pretty stupid, huh?"

I'd contemplated that very reasoning and grasped her by the shoulders to face her. "I know lonely, but it's never too late to change your behavior. You just have to want to change, And, in your case, learn the word 'no' and mean it."

We laughed and parted ways. I don't think Kathy called Justin regarding the not sleeping with me issue, but he did suggest we go away for Valentine Day's weekend. Even I realized that was code for "let's have sex." I was as ready as I would ever be to take the leap into intimacy, but I didn't pack a bag until the last minute. I assumed Cheryl would find a reason for Justin not to leave town, but she didn't page or call him with a fictitious emergency. I was excited about the weekend in the mountains of Blue Ridge and a touch anxious about getting back in the saddle, in a manner of speaking.

The two hour drive was occupied with friendly banter and debating what music to listen to on the radio. We stopped for dinner once we were out of Atlanta's Friday evening traffic before we checked into a beautiful country cabin. Although the cabin was comfortably warm, Justin lit a fire in the rock fireplace and found a soft-rock radio station to create a romantic atmosphere. He retrieved a bottle of wine from his bag and found two glasses in the kitchen while I changed into the slinky nightgown I'd packed for the occasion. Three glasses of wine later Justin led me to the bedroom where we tumbled onto a king-sized bed. The mood was perfect, but that was the only thing perfect about the experience, which was over before it began. There was no foreplay, no lasting sex, and we definitely weren't wrapped in the arms of afterglow.

Before Justin fell into a sound sleep, he rested his hand on my shoulder and mumbled, "Was it good for you, babe?"

Good for me? Hell, I wasn't sure anything had actually happened. I draped myself in a flannel robe and returned to the den to sit by the lingering fire that hadn't had time to die. I made myself comfortable on the sofa, tucked my knees under my chin, and mulled over on what had passed for sex. It had been a while since I'd made love, and my experience was definitely limited, but surely I hadn't forgotten what making love *should* have been. The ex-wife from hell hadn't interfered with Justin's plans to take me away for the weekend because she had a motive. Cheryl, the conniving bitch, wanted me to find out how totally inept Justin was when it came to sex. It was amazing she'd conceived two children with the man.

On the other hand, maybe Justin was tired from working all day and driving up to the mountains. Or maybe he'd had too much wine to "perform" in the bedroom. Or it could have been that he was as nervous as I'd been, and his anxiety had detracted from his ability to make love. Satisfied that there had to be an answer for his lack of expertise with women, I crawled back in bed and convinced myself that sex would be better in the morning, when we were rested and more comfortable with each other. Regrettably, that wasn't the case.

I was awakened by the aroma of fresh coffee. Justin was standing next to the bed holding two mugs. "Good morning, sweetie. I hope you slept as well as I did." He kissed my cheek and offered me the warm mug. "Have some coffee, and we'll hop in the shower before going to the lodge for breakfast. We need to fuel up for the day hike I have planned."

I smiled when he said we would be showering together and thanked him for the coffee. He set his mug on the nightstand and went to the bathroom. As soon as I heard running water, I gathered up my personal items and stepped into the steamy shower with him. I wrapped my arms around him and snuggled close to his back and waited for him to turn around so the fun could begin. Instead of turning to face me, he threw a wet washcloth over his shoulder—and in my face. "Hi, there. You're just in time to wash my back."

The man was clueless.

We arrived at Justin's home late Sunday afternoon because we'd taken my car. His ex and the girls were waiting for him inside; she had a key. Cheryl was clearly there to gloat, and asked with a smirk, "So Sheila how was your first weekend getaway with Justin?"

I wasn't about to let her have the last laugh. I wiped that smug smile off her face when I leaned forward and whispered, "Justin is the best lover I've ever had, an absolute lovemaking machine. We barely left the cabin all weekend. As a matter of fact, I can't remember the last time I was so sexually satiated. I honestly don't know how you could have let the man get away." Her jaw dropped, and for the first time since I met her, poor ole Cheryl was at a loss for words.

I excused myself, claiming to be exhausted, and flashed Cheryl a sly smile as I gave the girls a goodbye hug. Justin puffed up like a barnyard rooster and strutted past his ex as he escorted me to my car. Yep, he was definitely clueless.

Or maybe he was just lazy when it came to making love. Either way, it was a topic for discussion with my more experienced girlfriends. As soon as I got home I called friends Kathy and Kim and asked them to meet me at the Waffle House to hash over the weekend. They readily agreed and after tossing my bag on the bed, I climbed back in the car and drove to the twenty-four hour restaurant. I'd just ordered coffee and raisin toast when my friends arrived.

"Okay, spill it. How was Justin in bed? Did y'all screw like rabbits all weekend?"

"Not exactly, Kathy. It was more of a wham bam, thank you ma'am experience, except that there was no "thank you.""

She and Kim exchanged glances before Kim spoke. "That's hard to believe. The man is good-lookin', been around the block a few times, and exudes confidence. Are you sure he wasn't any good in bed?"

"Of course I'm sure. I was there, and the sex was definitely lacking anything close to what I remember it to be."

Kathy laughed and covered my hand with hers. "Oh, Sheila, I'm so sorry you're first time in years was with a dud. I know you're disappointed, but there are lots of men out there who know their way around in the bedroom. Ditch his lazy ass and move on."

"I agree," said Kim.

The waitress came back to take their orders of coffee and waffles. When she left the table, I shook my head in the negative. "There's a lot to be said for compatible companionship, and sex isn't all there is to a relationship. Things could improve with time. I just need to be patient."

Kathy snorted. "You can be patient all you want, but he's not going to change his selfishness for you. And if the man hasn't learned how to satisfy a woman by now, he's never going to. You deserve a man who realizes there are two people in bed. No damn wonder his wife divorced him."

There was no need to mention that Justin was the one who initiated the divorce—or that Kathy often settled for less than she deserved. "Maybe you're right. My niece Kim and I are going to walk at the rec department tomorrow afternoon, and I'll discuss the situation with her and get her opinion. In the meantime, let's talk about something, anything, else."

We discussed their own dating woes, and when I got home around eight, there was a message on the machine from BJ telling me to return her call. As it wasn't late I dialed her number, and she answered on the first ring. "So how was the big weekend? Was the sex good? Have you been thoroughly satisfied?"

I didn't know whether to laugh or cry. "No, BJ, afraid not. As a matter of fact, it was the most awful sexual encounter of my life. I can't even quote Kim's husband Bob, who said that the worst sex he ever had was still pretty good. Granted, my experience has been limited to one man, but Barry knew what he was doing. With Justin, the whole thing was over before I realized it had begun."

"I can't believe you've wasted all this time on a man who's bad in bed! How dare he string you along—"

I interrupted her outburst, "BJ, he didn't string me along. We both agreed to postpone a physical relationship until we were at ease with each other. I wanted to get to know him better."

"I'm tellin' you right now to get out of the relationship. We all know you deserve better, and you know it, too. What the hell is wrong with you?"

"Nothing is wrong with me, but I appreciate your feedback. Justin and I are compatible in other ways, and there's more to a relationship than sex." I realized I'd said the same thing to Kathy and Kim only an hour earlier and couldn't imagine why I thought it was necessary to defend Justin. I scribbled a note to call Patti in the morning for an appointment. Maybe a trained therapist could help me sort out my mixed emotions.

BJ was still on a rant when I told her that I needed to unpack and ended the conversation. I slept most of the night and woke up earlier than usual for work where I stayed busy. When the clock announced that it was four o'clock, I took my small bag to the office restroom and threw on jogging pants and a sweatshirt. I went straight to the track and was stretching when Kim wheeled into the parking lot.

She hopped out of the car and said, "I've got about an hour before I have to pick up the kids, so let's get a move on. I've been too busy to call you about your sexual escapade in the mountains, but you have my full attention. Let's hear it, and I want details. And I'm not talking about your hiking trip because I don't give a damn about streams and waterfalls."

I sighed and kept walking. "There are no details. Either I've forgotten what good sex is, or Justin is bad in bed. Really bad."

"Are you shittin' me? You waited for three months before climbing in bed with that man and he finished without giving you a second thought. Is that what happened?"

"Pretty much. I hoped the next time would be better, but it wasn't."

"I'd cut him loose right now. No need wasting time with a man who's a lousy lay. I mean, what if the two of you actually got married? Do you really want to spend the rest of your life with 'Jumpin' Jack Flash'?"

I laughed at her reference to the Rolling Stones hit from the late sixties. "I don't think that's what the song is about, but it's funny that you nick-named Justin by the title. Where marriage is concerned, I don't see Justin and me ever getting married. He's legally divorced, but for all intents and purposes he has a wife, and three in a relationship is one too many. But before parting ways, I'm going to take some time to think it over, try to figure things out. I'm actually meeting with my former grief counselor on Thursday to get her objective opinion."

She sighed loudly. "I can save you some time: dump his ass. Especially if marriage is not in your future with him. Mama, Cindy, and I are worried you'll get used to your rut of living alone and won't ever remarry. None of us want you to grow old by yourself, and you could live another forty years if you inherited Papa Joe's genes." She patted my forearm. "You're too good for the SOB and an ex-wife he lets control him." She picked up the pace. "We have to put this experience behind us and move on."

We? Us? Did she have a mouse in her pocket? "Kim, I realize y'all love me and want to somehow fix my life, and I appreciate your concern. But whether or not I remarry is irrelevant, so drop it."

Patti listened patiently on that rainy evening I sat in her office and dis-cussed my relationship with Justin. I told her everything, the good and bad of dating Justin and the opinions of a few friends with whom I'd confided. After half an hour of letting me ramble, Patti offered her advice.

"Sheila, if you're happy the way things are between you and the man you're seeing, then it doesn't matter what your friends think. However, I do want to caution you not to accept a less than satisfactory liaison simply because it feels familiar."

"Familiar? In what way?"

"In that he shares custody of two children. No matter how hard you try or how badly you want to recreate what you and Barry had, you can't go back. That's why God didn't give us a reverse."

We finished the session, and I drove home lost in thought while the windshield wipers swished against the downpour. I hadn't considered that I was involved with Justin in an attempt to turn back time. Was Patti right in that I'd gotten comfortable spending time with a man and his kids? I didn't think so, but I knew that it shouldn't have been that difficult to be in a relationship, a relationship that rocked along on the same tedious track until after the July trip to Myrtle Beach in South Carolina.

Justin had invited me months beforehand, when he reserved the three bedroom condo. We all had a great time, but who doesn't have a great time at the beach? After the trip Justin grew distant and indifferent, as did I. The change in Justin was gradual, almost imperceptible. He became moody and withdrawn. His plans became our plans, without consideration for what I wanted to do. We rarely went out to hear Backstreet because he was bored with partying with my friends, and I no longer enjoyed his company. Conversely, the first six months had been wonderful, and we'd spent most of our time together having fun—except in the bedroom. I came to the conclusion that any man could be on his best behavior for a few months. The relationship was over, yet neither of us was willing to pull the plug, so we stayed together, perhaps, because he didn't know how to be alone, and I didn't want to return to my loneliness.

BJ was the first to recognize how miserable I was. "Sheila, I don't know what in the hell is going on with you, but you need to dump his ass. You 're not happy and to prove it, use a calendar and record the days you're happy and the days you're not with either a smiley face or a frowny one. I'll bet you a hundred dollars that at the end of a month, there will be twice as many frowns as smiles. Stop putting off the inevitable and get out of the mess you've gotten yourself into."

I couldn't argue with her because she was right, and I didn't need a calendar. In hindsight, I'd wasted more than a year of my life on a relation-ship that wasn't. That wasn't entirely true. Justin showed me what kind of man I *didn't* want and reminded me that I liked my own company more than his. I didn't know what happened or when we fell apart and didn't re-ally care. I trusted that God would send me the right man—but not until I let go of the wrong one. And Justin was definitely the wrong man.

Nevertheless, we kept up the pretense until one day a couple of weeks before Thanksgiving, a holiday I was not invited to share with his family as I had been the previous year. The two of us had plans to meet for lunch at the Corner Café on the square in Carrollton, one of several restaurants in the area. I was a few minutes late because I couldn't find a parking place as the area was filled with hectic patrons who sought every inch of available space. I finally found a spot two blocks away and walked to the café among bustling shoppers. The smell of fresh coffee welcomed me, but Justin didn't see me when I entered the small eatery. However, I immedi-ately spotted him grinnin' like a jackass eatin' briars as he entertained two attractive women with his jokes and charm.

His enormous ego filled the cafe, and arrogance oozed from his every pore while he flirted with the younger women. I deliberated on why I hadn't seen sooner how highly Justin thought of himself. He was in the middle of another monologue, one I'd heard several times, one he thought was funny but wasn't. Nonetheless, the women giggled like they were teenagers. They would never guess that for all his charisma and playboy confidence, he was hopeless when it came to making love. Or that he would never love any woman as much as he loved himself.

I tapped him on the shoulder. "Excuse me minute man, but are you ready to sit down and order?"

He gave the women another captivating smile and excused himself. When we were seated out of earshot he glared at me and for the first time acknowledged that his lovemaking skills were inadequate, to say the least. "Did you have to call me 'minute man' in front of those women? Honestly, Sheila, I think you were trying to humiliate me when I was…"

He stammered for words I supplied. "When you were trying to pick up another woman while you waited for me? Considering the fool you were making of me, you're damn lucky I didn't refer to you as a one-pump-chump." I ignored his flushed anger and continued, "I'm not stupid, Justin, but I have been blind for a long time. Your older daughter was right when she told me I was just another girlfriend in a steady stream of them. What is it you want? What are you looking for in all the women you've dated and left behind? Evidently, the woman you married couldn't keep you committed to her, either."

He waited until the waitress was out of earshot. "I don't know what's wrong with me, Sheila. I can't make things work with any woman, and instead of trying I run away from anything that begins to feel real."

What a load of crap. Justin was the poster child for a man who couldn't commit. I almost felt sorry for him, but it wasn't my job to restore his wounded pride—or to psychoanalyze him. The waitress brought our sandwiches and coffee, and we ate in silence. I finished the meal, thanked him for lunch, and walked out of the café. I'd seen the light, and there was absolutely nothing left to say. I buttoned my coat against the chill as I walked to my car and contemplated love and life. It was possible that, as Carson McCullers maintained, "the heart is a lonely hunter."

A week later there was a mutual, unspoken agreement to let the relationship die a painless death. In retrospect things were never serious, and there wasn't anything to keep us together. Then again, I would miss our occasional weekend trips to the mountains where hiking was the highlight. I may not have had experience in getting out of a bad relationship, but once it was over I was relieved. More than relieved, I was happy and reveled in my reclaimed freedom.

Justin, on the other hand, continued to call me at work and at home to ask how I was doing and if I was dating anyone, as if that were any of his business. He told me that he wasn't seeing anyone, as if it mattered. Thanks to two years of grief counseling, I'd learned how to let go and suggested to Justin that he not call me again. He respected my wishes but showed up on Christmas night with a gift he'd bought before things ended between us, a gift he could have easily returned. I invited him in but didn't encourage him to stay. I quickly opened the impersonal gift of a tan hiking vest, thanked him, and stood to show him to the door. We were completely over, and I had no desire to remain friends.

The ringing phone was the perfect excuse to tell him goodnight and goodbye. I ushered him out the door and picked up the phone to hear Kim's voice wishing me a Merry Christmas. I returned the greeting. "Merry Christmas to you and your family. I'm looking forward to taking the tree down tomorrow. Thank goodness Janis' daughter Liz helped me put it up this year, though we didn't read the instructions or notice the order in which the tree limbs were placed in the box. We had the whole thing together before we realized it was inverted. Imagine. Anyway, it didn't take long to match the colored tips and throw on the lights and decorations. Did the kids get everything they wanted from Santa? I'll come see them in a day or two, after they've gotten over their excitement."

"Are you talking too much because you're upset? I happened to be driving home when I saw Justin's car pulling out of your neighborhood. I can come over if you need me. The kids have had a long day and are sleeping like logs, just like their daddy. The three of them left Mama's gathering earlier, and Cindy and I stayed to help clean up the mess. Why was the asshole there?"

"Thanks for the offer, Kim, but I'm not upset and there's no need in getting out this late to come and see me. I'm really fine, as I've told you a dozen times. Justin dropped by with a Christmas gift, but he was here less than ten minutes. Stop making more of the breakup than there is to it. He and I both knew it was a dead end relationship."

"Ok, as long as you're sure you're not down in the dumps on Christmas. Hey, let's go out tomorrow night and celebrate the end of your first serious, but bad, relationship. I can get together a few friends for a girls' night out to cheer you up."

"No, absolutely not. I don't need cheering up because all I feel is relief. And I've had a wonderful Christmas with my sons and daughter-in-law. We had Christmas Eve dinner before we exchanged presents, and today I visited with Daddy for a while. Now stop worrying about me and go to bed."

She grudgingly accepted that all was well but argued, "You're never going to find the right man if you don't keep looking. Those *Sex in the City* women are always on the prowl for a man."

I smiled at the absurdity of the comparison. I was by no means Carrie Bradshaw, and Bremen was a far cry from Manhattan. I thought about the women from the t.v. series and the singles bars and a song from an eighties movie, *Urban Cowboy*. The lyrics summed up the people who gathered at various watering holes for the sole purpose of finding someone to fill a void in their lives. Johnny Lee's hit "Lookin' for Love" lamented that he'd been lookin' in the wrong places and in too many faces in his quest for love. I wasn't searching for love when Justin and I met in such a place, a honkytonk, and he was nothing more than a stepping stone or, more aptly, a stumbling block.

I replied to Kim's comment, "I'm not looking. I'm waiting."

*Name changed

Part Three

"Life changes when you least expect it…"

Jim Valvano

Chapter Twelve

Timing was Everything

It was mid-January, which proved to be one of Georgia's milder winter months, and I was picking up a few groceries at Ingle's on a Friday afternoon. I didn't have plans for the weekend but had been invited to join friends to go dancing to the oldies Backstreet was known for. I hadn't decided whether or not to go since we'd all gotten together to ring in the New Year where in the midst of the crowded celebration, with its noise makers and confetti, I was lonely.

I strolled aimlessly among the aisles and wondered what the new millennium held for me. I also thought about the Chicken Littles who were convinced the sky was falling with the arrival of the year two thousand. Despite the Y2K warnings, the computer world didn't come crashing down around us, leaving a path of chaos in its wake. Nor had the world come to an end. The predicted crisis turned out to be more hype than fiasco. I shook my head over the catastrophe that wasn't and was reaching for a box of instant oatmeal when I heard a familiar voice.

"Hi, Sheila. It's good to see you again."

I turned around to see Tom smiling at me. We'd bumped into each other a few times over the past eighteen months since we'd met. It was inevitable in a town the size of Bremen, and he'd always been accompanied by his boys. He was alone, which prompted me to ask, "Where are Thomas and Levi? Did you leave them in the truck?"

"No, they're spending the weekend with their mama. It's not something they choose to do, but my mama said I shouldn't keep them from spending time with their mama. She thinks they could resent it when they get older, that I kept them separated from her." He tossed a large box of Cheerios into his buggy and abruptly changed the subject. "Are you still dating Mr. Carrollton?"

His inquiry about my personal life threw me off guard. "Excuse me? 'Mr. Carrollton'?"

He shrugged broad shoulders. "I don't actually know the man's name, but I saw the two of you at the annual Towne Festival back in October. I was with a friend who didn't recognize the man you were with, but he said he thought he was some guy from Carrollton, so…"

"Hence 'Mr. Carrollton'. I've dated more than one man from Carrollton, but that particular man I dated more than once—long enough to realize that he and I didn't have as much in common as I'd mistakenly thought. We ended things in November. How 'bout you? Are you dating anyone special?" I subconsciously held my breath as I waited for his answer.

"Nope. I'm so busy with work and raising my sons that I rarely have time to date, but I have gone out with two or three women over the past year, nothing serious They've since moved on to greener pastures, meaning a man without full custody of two kids." He added a large box of Pop-tarts to his cart. "I regretted that I didn't get around to calling you. By the time I had a few minutes between my job and the boys' school and sports activities, you were involved with someone else. I wanted to call and kicked myself for missing the chance to get to know you."

His gaze held mine longer than necessary, and for a moment or two it felt as if we were the only two people in the store. The spell was broken when a woman with a crying baby brushed past me to snatch a package of grits off the shelf before hurrying on her way. I smiled at Tom. "You haven't missed your chance. Not at all."

His smile widened, and he asked, "Would you like to go hiking on Sunday afternoon? I figured if you used to go camping that you might also enjoy hiking. I promised to help a friend work on his car tomorrow, and I'm not sure how long it will take or I would ask you to go on Saturday. Other than a date with piles of dirty laundry, I'm free on Sunday. Do you mind giving me your number?"

I momentarily thought about the book of ridiculous "rules" that Megan loaned me and encouraged me to follow, especially the one about not being too available. In defiance of an ill-advised book, I accepted the invitation. "I would love to and as a matter of fact, I do enjoy hiking." I found a pen and scratch paper in my purse and scribbled down my phone number. He reached for the note, and I said, "Call me on Sunday morning, and let me know what time you want to leave. Is there somewhere in particular you have in mind?"

Tom was still beaming. "I thought about Cheaha because it's only an hour away. Regina*, my ex-wife, will bring the boys home at five o'clock, and I don't want to leave them alone too long. Is that state park okay with you?"

"That's an ideal place for hiking! There are some good trails, especially a section of the Pinhoti just outside the park's entrance. I look forward to hearing from you, Tom."

I kept busy on Saturday but declined the invite to go dancing with friends and decided to rent a movie and get a good night's sleep. I woke early on Sunday to a beautiful morning filled with blue skies and anticipation. I showered, dressed, and threw a few necessities into a small backpack. I was enjoying a second cup of coffee when Tom called; it was barely nine o'clock.

His voice echoed his happiness. "Good morning! I hope I'm not calling too early. I didn't wake you did I? If you were out late last night, I can call back later."

"You didn't wake me. What time would you like to pick me up?"

"Anytime is good with me. I've been all set since daybreak. I have to get up very early to be on my jobsite by six a.m., so it's hard to sleep in on the weekends. I've already gotten a jump on the washin', so just tell me what time to be there. Whenever you're ready is fine."

I smiled at his eagerness. "Give me half an hour."

The weather was a January gift: sunny and sixty, an easy day for hiking. That time on the trails was the most enjoyable I'd had in quite a while. We hiked and laughed and talked—about everything. Tom was a good listener, and I told him about my upcoming escapade to Ireland. I'd wanted to make the trip ever since the first time I saw the movie, *The Quiet Man* with John Wayne and Maureen O'Hara. Tom was concerned for my safety when I told him the woman who'd agreed to accompany me on the spring trip had instead chosen to put the money towards a boob job after her recent divorce. I assured him that he didn't have to worry about me because I would be traveling with a group. The ten day tour was offered by a local travel agency at a discounted price to UWG alumni, which is how I could afford the indulgence.

We moved on, and our conversation consumed the hours that flew by like minutes. There was no tension, no need to impress each other, and no expectations other than reveling in the beauty of blue skies, hilly landscape, and sun-dappled trails that led to gorgeous overlooks. We both regretted that the day was drawing to an end, but the sun set early in the winter, and Tom had to be home for his returning boys—something I understood having previously dated a divorced dad. But he surprised me when he merged onto I-20, westbound instead of east. He called his ex-wife from his cell phone and asked her to keep the kids for an extra hour and to tell them that he would be home by seven. There were no arguments, or drama, or accusations of Tom putting a woman before his children. Given their circumstances, that would have been the pot calling the kettle black.

We stopped at a popular steakhouse in Anniston, and I offered to pay for my meal. Tom was offended and said, "The very least I can do is feed you supper after a lunch of granola bars, apples, and water." He smiled with eyes that were just about as green as the tall pines we'd left on the mountain, and his stare was intense, as if he were contemplating what to say. "I really had a good time today, and I hope you did, too. I'd like to call you again sometime."

"I had a wonderful day and would like to hear from you again."

Tom didn't call, but on Monday morning the florist delivered a beautiful bouquet of fresh flowers and a card thanking me for a great afternoon. The office receptionist, who had met Tom through a mutual friend, told me not to make too much of the flowers because Tom was just a nice guy. Despite her attempt to piss on my parade, the flowers lifted my spirits on a dreary Monday, and I resisted the urge to call and thank him for his thoughtfulness. Instead, I waited for him to call me again, if he was interested enough to pick up the phone.

'Again' was later rather than sooner. He called a week or so after our hike and invited me to a basketball game with him and the boys. The high school's team had made it to the final round of playoffs, and Thomas and Levi were anxious to go. Once again I ignored the asinine advice to act aloof and readily accepted the invitation. Tom's children were well-mannered and seemed to be much less mischievous than my two had been. His boys were close in age and resembled each other, but Levi wore a port-wine stain that covered most of the left side of his face, a birthmark that made him extremely self-conscious. I wanted to offer him solace and find a solution, but I planned to tread lightly and to not become attached to the boys the way I had to Justin's daughters.

Nevertheless, Tom and the boys arrived promptly, and twenty minutes later the four of us walked into the gymnasium. I could almost hear heads swivel in our direction. Tom explained that he hadn't met many people in town and that he preferred to keep a low profile. Evidently, he wasn't lying because when I'd asked around after we met, he was known only as the man with two little boys in a red truck. As whispers spread through the stands like the wave, Tom's days of anonymity were behind him. It wasn't that I was anybody distinctive, but I'd lived in Bremen all of my life and had worked in the school system in one capacity or another for twenty years. I'd met many of the students and their parents and was either friends, acquaintances, or related to most everybody else. Hence, most people knew that I was widowed more than three years ago, and for reasons I couldn't fathom they were interested in my dating life. I decided not to worry about the busybodies since Tom and I weren't actually an "item" worthy of such attention.

The ballgame was one of several dates, although I'm not sure "date" was the correct term. Tom always picked me up and delivered me safe and sound to my door, always paid my way, and was at all times a perfect gentleman who never made any advances. We attended basketball games where Thomas and Levi played on the same team, per Tom's request in order to have their practice schedules the same. Sometimes all of us had a bite to eat afterwards. He called me at the office one afternoon to tell me a coworker had given him four tickets to that night's hockey game at Philips Arena and that he very much wanted me to go with them to see the Thrashers. I accepted because if nothing else, Tom would be a trustworthy replacement for my redneck buddy who'd reconnected with his ex-wife, quit his job right after his daughter graduated, and moved to Memphis.

Adam was out of the picture, and Tom and I developed a friendship of our own. I acknowledged the relationship as such, even though I wasn't dating anyone else, and I didn't think he was either. Nonetheless, I was caught off guard when Tom called a few days before Valentine's Day and asked me to go to the dance at one of the clubs where Backstreet was playing. He sounded slightly nervous, as if unsure of my answer, when he elaborated. "I saw the ad in the paper and remembered that you like the band, but it did cross my mind that you might already have a date. I understand if I'm too late in asking and apologize for not asking sooner."

I was reevaluating our relationship but decided that I liked Tom very much and didn't want to keep him waiting for an answer. "I don't have a date for Valentine's and had planned to stay home with popcorn and an old movie. Thank you for thinking of me, Tom. I would love to be your date. What time should I be ready?"

He exhaled with obvious relief before he replied, "Great. I thought we would go somewhere to eat first, since the band doesn't start until nine. Of course, most restaurants will be crowded on Valentine's Day. I'll pick you up at six-thirty, which should give us time to drive to Carrollton, have supper, and make it to the dance. I'm looking forward to spending a whole evening with you, an evening that's ours and not sports related."

We laughed and wrapped up our conversation. I called Kim to tell her the handsome hunk asked me for a date, one without his boys. She was relieved that Tom and I hadn't fallen into the "friends" zone and told me

I would have to buy a new dress for the occasion and made plans. "We can browse Belk's tomorrow afternoon and if we don't find anything, we can run over to the mall on Saturday morning and see what Macy's has to offer."

"Why do I need a new dress? I have plenty of clothes, Kim."

"Well you sure as hell don't need to throw on a pair of jeans and a boring red sweater. Tom has finally asked you to go out to dinner and a dance, a real date. You need to splurge on something fitting the occasion."

I protested and told her it was just another date, but even as I said the words the butterflies in my stomach told me it was much more than that. Therefore, I conceded and agreed to shop for something special. Luck was with us because we found the perfect dress at Macy's, with twenty-five percent off, and only one in my size. The dress led us to the shoe department where we selected a pair of siren red high heels, the same color as the rosebuds that traveled from the hip to the above-the-knee slit on the right side of the body-hugging, sleeveless, black dress. Kim wanted to stop by the jewelry counter, but I assured her that I had jewelry to match.

I spent the afternoon primping and was inexplicably anxious as I applied makeup and pulled hot rollers out of my hair. I nervously fluffed my shoulder-length mane, tugged on pantyhose, and slipped the dress over my head. I was sliding on the red heels when the dingdong of the doorbell startled me. I fastened a simple, silver bracelet onto my wrist and hurriedly put on matching, heart-shaped earrings. I took a deep breath and paced myself as I walked to the front door.

Tom smiled and let out a whistle when he saw me. "You look beautiful." He shuffled from one foot to the other; apparently, I wasn't the only one who was nervous.

"Please come in, Tom, and welcome to my home. I have to grab a light sweater and my purse before we leave."

He helped me into the black cardigan with three-quarter sleeves and pearl buttons. "Is Applebee's okay with you? I didn't think to make a reservation at a nicer restaurant."

"Applebee's is fine. They have a dessert that's worth every calorie, and the walnut blondie with warm maple sauce is big enough to share."

I turned on the porch light, locked the door, and Tom escorted me to the car. He opened the door for me, as he always did, and an awkward silence settled in as our companion. What was wrong with us? We'd always had fun together and were never at a loss for words. Then it occurred to me that it was our first official date with all the tension of unforeseen possibilities between two adults who, up to that point, had been nothing more than friends. We each started to speak simultaneously, and our laughter broke the ice. We relaxed and enjoyed a delicious meal that included a glass of wine and a shareable dessert.

Tom paid the check and glanced at his watch. "We have more than an hour before the dance, and I'd like you to meet someone. It's not more than a few minutes out of the way."

"Okay, but who is that you're so anxious for me to meet?"

"My mama. The boys told her all about you, and she's been nagging me to bring you by the house to meet her. Our excuse to limit the visit will be that we're on our way to a dance."

His *mama*! Not only was I not ready to be introduced to her, I wasn't dressed for meeting a man's mana. It wasn't that I resembled a floozy, but my outfit was chosen for a first date with a man whom I wanted to impress. Sexy was not a look a man's mama would appreciate, so I tried to finagle my way out of the visit. "You know, Tom, maybe another time would be better, when the boys are with us. There's no need to rush things, and I can go with you some other time, when I'm dressed down a bit."

"Don't worry. You look gorgeous, and my mama, Charlcie, is going to love you."

My attempts at avoidance failed and when we entered Charlcie's home, he introduced the two of us. The look of love was not exactly the one his mama gave me as she scrutinized me from head-to-toe. Her gray hair was short and permed, and wire-rimmed glasses framed eyes that didn't miss a trick. She was a rather portly woman who sat in her recliner as if it was a throne; everything from a box of Kleenex to the phone to the t.v. remote was within easy reach. Charlcie muted the *Wheel of Fortune,* and the room filled with an awkward silence, broken only by the tick tock of a clock's black cat tail that swayed back and forth. The cat clock had green eyes.

Charlcie spoke first. "Have a seat, Sheila. Thomas and Levi didn't tell me how pretty you are. Of course, they probably haven't seen you dressed for a night at a juke joint. That dress is worth every penny you spent on it if your plan is to seduce my son. It certainly sets off your figure. Don't you think so, Tom?"

I blushed when Tom looked at me with a burning observation of his own. Her son dragged his eyes away from me to answer her. "Yes, Mama, it does. What's your point?"

Charlcie didn't beat around the bush. My butt had barely hit the sofa when she turned her attention to me. "You might as well know there are only two things the men in my family really enjoy. One of them is good cookin' and the other is, well, if you date my son long enough, which you probably won't, you'll figure out the other one soon enough. It's only fair that you know right up front that Tom needs a wife, a woman willing to take on a man and two boys who need a woman's touch. Tom does the best he can, but he's spread too thin and it's not easy to find a woman willing to help raise another woman's children, my grandchildren." She let out a frustrated sigh and continued, "Tom dated many, many pretty women and could have had his pick among them for a wife, but instead of heeding my warning he married that worn-out whore. That's all the breath I'm gonna waste on his ex." She gave me another once-over and said to Tom, "Sheila doesn't look like she's interested in marrying and raising two boys and another thing—"

He interrupted, "Mama, Sheila and I are just getting to know each other, so don't start anything. She doesn't want to hear about my past or my mistakes. We just stopped by for a few minutes so you could meet her. As a matter of fact, we should be going."

"Sit down, Tom, and hand me that high school yearbook from the bookcase, the one from your senior year. I want to show Sheila a picture of Renee*, your high school sweetheart. She's divorced, you know, and just as beautiful as ever. She moved in with her mama, now that her daddy has passed. God rest his soul. You did go by the funeral home last year and pay your respects, didn't you, Tom?"

"Yes, Mama, I did. You're being rude to discuss a girlfriend from decades ago in front of my date—and you damn well know it." Tom stood and offered me his hand. "We're leaving before we have an argument."

Charlcie disregarded her only son and asked me, "Do you have anything to say or has the cat got your tongue?"

I'd been put through the wringer and realized that if I let her and her abrasive personality intimidate me, any relationship with Tom would put a strain on the one he had with his mama. "No, ma'am, the cat hasn't gotten my tongue. I may or may not be the wife and stepmother to your grandsons that you would choose for Tom, but that's out decision, not yours. As for raising boys, I've raised two of my own and buried their daddy. I'm stronger than you think, Charlcie. Regarding Tom's old high school flame, that is evidently buried in the past or they would have reconnected at her father's funeral. Clearly, none of those women, including the one he married, was what Tom wanted. It's very possible he saved the best for last." I reached for Tom's extended hand while his mama sat speechless, no doubt a rarity. "And considering the two things men appreciate, I'm a pretty decent cook, and I've no doubt I can handle whatever else it is that Tom enjoys. Now if you'll excuse us, we have somewhere else to be. It was nice to have met you, Charlcie. I'm sure we'll see each other again." I sashayed out the door, with Tom in tow.

Determined to have the last word Charlcie called out, "Don't let the heat of your ass burn up your brain, Tom!"

The unplanned stop to meet his mama had been a bit of a downer, but the night as a whole was nothing short of wonderful. Tom and I danced almost every dance together, especially the slow ones. He held me close and caressed me but respected me enough not to let his hands wander. My friends readily accepted him and women gravitated toward him, hoping for a dance—or more. Tom could have had his choice of several women, but to him I was the only woman in the room. One bold woman shoved her phone number in his back pocket. He crumbled up the paper, tossed it over his shoulder, and whispered in my ear, "I'm already with the woman I want."

The date ended with a slow, sensuous kiss that left me breathless and held an unspoken promise. Gentleman that he was, Tom didn't ask to come in but left as soon as I was safely inside. I leaned against the closed door and hoped to hear from him soon. I didn't have to wait long. I was in my pajamas and brushing my teeth when the phone rang. I expected it to be Kim, but it was Tom. "I don't want to seem too eager, but I wanted to hear your voice again before I go to bed."

My heart fluttered. "Goodnight, Tom. Sweet dreams."

Monday held another delivery from the florist, beautiful pink and creamy roses mingled with baby's breath. The card was an apology for not re-membering to bring flowers to me on Valentine's Day. I was thrilled with the roses and had almost forgotten how nice it was to have a thoughtful man in my life. As if dinner, dancing, and roses weren't enough, Tom and the boys waved me down at the track where I was walking with Kathy after work.

The truck inched along, and Tom said, "We drove to your house, but your car wasn't there, so I took a chance that you were over here walking." He, Thomas, and Levi were grinning slyly as Tom pulled the truck over to the edge of the road. Thomas handed him a bag, which he opened and pre-sented me with a huge box of chocolates. Levi piped up, "We got the candy for half price since Valentine's Day is over."

Tom admonished Levi and said, "My sister Nita told me that I should have showed up at your door with flowers and candy on Saturday night, but I'm a little out of practice when it comes to wooing a woman."

I leaned into the truck and lightly brushed his lips with mine, which extracted snickers from two young boys. "There's absolutely nothing lacking in your wooing skills."

Kathy broke up the romantic moment. "Good Lord, you two need to get a room."

I shushed her and thanked Tom and the boys for the candy before I ripped open the cellophane-wrapped box and offered to share with everyone. Tom passed, but the boys grabbed two or three pieces before Tom stopped them and reminded them the candy was for me. He propped his elbow on the window frame and said, "We're going to get a bite to eat as soon as the boys' basketball practice is over. Would you like to join us?"

I didn't want to decline, but had already committed to eating at 302 South Street with Kathy. "Thanks, but I'll have to take a raincheck. Kathy and I already made plans to go to a restaurant in Carrollton. Maybe next time."

His disappointment was visible, but he resigned himself to the fact that I couldn't accept his invitation. "That's okay. I'll call you tomorrow." He waved goodbye to both Kathy and me and said, "Enjoy the rest of your walk."

I watched him drive away before I walked the chocolate to my car and fell back in step with my friend, who expressed her opinion. "I know how you like to get to know a man before you sleep with him, but I'd tap that before someone else does. I noticed more than one woman hittin' on him at the dance, not that other men didn't notice you, but a few of those hussies would have torn Tom's clothes off in the parking lot. Brazen bitches."

I laughed at her bluntness. "Kathy, I'm not going to sleep with Tom just to beat another woman to the punch. If things are meant to be, then it will work out between us. If not, I won't have to be embarrassed if I see him at the grocery store because I slept with him too soon. We're taking things slow."

"Well, don't make him wait too long or some other woman may wheedle her way straight into his bed."

I brushed her comment aside. "I don't think so, Kathy. I get the impression Tom sowed his wild oats in his younger days and isn't interested in a one night stand. Either way, I can't worry about what will or won't be between us."

Only time would tell if our destinies were intertwined. In the meantime, Tom and I spent almost every afternoon walking together while the boys played ball or rode their bikes. Every other weekend was spent together hiking or riding bicycles on the Silver Comet, a network of paved trails named for the *Silver Comet* passenger train that rode the rails from the mid-forties to the late sixties. Construction of the "rail trail" provided many outdoor enthusiasts the perfect place to walk or bike with a variety of scenery; one of my favorite rides was west where the Silver Comet connected to the Chief Ladiga in Alabama. On alternate weekends, when the boys were with their mama, Tom and I went on dates or stayed home and watched old movies. He continued to send flowers to the office on a regular basis, to the vexation of the receptionist Debbie Downer. I didn't let her steal my joy when I felt as if I were being "courted," a term Mama would have used.

My friend Emily, who never sugar-coated anything, put it another way: "What the hell are a few flowers when a man needs a woman to help him raise two boys?"

I didn't consider the flowers a bribe and told her as much. Besides, I delighted in the weekly bouquets that brightened both my office and my mood. It was late March, and Tom had made plans to go with Levi on the fifth grade class trip to Washington, D.C. and Williamsburg, VA. Thomas had gone the year before, but it was the boys' first year enrolled in Bremen City Schools, and Tom hadn't realized that most of the parents accompanied their children. He regretted that he'd sent Thomas without him, entrusted with a chaperone, so he mailed a check to the school for both him and Levi when he received the informational letter the previous fall.

It was agreed that Thomas would stay with me during Tom's absence because he didn't want to spend almost a week with his mama and her current boyfriend. I was looking forward to the company and getting to know

Thomas better. We dropped Levi and his daddy off at the designated area where they would board the Greyhound bus. Tom held me close and told me how much he appreciated me taking care of Thomas and how much he would miss me. "If I hadn't promised Levi that I would go, I'd cancel right now and send him on his way without me. I can't wait for the trip to be over and I'm back here with you. I'll call you every day, twice a day if I have cell service."

I returned his hug and assured him that I didn't mind helping out with Thomas and that I would miss him, too. "I made the trip with both of my sons and don't regret it for a minute. Have fun and enjoy the time with Levi. This is the last school trip on which parents are allowed to go. In May Thomas will be going to Skidaway Island State Park in Savannah with the sixth grade class, and only faculty members are allowed to make the excursion. There are also seventh and eighth grade expeditions, without parents. Don't worry about us and call me if you get the chance. Thomas and I will be here when you get back, so don't dwell on hurrying home."

As promised, Tom called every night to speak to Thomas and me and to give us an update of the day's events. One night the call didn't come but I wasn't worried because if anything had happened the school would have been notified, and I would have known immediately. I told Thomas that his daddy probably got hung up somewhere on the trip and to go to bed since it was a school night. I waited for Tom's daily call until after eleven before I climbed in bed and was on the edge of deep sleep when the phone disrupted my slumber. I clumsily reached for the receiver and groggily mumbled, "Hello. Who is this?"

"It's me, Tom. I'm sorry its past midnight, but we were caught in a traffic jam and my cell phone was dead. I left it charging in the room with Levi and the other two boys chaperoning on the trip. They're all sleeping like logs, so I walked to a pay phone a few blocks from our motel."

I was happy at the sound of his voice but heard rain in the background. A clap of thunder reverberated through the phone line. "Why are you in a phone booth in the middle of the night in a thunderstorm? Are you crazy?"

"No, but I am lonely."

I adjusted my pillow and asked, "How can you possibly be lonely when you're traveling with three busloads of other parents, teachers, and students?"

His voice was low and sexy. "You don't understand. I'm lonely for you."

Pat, Cindy, and I finished our regular Tuesday lunch at Bilbo's and walked outside to park ourselves on a bench where Pat promptly lit a cigarette— or as Daddy referred to them, "cancer sticks." She took a long drag and exhaled slowly. "So, Sheila, you're traipsing out of the country again, to Ireland this time. Daddy's worried about you. He read an article in *Reader's Digest* about Ireland and the skirmishes always going on there. By the way, make sure you bring me a copy of your itinerary and call me every day, and I mean every day. What's the time difference?"

"Yes, I am 'traipsing' out of the country again, and Daddy needn't worry about me. Ireland's history is filled with conflict, but I'll be perfectly safe. If I remember correctly they're five hours ahead of our time. I leave on Friday, around six p.m. Tom and the boys are going to drive me to the airport and will pick me up when I get back Sunday week. That reminds me, I have cards addressed and stamped for Tom. I'll bring them by your office before I go so you can drop one in the mail every day. They're just to let him know I miss him and will be thinking of him, so please don't forget to mail them."

"Well, how sweet," she smirked sarcastically. "Why are you sending him damn greeting cards when you ought to be jumpin' in bed with him and really give him something to miss? He's a handsome, romantic, and good man who treats you like a princess, and you're wasting time with cards." She inhaled another draw from her cigarette and blew the smoke away from Cindy and me, a courtesy I appreciated. "What if your plane crashes on this trip and you die without ever having had sex with Tom? Now that, baby sister, would be a tragedy."

I shook my head over her misplaced concern. "Let me make sure I understand your position in the event I'm killed in a plane crash. If the plane goes down during its eight hour flight, possibly in the ocean where my body would never be found, the 'tragedy' would be that Tom and I never made wild, passionate love?"

"Since you put it that way, then, no, that wouldn't be my first concern, but you can't deny you've thought about having a roll in the hay before you go."

Cindy entered the conversation. "Mama, when she's comfortable with Tom and sure of their relationship, she'll make her own decision about sleeping with him. Really, it's none of our business."

Pat looked at Cindy as if they'd never met. "Of course it is, and who *are* you? Truth be told, you're just as anxious as I am for her to move things along. Then she can tell us all about it. After the last dud she slept with, she deserves a good time in bed."

Cindy rolled her eyes and dropped the conversation with a glance at her watch. "I've gotta get back to work, and so do the two of you." She hugged me tightly. "Have a great time and stay safe. Love you."

"Thanks, love you, too."

We three women were family and friends who scattered our separate ways, but I couldn't stop thinking about Pat's suggestion that I not waste any more time and sleep with Tom before I got on that plane. We were, after all, unattached adults who were very much attracted to each other. It wasn't that I didn't trust Tom or that I worried he would take me to bed and never call again. I just needed more time, time for us to get to know each other better. Although I'd known Tom for well over a year, we'd been dating for less than two months. Besides, there was no rush. Resolve restored I finished the work day, met Tom at the rec to walk, and went home to finish packing for a trip I'd longed to take for decades. A trip that, luckily, coincided with spring break.

Hartsfield International Airport was the hub for Delta airlines and had recently been named the "World's Busiest Airport." It was certainly living up to its claim to fame, and Tom allowed plenty of time. Thirty minutes after arriving we found a parking place so that Tom and his sons could go with me to the gate and insure that I made it safely onboard. The kids grabbed my luggage and wheeled it to the curb for check-in at the Delta kiosk, and I noted the concourse, gate, and departure time on the boarding pass. The four of us proceeded to the tram, and I waved to several of my fellow travelers. I'd met them a week ago at an orientation hosted by the travel agency where we were given our plane tickets and itinerary. They lollygagged, but Tom hustled us along to secure spots on the first tram that stopped. We swooshed along to Concourse E, from which all international flights departed. It was a hike to Gate 35 where we found plenty of available seating. In fact, we were the only four people at the gate.

Fifteen minutes passed, but no one else showed up to join us. I wasn't concerned, but Tom was beginning to fret. "Sheila, are you sure we're at the right gate?"

"Of course I'm sure."

"Don't you think it's strange that no one else is here, waiting to catch a flight to Ireland? What about those people we saw who are part of the group? Where do you think they are?"

"Oh, I don't know. They're probably running late or at the wrong gate."

Levi observed, "I don't even see a plane taxiing across the tarmac."

Tom stood up and paced for a few minutes. "Just to be on the safe side, would you mind checking your boarding pass and ticket again?"

I retrieved the ticket stub from my oversized purse and pulled the boarding pass from my pocket. I scanned the information. "Hey, what a coincidence. What are the chances my seat assignment is the same as the gate number?"

Tom furrowed his brow. "Slim to none." He took the slips of paper from my hand and compared the two. "Oh, hell, Sheila! We're the ones at the wrong gate. You must've misread the information when we checked your luggage. Thank goodness we're at the right concourse, or you would miss your flight."

He motioned for the boys to follow us, and we all scurried down the wide corridor to the other end of the concourse to Gate 6, where the rest of the group was in line for boarding. A tall man with gray hair saw me running to join the end of the line. He pointed and said, "There she is! I knew I saw her in the terminal."

The travel agent who'd coordinated the trip approached me with a stern look and admonished, "Sheila, I stressed the importance of staying together and of not being late. Was there an emergency that delayed you?"

Properly reprimanded, I replied, "No, no emergency. Just a little confusion as to which gate I needed to report for our flight. I'll be more careful for the duration of the trip."

He walked away in a huff. Quick hugs and goodbyes were exchanged among Tom, the boys, and me with a promise to call and let them know that I'd arrived safely. It was Thomas who expressed the worry I had no doubt they shared. He turned to Tom and asked, "Daddy, who's going to take care of her in Ireland?"

Tom absentmindedly patted Thomas' shoulder. "I don't know, son. I don't know."

Carry-on luggage was stowed as we located our seat assignments and settled down with books or magazines for the long flight. A light snack of cheese, crackers, and a beverage of our choosing was served at nine o'clock, followed by the distribution of blankets and pillows. One of the flight attendants announced that it would be lights out in fifteen minutes and recommended that we close the window shades and use the facilities beforehand so as not to disturb the other passengers. I felt like I was in preschool. My seatmate Melissa, a striking brunette with brilliant blue eyes, and I introduced ourselves as soon as we sat down. She echoed my feeling of being treated like children and added, "I'm glad I dressed in sweats instead of the jeans and shirt I'd planned to wear. I wonder if anyone else is considering putting on their pajamas."

"I don't know, but I'm not changing out of my leggings and long-sleeved t-shirt. I dressed comfortably so I can sleep. I just need to take off my Nikes, which are great for walking but not so much for sleeping."

Melissa laughed. "I know what you mean."

Thankfully, we hadn't landed in the middle row of four seats. It was the two of us, and she preferred the aisle seat. We barely made it back to our seats after waiting our turn for the restroom when the main lights were shut off, leaving us in semi-darkness. We reclined our seats as much as possible, but neither Melissa nor I could find a comfortable position in which to sleep. I stretched and yawned but nine-thirty was too early for me to bed down for the night. I turned towards Melissa, who was also wide awake and asked in a lowered voice, "Are you traveling alone, too?"

"No. Those two snoring in the seats in front of us are my parents. My fiftieth birthday is in a few days, and Dad wanted to treat me to something special, especially since my divorce was final last month."

"Oh, I'm sorry you're marriage ended in divorce. How long were you married?"

"Almost twenty-seven years, but it was a mistake from the beginning, which is another reason Daddy is paying for this trip. He feels responsible."

I was confused and couldn't imagine how her daddy could hold himself accountable for his daughter's failed marriage. "How can he blame himself?"

She sighed and even in the dim light I could see the regret that hung on her shoulders like a worn-out winter coat. She explained, "Jim and I met in college and fell in love, or so I thought. My degree was in marketing, and I had dreams of moving to New York and finding a job in advertising. Jim, on the other hand, had different dreams that didn't involve moving anywhere. He'd been a high school football star that earned him a college scholarship. With his teaching degree, he easily secured a position as assistant coach at one of the local high schools." She paused to make sure her parents were still sleeping soundly. "On my wedding day I realized I was making the biggest mistake of my life, but when I broke down in sobs my mother consoled me and convinced me it was nothing more than premarital jitters. To further add to my guilt at wanting to cancel the ceremony, she reminded me how much money Daddy had shelled out in order for his only daughter to have a lavish, fairy-tale wedding. It wasn't that Dad couldn't afford the wedding, but to keep the peace I ignored my instincts, pasted a bride's smile on my face, and was escorted down the aisle by my beaming father."

Hers was a far cry from the elopement Barry and I had in a courthouse and yet only death could have separated us. I was curious to know how her marriage fell apart. "What happened after twenty-seven years of marriage that prompted you to finally divorce a man you never loved?"

She shrugged. "Nothing specific. We stayed together because it was expected of us, especially after the children came along. Jim's career was well-established when he was promoted to head football coach. We moved up the social ladder that included a bigger house in a better neighborhood. I was a stay-at-home wife and mother to two boys who are now grown and married. They each live in different states and rarely come to visit. I made the decision to end the marriage because it had outlived its purpose. Daddy was devastated. He thought of Jim as another son and tried to talk some sense into me. I finally caved and told him about how I'd wanted to call off the wedding the day I was married, but felt obligated to him for the expense. And, of course to spare Mother the humiliation of having a runaway bride for a daughter. Her hoity-toity country club friends would have never let her live it down."

I reflected on our similarities and our differences and elaborated, "I also raised two sons, but I worked from the time the younger one entered Pre-K and was fortunate to find a job in our school system, where I was promoted several times over the years. My sons both married almost three years ago, but the younger one divorced soon afterward. They live nearby, and I'm grateful for that." I skipped the details but summarized my story. "I was widowed at forty-three and was not prepared for a life without my husband, my high school sweetheart. But I came to terms with his death and accepted what couldn't be changed. I started dating a couple of years ago and have met a very nice man who's raising two boys of his own. I don't know where the relationship is going, but I'm happy where we are right now. And for what it's worth, we can always be what we might have been. This could be your opportunity to move to New York and find a new life, a new career, and a maybe a new man."

Melissa offered her condolences for my loss but didn't pry. She balked at my suggestion of starting over. "I'm happy for you, that you met someone, but it's way too soon for me to considering putting myself out there again. As for old dreams, that ship has sailed. There aren't many advertising companies interested in hiring an over-the-hill, divorced woman with a dusty degree whose résumé is limited to housewife."

I didn't know how to encourage her to pursue her dream in the face of logic, but we talked for another half hour before submitting to sleep. It seemed I'd barely closed my eyes when shades were pulled up and bright sunshine filled the plane. Bleary-eyed, I checked my watch. It was two a.m. An attendant clapped her hands to further rouse us from slumber. "Rise and shine! Breakfast will be served in fifteen minutes."

"What the hell?" grumbled an annoyed traveler. "It's the middle of the night!"

"Not in Ireland," replied the chirpy attendant. "It's seven a.m., and we land in an hour. I suggest you wake up and prepare for landing." With a smile she asked, "Coffee or tea?"

We landed at the airport in Shannon, located halfway between Ennis and Limerick, and retrieved up our carry-on bags. An undersized tour bus was waiting in the designated area to carry us east to Dublin, which rested on the coast of the Irish Sea. Our group was ushered aboard for the three hour ride by the guide who would be with us for the duration of the trip. A blue uniform hung on his tall frame, accessorized by a large, friendly smile and the Irish characteristic blue eyes and copper hair. In a charming Irish brogue Sean O'Brien introduced himself and welcomed us to Ireland. I noticed he was overly friendly to the females in our group, and I summed him up as a ladies' man. Then again, perhaps a flirtatious nature was part of his job description or his personality—or cultural upbringing by his beloved "Mammy."

As I sometimes suffered from motion sickness, I requested a seat near the front of the bus rather than sitting in the back where the bus swayed more. I ignored Sean's forwardness and dozed most of the ride but noticed the weather was overcast as we made our way into the Republic of Ireland's capital. Sean was a confident driver but drove faster than I would have preferred, especially when he circled the bus through the roundabouts that replaced the four-way stops to which I was accustomed. Time in Mexico had taught me to accept drivers on the left side of the road who could be more than reckless, so I relaxed my grip on the seat in front of me and focused on the scenery en route to our hotel near the Temple Bar district.

Along Dublin's Georgian streets the doors of several rows of red-brick townhouses were all brightly painted, each a different color. They resembled a box of crayons with only the heads visible rather than the multi-colored hues that bathed the restored Georgian houses of Rainbow Row in Charleston, South Carolina. I was curious about the doors in Dublin and recalled that when Sean introduced himself he told us to ask any questions we might have. I leaned forward and tapped him lightly on the shoulder. "Excuse me, but why are the doors painted in varied, vibrant colors?"

He laughed and answered, "Ah, 'tis a simple answer. We Irish enjoy our whiskey, often to the extent of a completely inebriated condition. Finding our way home can be a challenge, but if we can make it to the right street and remember the conspicuous color of the front door, then we can enter the home without worry that it's the wrong house. To be sure, more than one drunk has staggered into a bedroom that wasn't his and not always by mistake." He turned his head slightly, winked and grinned. "Do you enjoy a bit of whiskey now and again?"

"No, that's not my drink of choice, but I do indulge in an occasional glass of wine."

"Then might you join me in a glass of wine this evening? I promise to behave myself, even if you aren't wearing a wedding band."

Sean proved my first impression of him as a player to be accurate, but before I could turn him down he braked and the bus screeched to a halt in front of the Gresham Hotel located on the famous O'Connell Street. The hotel wore its age on its weathered exterior and because the trip was incredibly reasonable, I expected the lodgings to be less than stellar. But when we retrieved our luggage and straggled inside to register, I was surprised at the beauty of an old European hotel that was renovated to include modern conveniences. I walked across the marbled lobby and took in the sweeping staircase with carved mahogany banisters that curved outward on each end to accommodate the wide stairs. The walls were covered in damask wallpaper with a rich texture that highlighted red velvet drapes, and what appeared to be the original chandeliers glowed with the beauty of old world charm. Large vases of fresh flowers were strategically placed to add inviting warmth to the overall ambience of opulence. The exchange rate for U.S dollars to euros wasn't separated by much, but undoubtedly our American currency was valued in Ireland. Then again, it was the off-season, and the weather was windy, wetter, and colder than in the warmer months of summer.

Once we all assembled in the lobby, our group was informed by the manager that our rooms were not yet available and that they would be assigned alphabetically by our last names. Mine was near the end of the alphabet, so there was nothing to do but find a place to crash and wait until my name was called. I made myself at home on one side of an oversized sofa and was drifting off to sleep when Melissa nudged me. "Hey, wake up. It's taking longer than expected to hand over the keys to our rooms, so lunch vouchers were passed around. Let's go to the bar and have a sandwich. Dad and Mom met another retired couple and are having lunch with them."

I stretched when I stood up. "Where did you stash your suitcases?"

"The manager offered to lock our luggage in the storage room adjacent to the front desk. Grab yours, and I'll show you the way."

Luggage secured, Melissa and I walked into the hotel's tavern where a group of men lined the bar like ducks in a row, attention focused on what appeared to be a soccer game of sorts. Nonetheless, when we were led to a table, the men turned as if on a rotisserie and greeted Melissa and me with a rowdy cheer and raised glasses. Three immediately approached us, introduced themselves, and asked our names. When I told them mine was Sheila, they cheered again and the tallest one smiled at me. "Your accent tells me that you are from one of the southern states in America, but Sheila is an old Irish name. Then, lass, is there a wee bit of Irish in your ancestry?"

His charming manner was polished to perfection, but when the men asked the waiter to bring extra chairs, I protested. "I don't know if my heritage is Irish, and I'm not interested in anything other than lunch. Please return to your game and Guinness, gentlemen."

Disappointed but not dissuaded he turned towards Melissa, who was being pursued by the other two men. She, too, was having none of it and brushed them aside. "Not interested, either. Move on, guys."

They good-naturedly shuffled back to the bar but gave us both a look of longing for what might have been. Melissa admired their muscled physiques but maintained her stance that it was much too soon to become involved with another man, even for a brief affair. We chalked up the encounter to nothing more than a playful attempt to break the midday monotony of businessmen.

We finished our delicious roast beef sandwiches just as names were being called for room assignments. I was, once again, pleasantly surprised by the luxurious suite where I would spend my first night in Ireland. The group would be leaving at eight a.m. for the first full day of touring, so I unpacked only the basics. There was a phone on the nightstand, and I called Pat on the toll free line at her office and assured her that I was safe and sound. I then used my credit card to call Tom's cellphone and loved hearing the sound of his voice but kept the call brief. The bed was beckoning me to indulge in a nap when there was a knock on my door. I looked through the peep hole and saw Melissa and welcomed her inside.

"Hi, Sheila. Wanna go exploring with me? Dad and Mom are taking a nap, but I'm too restless to sleep. I left them a note that I was out sightseeing and would be back in time for dinner." She pulled a brochure from her purse. "I found this info on a stand in the hotel lobby and thought we could check out some of the local tourist attractions, if you're up for it."

I could sleep anytime, and it wasn't likely I would be in Ireland again. "I'd love to join you. Thanks for thinking of me." I hung my bag over my shoulder and tucked the room key inside a zippered compartment as I locked the door on our way out.

The morning's clouds had dispersed, leaving a blue sky and cool breeze behind. Dublin was a laid-back city surrounded by Dublin Mountains and Dublin Bay; music permeated the air to create a happy-go-lucky environment where the residents were very friendly. We were within easy walking distance of Ha' Penny Bridge, so-named because before 1919 when the toll was lifted, there was a half-penny charge to cross the bridge. Next on the list was Dublin Castle, a major government complex where the most current construction dated from the eighteenth century, but a castle had stood on the land for centuries. The brochure was very informative and led us to the last stop of the day, St. Patrick's Cathedral, built in 1911; it was the National Cathedral of the Church of Ireland. I was in awe of the hundred and forty-one foot spire and the intricacies of the centuries-old structure that reeked of Ireland's past. The timelessness of those places seemed oddly out of place amidst the traffic and crowds.

Dublin was Ireland's capital, but there were small villages tucked within the county. Melissa and I debated as to whether or not we had time to catch the bus for the short ride out of the heart of town to the coastal village of Dalkey. The village was located in south county of Dublin, and the pamphlet made the charming village with its crooked, narrow streets that led to the sea inviting. In the end we decided against that destination as it was nearing sundown, and neither of us wanted the Irish cavalry to come in search of two American tourists. We returned to the hotel in time to shower and change for dinner at a nearby restaurant where reservations had been made for the entire group. Ben and Diane, Melissa's parents, graciously invited me to join them at their table, and I graciously accepted.

I slept like the dead, and it was several minutes before I was awakened by the tiresome clang of the alarm clock. I'd glanced at the itinerary a week ago, but it didn't matter what the travel plan was as I was traveling with a group of thirty other people. My responsibility was to show up at the designated place and time, and I'd promised the travel agent who coordinated the trip not to be at the wrong place at the wrong time. I made a cup of tea (coffee wasn't provided) in the room, showered, dressed, re-packed, and met in the hotel's restaurant for breakfast. I was offered porridge, but declined and requested grits—a slim chance. The waitress was puzzled and asked, "What is a grit, ma'am?"

I laughed because "a grit" all by itself wasn't much of anything. I told her if she ever made it to America to find a Waffle House and order up a bowl of grits. Despite the absence of a steaming bowl of grits, we enjoyed a large, scrumptious breakfast that was, amazingly, included in the cost of the room. Sean greeted us with a smile and, "Top o' the Morning to Ya," as he loaded our luggage into the belly of the bus. He had accepted that neither Melissa nor I was interested in a holiday fling but seemed to have found a woman who was. Jackie couldn't stop smiling at him.

Sean's personal life was none of my business. While there was much to see and do, we were promised stops along the way at shops where souvenirs could be purchased. Valerie asked me to bring her a Waterford crystal bowl as "Waterford" was named after the city of Waterford, Ireland; friend Jeani was Catholic and asked for Rosary beads made in Ireland. I'd have to figure out the other purchases I intended to make, including souvenirs for Tom and the boys and a memento for myself. Perhaps a pair of Claddagh earrings would be a perfect remembrance.

Shopping aside, each day in Ireland proved to be an adventure. We visited Blarney Castle where I waited in line to kiss the Blarney Stone, as almost every tourist did, including celebrities. It wasn't until after I'd hung upside down like a bat to gain access to the infamous stone that I considered how germ-ridden the stone actually was. We stopped at several castles along the route, and I was surprised by the design of the very narrow and twisty stairwells. On Melissa's birthday we all celebrated with her at a castle where supper was served and where we were treated to a jousting tournament.

Another day escorted us to a working sheep farm where we enjoyed a lunch of Irish stew and homemade soda bread, hot from the oven, served in a large dining hall which had evidently been added to the original structure. The farm was a postcard setting that came to life with its whitewashed house that carried a thatched roof and an emerald green front door and shutters; a large barn housed livestock, and chickens roamed freely about the yard. Beneath a rare, sunny, spring day the pasture where sheep dotted the hillside was greener-than-green and studded with large rocks. I learned that the sheep dog controlled the sheep not by barking but by making eye contact and steering the sheep to keep the herd together. As it was shearing season, we watched the process and touched the downy softness of the fleece. I enjoyed the day, especially feeding a lamb with a baby bottle, but I was ready for a shower as we made our way to that night's accommodations.

After checking in at another luxurious hotel and freshening up, several of us strolled to a pub down the street where locals frequented to share a pint of Guinness and tall tales. One of the elderly men made music with spoons as his only instrument. He looked like my notion of a leprechaun, a small man with shaggy gray hair and beard, twinkling blue eyes, and rather large ears that were pointy at the tip. At my request, the kindly gentlemen tried to teach me how to "play" the spoons. I quickly realized it most likely took years of practice to illicit a tune from cutlery, but I delighted in the experience and dropped ten euros into his tip bucket. It was easy to denote monetary values because the currency was a different size and color for each denomination. My gesture of appreciation was rewarded with a smile and an Irish blessing that joy and peace surround me. I certainly slept peacefully.

Morning led us along the Ring of Kerry, which offered some of the most stunning views of mountains, countryside, and ocean that I'd ever seen. Ireland was Europe's third largest island and was surrounded by several bodies of water that included the Atlantic Ocean. I hoped to return one day and travel off the beaten path, but tomorrow was our final day, and I was ready to go home. Our excursion took us full circle to County Clare, about an hour's drive from where we began—the airport in Shannon. It was after six when we arrived at the charming Atlantic Sunset House where I was amazed at the large set of rooms provided for me. I'd learned to ask for coffee at the front desk, and a pouch was readily provided. I showered and joined Melissa and her parents for dinner, as I had for most of the trip. It was Saturday night, our last night in Ireland, but I declined the invitation to scope out some of the local bars.

Instead, I excused myself after dinner. The morning's fog had lifted so we'd been able to spend the afternoon rambling over the majestic Cliffs of Moher where the sea cliffs provided magnificent views of the ocean. As a result I was dog-tired and anxious to escape to the solitude of my suite where I called Tom. Instead of bar hopping I preferred to hear Tom tell me how much he missed me and that he would be waiting at the gate tomorrow afternoon. After we hung up, I changed into warm pajamas and thick socks and wrapped myself in a flannel robe before I ventured outside to the private patio that was part of the B&B's appeal. It was already dark but I could hear the surf and smell the salt air as I took pleasure in the setting of the North Atlantic. A chilly breeze brushed over me, and I pulled the robe closer and nestled in its warmth. I thought about all that I'd seen and done over the past ten days, a thousand mile loop that weaved along the island. As wonderful as the trip had been, I wished Tom had been there to make those memories with me. The realization that I wanted Tom, not Barry, to share those experiences shocked me. Until that night, it was Barry I'd missed and had longed for him to be a part of my new adventures. I didn't know what to make of my confusing emotions and climbed into the arms of the sleep to let my dreams sort them out.

*Name changed

Chapter Thirteen

Two Sides of the Same Coin

When our group exited the plane we exchanged goodbye hugs, knowing our temporary friendships would fade into the past. We dispersed, and I spotted Tom, Thomas, and Levi waiting at the gate; Tom was holding a bouquet of flowers to welcome me home. I eagerly embraced him and when he pulled me close to his chest and kissed my forehead, I savored his touch, his smell. For the first time in a long time, it felt like I was home.

I hugged the boys and promised there were souvenirs for each of them. We made our way to baggage claim and chatted as if none of us had seen each other for weeks instead of days. Thomas and Levi told me about their camping adventure and how many fish they'd caught as we propelled our way through the busy airport and to an even busier parking lot filled with weekend travelers. We were finally on Camp Creek Parkway, and the boys were occupied with Nintendo games. Tom took my hand and kissed each fingertip. "I missed you more than I ever thought I would."

"I missed you, too, Tom." I didn't elaborate on how much I'd missed him or that I wished he'd been with me. For some unknown reason I held my emotions in check. I cared deeply for Tom and trusted him with my heart, but a vague feeling of fear gnawed at me. I pushed whatever it was to the deep recesses of my mind and enjoyed supper with my trio of handsome dates.

My life fell into a familiar routine, a déjà vu of sorts. A neighbor of Tom's, Kathy, kindly offered to take the boys to school each morning when she took her kids. Sadly, the boys' mama wasn't the most dependable when it came to picking up her sons after school and dropping them off at the home they shared with Tom. Many days she didn't bother to show up at all. If Tom had to work late or got caught up in the web of Atlanta traffic, Thomas and Levi were left stranded. I took the situation by the reins and suggested the boys walk across the street to my office where they could do their homework and wait for their daddy. If Tom wasn't there when I left for the day, I volunteered to take the kids home.

It proved to be the ideal situation, and I was able to help the boys with homework questions. To express his gratitude at not having to worry about his sons, Tom invited me to eat supper out with them after our daily walk, and unless I had other plans I accepted. The boys were involved in baseball, so cooking was optional as time allowed. When there was no game I often prepared a much appreciated home cooked meal and was reminded how much growing boys eat. When a game was on the calendar, I attended those games, rain or shine, and cheered them on from the sidelines. We took them to several Braves games, and although I protested that I was intruding on their father-son time, they genuinely welcomed me and persuaded me to accompany them.

Tom and I had fallen into an unlikely friendship and somewhere between bike rides and hiking and baseball and dating, we slowly, almost imperceptibly, fell in love. A fact of which we were both aware but didn't verbally express, perhaps for the same reason: fear. I was afraid to acknowledge that I was in love for the second, and last, time in my life. That fear sent me to my long-time therapist for a discussion I wasn't prepared to have.

Patti greeted me warmly, "Hello, Sheila. You look happy, though perplexed. I'm assuming your confusion is what brought you here. Please have a seat."

I perched on the edge of the oversized chair and blurted, "I'm almost certain I'm in love. That is, I am in love, and I'm terrified."

"Okay. What about being in love has you so distressed?"

I stood and paced the elegantly appointed room, a room designed to create a relaxing environment. "I'm not sure, but maybe it's because the only other relationship I've had since Barry's death was a disaster, and I was depressed without realizing why. Or maybe I'm petrified that if I acknowledge out loud that I love Tom, then he'll die and I'll have to suffer the pain of losing him."

Patti watched me for a few minutes before she spoke. "Sit down and let's discuss this matter. Or have you forgotten sitting in this very room four years ago and tearfully telling me that you wanted what you had? It seems that God heard you and sent you what you had: a good man and two young sons. So let's compare your relationship with…what was his name?"

"Justin."

"According to what you told me in one of our last sessions, your relationship with Justin made you miserable because he took and you gave. If you remember, I advised you to tread lightly. How does your relationship with Tom measure up?"

I returned to the comfort of the recliner and smiled. "There is no comparison. Tom is kind, patient, and considerate of my feelings. I'm included in his life, and he is sensitive to my moods—especially during my PMS from hell. He sends me flowers for no reason and always opens the car door for me, even if it's pouring rain. It's those thoughtful gestures that mean a lot to a woman. In short, he makes me feel cherished." The smile slid from my face when I became aware of the fact that I could have been describing Barry instead of Tom. Another irrational fear reared its head. "Patti, what if I'm in love with Tom because it's like turning back time?"

"What do you mean?"

"Well, you did caution me that my attraction to Justin could have been that he had two young daughters, children to whom I became attached. You warned me not to accept an unhappy relationship based upon what resembled my past."

"Yes, I recall that advice, but you've assured me that the two men are nothing alike."

I wasn't satisfied and pursued the topic. "No, but Tom and Barry have very similar personalities. Barry loved me unconditionally, and unless I'm mistaken, so does Tom. Not only that, I've taken the boys under my wing to the point that their own mama tearfully told them that I was trying to take them away from her. That notion is ridiculous given that she chose to walk away from the responsibility of raising them." I mulled things over in my mind before I continued, "What if the familiarity of things with Tom is an attempt to recreate the life I had with Barry and our sons?"

She studied me carefully before she addressed my concerns. "Sheila, you've long accepted Barry's death. You also realize that your sons are now grown men with lives of their own. And most importantly, you know what love is and what it isn't. You never once expressed that you loved Justin, who was apparently arrogant and self-centered. If Tom reminds you of Barry, then isn't that a positive thing? Why would you be attracted to a man who isn't kind and considerate? Why would you settle for less than what you want in a relationship?"

I sat still and listened to the ticking of the clock as dusk closed in around us. Patti switched on another lamp. Her reminder for me not to settle was something both Daddy and Valerie had agreed upon. They couldn't all be wrong in that advice. "But Patti, what if Tom and I marry and he's killed in a car wreck or is stricken with cancer and dies? I don't think I can survive the grief that follows heartbreak. I can't go through that darkness again. Not only would I lose Tom, but Thomas and Levi as well because they aren't my children."

She gathered her response. "And what if Tom doesn't die? Or what if you die before him? Or what if you throw away the chance for years of happiness? Some people die young and leave behind heartache for their loved ones. Many couples divorce, recover, and move on. Other couples grow old together and live happily ever. The point is that love itself is an act of trust, trust in another person and trust that you will handle the uncertainties of love." She leaned forward and placed her hand compassionately on my forearm. "Barry was and will always be your first love, but he doesn't have to be your last. I can't foresee what will happen between you and Tom, but I can ask you if love is worth the possibility of what could be?"

I reflected on her words and realized that love was a gift worth the gamble, and I needed to stop overthinking the pitfalls. I decided instead of feeding my fears it was time to listen to my heart. With a newfound sense of peace I answered, "Yes. Thank you for reminding me that we can't live our lives on 'what if'. And that love is worth whatever risks it brings with it."

It was a rainy weekend in May that Tom's and my relationship changed. The boys were with their mama, and we'd gone out dancing with friends where our favorite band, Backstreet, was playing. When Lonestar's hit song "Amazed" surrounded the dance floor, Tom held me close and whispered, "We've found our song, babe." He gently stroked my back. "I know that's corny, but the words sum up how I feel about you. And I don't think it was a coincidence, but I'm amazed our paths crossed that first afternoon at the ballfields."

His cologne was intoxicating, and I melted in his arms but didn't reveal that I was amazed I'd been given a second chance at love. We stayed until the band was winding down, and it was after midnight when Tom drove me home. Despite the hour I invited him in to have a glass of wine and to join me on the screened porch. We slipped off our damp shoes at the back door and while I poured the wine, he lit a few candles on the porch and switched on the portable radio to a soft rock station. When I joined him, he'd already made himself comfortable in the chaise and scooted over to make room for me. In an *Ally McBeal* moment, I imagined Tom belting out the lyrics of Rod Stewart's "Tonight's the Night." But there was no need to spell things out.

I nestled next to him, rested my head on his shoulder, and savored the fragrance of his musty cologne, or maybe it was the scent of him that I savored. The pitter-patter of an approaching storm enveloped the porch in a cocoon and brought with it the scent of a summer rain. The candles burned slowly and cast a soft glow while melodies of love eased from the radio as we sipped the Merlot. For several minutes we sat quietly in the romantic setting before Tom lifted my chin and kissed me with a hunger that matched my own. My body yielded to his demand for more. It was as if we'd survived a drought only to find ourselves drowning in a riptide, and we clung to each other in its powerful current. Tom lifted me with broad shoulders and carried us from the chaise to the plush, oversized rug.

I was aware of the lyrics from Savage Garden's "Truly Madly Deeply" that slid from the radio as the rain began to come down in a deluge. Tom kissed me tenderly as he leisurely undressed me and began his slow, tantalizing journey of arousal, a journey that left me lightheaded and longing for more. His sensual lips, his gentle caress ignited a fire that had been dormant for a very long time. Thunder reverberated as our passion reached an uncontrollable yearning, and he peeled clothes from his eager body. A flash of lightning illuminated the porch, and the storm faded to a steady rhythm that matched our own. We made love without trepidation, without worry of what tomorrow might bring. Nothing mattered except the two of us lost in long-awaited lust.

I didn't know how much time passed but the rain had dwindled to a drizzle, and thunder rumbled in the distance. We relaxed, spent and breathless, in each other's arms. Tom traced my cheek with one finger and kissed me from the top of my head down the length of my neck and shoulders, lingering kisses that sent shivers down my spine. He pulled an afghan from one of the chairs and wrapped us in its softness. I sighed contentedly and was basking in the afterglow of our lovemaking when Tom propped himself up on one elbow. He leaned down and kissed me. "I don't want to jinx whatever is going on with us or scare you away, but I'm pretty sure I'm in love with you."

I pulled him closer, as if I couldn't get enough of him, and said without hesitation, "I think I'm falling in love with you, too."

Another passionate kiss later he retrieved the wine bottle, refilled our glasses, and smiled playfully in the fading candlelight. "Give me another twenty minutes, and I'll be ready for round two."

Oh me. It was not the man's first rodeo.

Pat was the first to notice my cheerful demeanor. We'd finished lunch on our standing Tuesday date and were sitting on a bench outside Bilbo's so she could smoke. She narrowed her eyes and gave me the once-over. "Oh hell! Why haven't you told me that you've been laid? And from the looks of it, more than once."

"I'm not one to kiss and tell. Besides, it's not something that came up in conversation."

"Then you should have brought it up! So how was it? Is Tom good between the sheets? Spill it, girl." She glanced over at Cindy. "Did you know about this?"

"No, I didn't. If I had I would have told you." Cindy faced me. "What about Kim? Have you told her?"

I shook my head in disbelief. "Y'all act as if my sex life is your business, which it's not, but since you brought it up the sex is incredible. I'm tellin' you the man is insatiable. One night he reached for me for the third time, and I had to tell him the shop was closed for maintenance."

Pat exhaled a flume of smoke. "How old did you say Tom is? I know he's a few years younger than you, fortyish, which seems to be a plus where sex is concerned. No damn wonder you've been walking around on cloud nine for the past couple of weeks. Spill it."

Betty, a walking companion from years ago, interrupted my sister's interrogation when she stopped to chitchat for a few mimutes. I could feel Pat's impatience, and the second Betty was out of earshot the grilling continued. But they wanted details I refused to provide, and I hated to disappoint them, but I blushed at the mere thought of sharing specifics. "Give it up, y'all. Some things are private. Or have you forgotten Aunt Sues' favorite country song, that old one by Charlie Rich, 'Behind Closed Doors'? Some things are best kept in the bedroom, secrets not to be discussed, even with you." Nonetheless, I wanted to shout from the rooftops that my sex life was not over—not by a long shot.

My birthday was approaching, and Tom and the boys wanted to make it special. It was decided that we would take the '71 Olds Cutlass convertible Tom bought to restore to Panama City Beach to celebrate both the Fourth of July and my birthday. I was always game for going to the beach and was excited as I packed my suitcase. The car was big enough to fit the four of us comfortably and had a huge trunk for our luggage. Tom had wisely planned ahead and reserved an ocean-front condo before everything was booked for the holiday week.

We all enjoyed the ride and honked at other vacationers who gave the thumbs up as they passed the Cutlass. Once settled in the condo we explored nearby shops and restaurants and decided on places to eat and what we wanted to do with our time. Tom and I held hands while we took romantic walks on the beach, and the boys chased sand crabs in the light from the boardwalk. The four of us snorkeled in the calm, clear blue waters of the Gulf of Mexico and played in the surf when the ocean came to life. On one of the carefree afternoons Levi and I got seasick from riding the rolling waves on a float and had to sit on the beach to recover under the oversized umbrella Tom had rented, along with lounge chairs.

Some boys about Levi's age sauntered by and made a point of staring at Levi's birthmark. One of them pointed and snickered, and the others joined in the taunting laughter. I wanted to jerk a knot in their asses but didn't want to further embarrass Levi, who dropped his head, wrapped his arms around his knees, and folded himself into the fetal position. Like a hermit crab he retreated into a protective shell. I recognized Levi's pain as my own at being made fun of because of the Bell's palsy I suffered as a high school freshman. I filed a mental note for future reference to research treatment options.

My fretfulness found its way to Chuck and his new relationship, which I hoped turned out better than his last. He'd found a job and moved out of Daddy's house, right into Geri's with her mama and stepdad. I thought he needed more time before moving on, but…My mother hen worries were sidetracked by Tom and Thomas running across the white sand that sizzled under a sweltering sun, and I laughed at their hop-scotch to the shade.

It was too hot to drop the ragtop during the day, but it was wonderfully refreshing when the sun took the heat of the day beyond the horizon, and we cruised the Strip. The stretch of highway known as the Strip was conned due to its proximity to the Miracle Strip Amusement Park, the same park where I'd first ridden "The Starliner" roller coaster as a young girl. It was hard to believe the old coaster was still up and running and continued to attract tourists to the theme park. Tom and Thomas opted out, but Levi and I couldn't wait to climb aboard the thrill ride. Levi was amazed at our good luck in landing in the very last car. However, after the rickety, bouncy, near heart-stopping ride over tracks that curved and climbed and dropped like a rock in a cart that jumped off the rails more than once, I decided "good luck" was a matter of opinion.

We finished making the rounds of rides, with me as a spectator, and left the park's bright lights, carny games, and the sweet smell of cotton candy and caramel apples behind us as Tom eased the Cutlass into the river of headlights. We joined those cruisin' under the stars where the sound of the surf a few yards away combined with an eclectic blend of tunes from a variety of radio stations—everything from country to pop to rock to rap. The boys waved from the backseat at passersby and laughed hysterically when a clueless teenager in a pick-up truck pointed to us in the convertible and excitedly declared, "American muscle car! Mustang!"

Tom was an excellent driver and flowed with the traffic until we reached a gas station on the right side of the road. He wheeled us in and parked under the glare of fluorescent lights. He'd barely climbed out of the car when four boys hangin' out of a beat-up, blue Jeep displaying a bumper sticker that read, "Ass, Grass, or Gas. Nobody Rides for Free" pulled in beside us. They were wearing the typical shorts, tank tops, and strings of Mardi gras beads, which guys gladly traded for a look at a girl's boobs. If there were girls walking around wearing string after string of beads, the assumption was that she didn't mind providing a peak.

The driver hopped out next to my car door and asked Tom for permission to have a look under the hood. In exchange he and his buddies would give me any number of the cheap, colorful beads. Being aware of the "barter" system of young beachgoers, I mistook a "look under the hood" as slang, meaning that the teenagers wanted me to lift up my shirt and expose my breasts to their eager eyes. I was about to flatly refuse when Tom said, "Sure, no problem."

I was appalled. "Tom! What is wrong with you? I'm not showing them my boobs for a few strings of tacky, plastic beads, or any damn thing else. I can't believe you would even consider such a thing!"

By then all four of the boys were standing around, presumably waiting for a gander at my naked torso. I couldn't have been more wrong. The tallest of the four stammered and stuttered, "Oh, no ma'am! No, hell no!" He covered his face protectively with his forearms and backed away from the car as if it might burst into flames. "There's been a *huge* misunderstanding. We don't want to see your…your bosom, ma'am. PLEASE keep your tatas covered up. When Tony there asked to see under the hood, he meant we'd literally like to see the motor that runs this big Oldsmobile."

The blush that raced over me was as red as the car. Fortunately, I found a tissue to wipe the shit off my face. Tom reached under the dashboard to pop the hood so the boys could ooh and ah over the original 350 Rocket Engine with its distinctive golden valve covers. The boys thanked Tom and piled back in the Jeep that squawked onto the road. Tom walked around to me, leaned over, and gave me a seductive smile. "Hey, don't feel bad. Those guys are too young to know what they're missing. I'll give you all the beads you want for a peepshow."

He was good-naturedly enjoying my humiliation, but I was not in the mood to be teased and muttered through clenched teeth, "Nobody likes a smartass, Tom."

The week after we returned from our idyllic beach escapade, there was a commotion in the lobby of my office building. I heard traces of crying and an unfamiliar voice explaining to the receptionist that Levi had a bicycle wreck and that he'd stopped to help. "I saw the accident, which was a bad one. He said he's okay, but it's pretty obvious he broke his arm when he slammed into the concrete curb. I offered to call his parents, but he asked me to bring him here, to somebody named Sheila."

I immediately left my office to find Zack, a student whom I recognized, and Thomas and Levi gathered in the lobby. Thomas was pale but unharmed and stammered, "We were riding our bikes, and Levi got his feet tangled up coming down the big hill over by city lumber. He was screamin' about his arm when Zack pulled over and offered his help. We threw the bikes in his trunk and asked him to bring us to your office. Should we call Dad?"

I assessed the condition of Levi's rapidly swelling arm and had no doubt that it was broken, severely broken. "Yes, we'll call Tom, but first things first." I thanked Zack and sent him with Thomas to take the bikes home with a promise to update a worried Thomas later. I pulled out the first aid kit from a cabinet in the kitchen area and handed Levi two ibuprofens and a glass of water. He sat down and cried in pain while I threw ice cubes in a baggie and applied it to his arm. My experience with Brad and Chuck's mishaps came in handy.

He gave me a weak smile filled with pain. "Do you think it's broken? If it is, how long will it take to heal? I made the middle school football team but don't want to sit on the bench. The coach is gonna be mad at me for missing practice. Do you think I'll be able to get in a few practices before the first game in September?"

It amazed me how young boys prioritized events in their lives. His arm continued to swell, and all he could think about was football, which was the last thing on my mind. "I don't know how long it's gonna be before you're back in the game, but right now I need to get you to an orthopedic to determine the damage and subsequent treatment. Give me a minute to call your daddy and tell him to meet us in Carrollton."

Tom's cell phone went to voicemail, so I left a brief message of current events and that I would call him from the doctor's office. Vicki, the new receptionist and an old acquaintance, assured me that she would explain the emergency circumstances to our boss, but Dr. McCain walked in as I was leading Levi towards the door. "I'm glad I ran into you. As you can see, I've got an emergency on my hands and have to leave work early to deal with this situation. I've left a message with Tom, but Levi's in too much pain to wait for him to make the drive from Atlanta."

He and Melissa had three sons of their own, so he understood that active boys and accidents go hand-in-hand. "It's good you're here to take care of Levi. Don't worry about leaving work early. See you in the morning."

"Yes, in the morning and thanks." Levi slowly slid into the passenger seat and winced when I gently fastened his seat belt. I grabbed a blanket from the backseat and rolled it up as a prop for his wounded arm. I drove as fast as I dared to the orthopedics' office where I quickly located a parking space. But when we entered the office, and I signed Levi in as a work-in, the rude and unreasonable receptionist was a hindrance.

She glanced downward through bifocals at the sign-in sheet and checked her computer. "Levi does not have an appointment and can't be seen today." She noted his arm covered with the makeshift ice pack. "You'll have to take him to the emergency room."

Ordinarily, I was a reasonable person, but the nurturing instinct kicked in and I turned into a protective mama bear. "Let me assure you that I'm not taking Levi to the emergency room where we'll have to wait hours for the on-call doctor to determine that he needs to see an orthopedic surgeon, which I already know. What we are going to do is have a seat in the waiting area, and you're going to get us in to see the first available doctor." I snapped my fingers to make my point. "And don't drag your ass."

She was slightly taken aback but held her ground. "He will have to be seen by an ER doctor who will then refer him to one of our surgeons. The doctor on call will see him then and only then so as not to inconvenience our patients who *do* have appointments. In this office there is a medical protocol in place for a reason."

I found a seat for Levi and made him as comfortable as possible before I returned to the window. "Let me recap for you: We are NOT leaving this office until Levi is seen and treated. As for 'medical protocol', the well-being of the patient is always the first priority. I'm not going to the ER and jump through hoops wasting time and waiting hours for an orthopedic surgeon while Levi suffers needlessly. We both know that's not necessary because there's a staff of doctors here, so we're gonna bypass the bullshit. I've already raised two older sons who were active in sports and who rode dirt bikes, so this isn't my first trip to this office. I can't tell you how many times our appointments were delayed by emergencies such as we have here. Therefore, it would be in your best interest to show us to an exam room before I really get mad."

Her jaw dropped at being addressed in such a manner, but she got her ass out of her chair and disappeared to the back of the office. In a matter of minutes, she returned through a door that led to several exam rooms. Her voice was as cold as ice, but making her my friend was not my objective. "You and Levi can come back now. The PA will examine Levi, administer something for his pain, and order x-rays before he sees the doctor."

I smiled sweetly at her anger. "Now really, was that so hard?"

She slammed the door behind us and returned to her domain behind the Plexiglas partition. The PA, Dennis as he introduced himself, glanced at Levi's swollen arm and assisted him onto a gurney and removed the ice pack. "Well, it's definitely broken and may require surgery, but we won't know until we take a few x-rays." He patted Levi on the knee. "In the meantime, let's see if we can make you a little more comfortable. I'll be back shortly."

He left the room, and the nurse handed me a clipboard filled with numerous forms to be completed while she administered the ordered injection of Demerol. I answered the questions as best I could, but I didn't have the insurance information. "His daddy is on his way from Atlanta and should be here in the next half hour with the insurance card. I've filled out the rest of the blanks as accurately as I could."

"That's fine. Just have a seat while a tech takes Levi down the hall for x-rays."

I sat in one of the chairs provided and was startled by a knock on the door. It was my favorite person with a message for me. "Levi's mom is on the phone and demanding to speak to you." She pointed to the phone on the wall. "You can take it in here, line two."

I had absolutely nothing to say to Regina and ignored her call. I gently hugged Levi and assured him that I would be waiting for him when he got back to the room. He nodded drowsily, but I was acutely aware of the stricken expression the nurse was wearing. I don't think the woman breathed until the technician wheeled Levi down the hall. She was as pale as the white sheets stacked neatly on a shelf, and her mouth was opened so wide that a softball could have easily fit inside. Brown eyes bulged beneath beads of sweat that decorated her brow. She gasped for air as she fought to speak. "Are you *not* Levi's mother?"

I answered, "No."

"Stepmother?"

"No."

"Guardian?"

"Sorry, no."

"Aunt?"

"No."

She braced herself against the wall. "Then exactly what is your relationship to this child?"

"I date his daddy."

Her knees buckled slightly, but she propped on the desk. It occurred to both of us that she had dispensed a narcotic to a minor without parental consent. Before she could pass out cold and hit the floor, I assured her that Tom had custody of Levi and that he would have given her permission to do whatever necessary to relieve his son's pain. She pulled a tissue from a dispenser and wiped her forehead. "Please call him and let me speak to him. Now."

"Okay." I picked up the phone and noticed Regina was no longer on hold, which was just as well. I used the open line to dial Tom's mobile number, and he answered immediately. I explained the dilemma and handed the phone to the nurse.

"Hello? This is Brenda, and I've given a shot to Levi for pain because I mistakenly assumed that the woman who brought him in was his mother. Given that she has no relationship to your son, I need your verbal approval to provide medical treatment."

"Yes, of course I agree. I'll give you my insurance card and sign whatever forms you need as soon as I get there, which should be less than fifteen minutes. In the meantime, I trust Sheila's judgment regarding what's best for Levi."

Shaken but relieved she thanked Tom and hung up the phone. Brenda didn't say another word as she left the room and almost collided with the receptionist who angrily announced, "Let me be clear about this: I am not your personal secretary. Levi's mother is on line three and adamant that she speaks to you immediately." Her teeth clinked like icicles, and her words dripped with frosty sarcasm. "If you would be so kind as to take her call, I won't have to interrupt you again."

"I don't want to take the call, but if it will make you happy…"

She slammed the door behind her, and I snatched up the receiver and pushed the button that was flashing impatiently. "This is Sheila. Why are you calling, Regina?"

She lit into me like a madwoman. "I'll tell you why I'm calling. I resent the fact that I had to find out from Thomas that his brother had an accident and broke his arm. Who the hell do you think you are? I'm Levi's mama, and I should have been called instead of you. It's my place to get him the medical attention he needs, not yours. It's clear that your sneaky plan is to replace me and take my sons away from me. You need to damn well remember—"

I'd heard enough. "You weren't called because neither of the boys know how to get in touch with you or even where you're living, this week. Given that you've left them waiting in the cold and rain because it was inconvenient for you to pick them up after school, Levi asked for my help. Of the two of us, I'm the more dependable, stable one, and my 'sneaky plan' to take your sons away from you is ridiculous. Let me remind you that you packed up everything they own, dropped them off on your mama's doorstep, and called Tom to pick up his kids. You made it clear that raising them interfered with your with your flavor of the month boyfriend. So don't jump my ass for the choices *you* made."

She continued to scream, and I wondered how Tom had gotten tangled up with a piece of work like his ex. I asked him once, and he claimed he'd met her back in his pot smokin' days. I never knew if he was being honest or if he was joking, but it didn't matter because the one positive result of his broken marriage was his boys. Lord only knows where they would have been without him. Thoughts of Tom's past were interrupted when he was escorted to the exam room by the receptionist, and I held out the receiver so that he overheard the venom his ex-wife was spewing. The hussy jumped on my last nerve, but she failed to ruffle Tom's feathers.

He took the receiver from my hand and said, "Go to hell, Regina." He hung up the phone just as Levi was carted back in, followed by a relieved Brenda waving the forms Tom needed to sign.

The doctor reviewed the x-rays with both Tom and me and admitted that while it was a bad break, surgery would not be necessary. The arm was set and a plaster cast applied, which would be replaced in four weeks with a soft cast. Football practice was on hold, but the doctor assured Levi that his arm would heal in time for the first game. We walked to the parking lot to separate vehicles, and I reminded Tom, "Call Thomas with an update, and don't forget to swing by Garrett's and have Levi's prescription for pain meds filled."

Tom wrapped me in a strong embrace and whispered, "Thank you."

It was only a few more weeks until school would begin when I noticed that every time we rented a movie at Blockbuster, Thomas and Levi both sat in the floor, very close to the television. Given that I'd already crossed parental boundaries with the broken arm incident, I asked Tom how long it had been since the boys had had an eye exam. He couldn't remember, and I suggested that it might be a good idea to have their eyesight checked before they began the first day of classes. He agreed, and when the three of them showed up at my door a week later, Thomas and Levi were sporting spectacles. The boys were so proud of them and thanked me for realizing they needed glasses, although they were more excited about transitioning to contacts when their eyes matured enough. Tom thanked me, too, and felt guilty that he hadn't noticed and taken care of the boys' trip to the optometrist sooner. I didn't mention that his next expense would be braces. Instead, I reminded him that he wasn't by anyone's definition a neglectful daddy, but that he had a lot of irons in the fire and had simply overlooked a minor problem.

Another minor problem arose a few weeks into the school year when the fad was for boys to dye their hair bright colors to supposedly separate them from the pack. The trend of nonconformity was ironic considering the middle schoolers wanted to follow the very crowd from which they professed to distinguish themselves. The boys pleaded with Tom to let them color their hair, but he flatly refused. "No, period. I'm not gonna have the two of you walking around looking like a couple of circus clowns. The subject is closed!"

Except the subject wasn't closed. Tom had listed me as a contact when he registered the boys for school since he worked in Atlanta, and I was conveniently located to the campus. It was after nine the next morning, and I was busy at my desk when Janis, who'd been promoted to the position of middle school principal, called and asked me to walk over to her office. I pushed paperwork aside and complied with her request. When I entered, two boys were sitting quietly with their backs to me. It was their hair that first caught my attention. Janis waited for the realization that the boys were Thomas and Levi to hit me.

"Oh, no! What have y'all done to your hair? Did your mama do that?"

They'd spent the weekend with their mama and played one parent against the other when they innocently asked her to color their hair. Other than disobeying Tom, the problem was that their mama hadn't realized that the other kids used temporary dye that could be easily washed down the drain. Regina had failed to comprehend the importance of that major detail and had used bleach on Thomas' jet-black hair, bleach that took the color to a glow-in-the-dark orange. Levi chose to have royal blue and bright green stripes scattered randomly through his thick brown hair. Their new dos were not revealed until the following day because they'd begged to spend Sunday night with their mama, an unusual request that should have been Tom's first clue that something was amiss.

I didn't tell them that Tom was going to kill them, a fact they were aware of based on the look of fear in their eyes. Thomas spoke first, "We just wanted it colored for the weekend, but it won't wash out. We didn't mean for Daddy to find out."

I sat down and sighed. "I'm pretty sure he's going to notice. Why would you deliberately defy him?'

Levi hung his head dejectedly but chimed in, "We thought it would wash out before Dad saw us."

Janis shuffled some papers on her desk. "Sheila, it's stated in the hand-book that body piercings, tattoos, outrageous hair colors, anything that is distracting in the classroom is not allowed. Not that it helps, but these two are not the first to challenge those rules. You can take them home, but they can't return to school until this situation is resolved. Or I can send them to in-school suspension for today where they'll be given classwork to be completed by the end of the day."

I wanted to call their dumbass mama and rake her over the goals, but what was done was done. I gave them one last look and addressed Janis. "I need to call their daddy. This decision should be his, not mine. If you'll excuse me for a few minutes, I'll step out to the receptionist's office and use Pam's phone."

Tom answered on the second ring. "Well, good morning. This is a pleasant surprise."

"Not as pleasant as you might think. I hate to be the bearer of bad news, but—"

He cut me off in a panic. "Is everything all right? Are the boys okay? Did they make it to school this morning?"

"The boys are fine, nobody is sick or hurt, but they did show up with wildly colored hair, compliments of their mama. The principal said they can't stay in the classroom today. The choices are for me to take them home, or she can send them to ISS for the day. I'm calling you because it's your decision."

I could hear him pacing and fuming on the other end of the line. "Hell, no, don't take them home. They're not gonna have a day to play video games and watch television all day. Will they get lunch in ISS?"

"Of course they will. It's not a prison. But they will have to stay quiet and work diligently to finish all the work the teachers will send with them."

"Then have Janis send their little asses to ISS."

"Ok. Do you want to talk to her or to the kids?"

"No. I'm too mad to deal with this over the phone. Tell my sons I'll take care of them when I get home. My next call is to their idiot mama for her part in their shenanigans. She could have checked with me first."

"Ok, but calm down. It's really not that big of a deal, and I'm sure they've learned their lesson. A day of in-school suspension will be a reminder not to rebel against the rules again."

"Oh, when I get home and tan their hides, they'll understand the consequences of their actions and won't pull another stunt like this."

I walked back to Janis' office and relayed the message. She motioned for the boys to stand and escorted them to the dreaded ISS room; they hung their heads like they were on the way to the guillotine. I returned to my office for a long day filled with distractions. As soon as the boys got to my office that afternoon, I left to take them home. They were eager to wash their hair another several times before Tom got home, and I didn't have the heart to tell them that their attempts would be futile. I hugged them both and promised to be back a few minutes before Tom was scheduled to arrive home so that we could find a solution.

Tom thought the solution was a good spanking, but I intervened. "Tom, settle down. Coloring their hair is not the worst thing they could have done. At eleven and twelve, they're not old enough to think things through and make a judgment call. It's a mistake their mama allowed. After all, she's the adult and should have known better."

"Thomas and Levi knew better because I already told them flat out no!" He turned his anger towards the boys. "What part did I not make clear?"

Neither of them said a word, so I continued, "Tom, there's no need cryin' over spilled milk, so stop yellin'. Let's take them to one of those walk-in salons in Carrollton that stay open late and have their hair dyed to the color it was so they can go back to school tomorrow." I rubbed his broad shoulders and felt the tension ease. "Don't tell me you never screwed up when you were their age."

He actually smiled. "I guess you're right, Sheila. It's not a life-changing blunder. But Charlcie would have worn me out if I'd pulled a stunt like this."

"Thankfully, you're not your mama," I muttered as we piled in the car and headed to one of the strip malls in Carrollton. We located a Great Clips and breezed in to sign in with the first available hairdresser. Stella motioned for Thomas to have a seat and adjusted her chair as she ran her fingers threw his goldenrod hair. "Well, it's fixable. I can use a permanent black dye to cover the orange, but he may need another touch-up before it grows off completely." She nodded towards Levi. "His can be covered with dye as well, and I'll do my best to match his natural color."

I sighed with relief, but Tom had a question. "What's this gonna cost me?

The young girl swayed her head back and forth. "Oh, I dunno. Maybe fifty to seventy-five dollars each. If you're lookin' to come out cheaper, I can shave their heads for fifteen bucks apiece."

The look of sheer terror on the boys' faces was almost comical. It was the same look they had when Tom dropped a quarter in the jukebox at the Waffle House and asked me if I wanted to dance to our song. Those two would have crawled under the table if I'd agreed to dance.

Tom put his hands on his hips and pursed his lips. "That would serve them right. It's not that I can't afford to pay for the dye job, but my sons need to be taught a lesson."

I jumped up from my chair and all but screamed, "Tom! You can't be serious. They would look like cue balls with glasses. Middle school is brutal even on a good day, and you can't send them to school with their heads shaved. Trust me when I tell you that you can't pay for enough therapy to get them through the trauma."

He wavered and relented. "All right, I'll pay Stella to do her best to put their hair back to the way it was before they—"

Hugs interrupted him. Thomas said, "Thank you, Daddy. We won't disobey you ever again. Promise."

Tom may have believed them when he returned their grateful hugs, but I suspected they'd made a promise they couldn't keep. The teenage years were waiting and would be a challenge. On the positive side, when Thomas and Levi told Charlcie about the incident and how I'd spared them a butt whipping and bald heads, she called to thank me. The two of us had reached a truce where Tom was concerned and didn't tread on each other's time with him. He could visit her anytime he wanted as long as I wasn't expected to go with him, which made us all happy.

The school year moved forward, and I was busy and happy. Both Thomas and Levi were involved in middle school football, and Tom and I were always in attendance at their weekly games. I became familiar with some of their friends and acquainted myself with a few of the parents. At one of the games I introduced myself to a woman named Beverly*, who sat down next to me to watch her cheerleader daughter. As the game was approaching halftime, I struck up a conversation with Beverly and found out she was a nurse in Dr. Kahler's office, the only plastic surgeon in Carrollton. As I'd researched port-wine stain removal, I decided to take the opportunity to discuss the matter with a professional. Her knowledge was very beneficial, and she encouraged me to schedule an appointment.

After the boys showered and disappeared in their room, I approached Tom about the subject of having the discoloration treated, but he shrugged indifferently. "Levi has learned to live with the birthmark, so I don't see any reason to have it removed."

I was persistent. "Maybe Levi has accepted something he thinks can't be changed. I've watched him around rude strangers and peers who stare at him, and I know they make cruel remarks. Please think about it, Tom. It would do wonders for his self-esteem."

"How do you know he's being teased at school? Have you seen or heard about anything like that going on?"

I hesitated to share what Thomas told me in confidence, but it was important for Tom to understand Levi's pain. "I know because his brother told me how self-conscious Levi is and how he's hurt and humiliated when some of boys make fun of him. He wanted to ask a girl to the middle school fall dance but was too embarrassed and afraid of being laughed at." I hesitated a moment before I continued, "And I know because I was a victim of bullying when I was a high school freshman and mocked of on a regular basis."

"You? Why?"

"Because I was afflicted with Bell's palsy. The facial paralysis made me an easy target, and I was tormented by several of my classmates. I wasn't lucky enough for there to be a cure since steroids hadn't been discovered yet, and I didn't recover one hundred percent. Surely you've noticed my slightly lopsided smile, which is a reminder of the residual paralysis. Let's circle back to Levi, who has treatment available to him that is worth looking into."

Tom replied, "I noticed your slightly crooked smile. I noticed everything about you. You never brought up the subject, so why should I have when it doesn't matter to me?" He put his arms around me and planted a kiss on my forehead. "If you think it's important to Levi, then schedule an appointment with Dr. Kahler, but don't get Levi's hopes up until after we find out if anything can be done."

I gave him an appreciative hug. "I would never give Levi false hope."

False hope wasn't a concern since two weeks later Dr. Kahler examined Levi and confirmed that the birthmark could be removed. Even though, as he explained to Levi, the procedure would take several laser treatments to reach the clear skin beneath the purple stain. Additionally, the treatments would be extensive and recovery would be uncomfortable, but Levi didn't care. Tom left the decision up to Levi, who readily accepted that the process was lengthy and painful. The next challenge was to obtain approval from Tom's insurance as they didn't cover what was deemed "cosmetic surgery."

To assist in securing approval for payment, Dr. Kahler wrote a letter to the insurance company. He explained the necessity of removing the port-wine stain at a young age because it would become denser with age, which would make removal much more difficult. The insurance company eventually approved the expensive treatments but would cover only eighty percent of the costs. Tom willingly agreed to pay the remaining twenty percent, which wasn't cheap but was money well spent. Appointments were scheduled, and after the first surgery Levi's face looked as if it had been stuck to hot coals, but we were assured that was normal. Subsequent appointments were scheduled at four week intervals in order to allow time for healing between treatments. Over time, as the offensive blemish faded, Levi's confidence soared and he blossomed with a whole new personality filled with a sense of humor.

It was on one of the follow-up appointments that something Beverly told me was apparent. Dr. Kahler performed one elective surgery on each of his employees per year at a greatly reduced rate for his services, something Levi overheard in a conversation between Tom and me. Levi and I were standing at the check-out window where a young woman wearing enormous breasts and a tight, V-necked sweater pulled Levi's chart to determine the balance due that day, for which Tom had given me a check. To his credit Levi did his best to avert his eyes, but the breasts seemed to have a power all their own, a power not to be ignored by an adolescent who'd just turned the corner of puberty. Poor Levi never stood a chance, and his gaze was repeatedly drawn to the woman's river of cleavage like metal to a magnet. I paid the bill and pretended not to notice the attraction so as not to embarrass him.

He didn't say a word until we were in the elevator. "It's pretty dang obvious which procedure she chose."

"Yes, Levi, it certainly is."

The holidays were filled with family as Tom and his boys joined Brad, Valerie, Chuck, and Geri to celebrate our blessings. Tom and I prepared a traditional Thanksgiving dinner, and a mountain of food was consumed. Christmas dinner was a smorgasbord that included everybody's favorite. Gifts were exchanged, and laughter filled my home for the first time in years. My sons liked Tom very much and as grown men, they appreciated that he was a single dad raising his two sons. They were also grateful they didn't have to help take down the tree and pack up decorations on the day after Christmas. Thomas told me it might be the end of January before they got around to doing the same at their house. Thomas was also the one who'd told me there weren't enough baskets when I'd tactfully suggested that they just needed to organize the clutter.

Nonetheless, they managed the household together. The haphazardly lifestyle the three of them shared would have driven me crazy, but I didn't live with them. Coincidentally, one of my sisters-in-law thought I was crazy. It was almost New Year's Eve when I received a call from Shelby with well-intentioned advice from a friend. "Sheila, are you serious about Tom?"

"Yes, I think I am. Why do you ask?"

"Because he's in a different place in his life than you are. You've already raised two boys, and the thought of two more is overwhelming. Have you considered the homework, science projects, and term papers—not to mention all those time-consuming sports—added to hundreds of meals to cook, piles of laundry, and housework? The list goes on and on, and just thinkin' about it is enough to give me a nervous breakdown."

"I realize Tom and I are in different places, but it doesn't matter. A road paved with all the things you mentioned is a road I've already traveled, but let's not put the cart in front of the horse. Tom and I haven't discussed marriage and a future together."

She sighed. "Donnie and I are worried that you'll get in too deep and take on more than you bargained for, especially when you don't have to. A friend of mine, who was in a similar relationship a few years ago, told me to pass along her advice to run as fast and as far away as you possibly can. She now lives in Canada."

I couldn't begin to explain to her the colors of love, especially those of an unexpected second love. "Shelby, it's already too late for me to run. They need me."

I was too full of myself to realize that God didn't send me to save them. He sent them to save me.

*Name changed

Chapter Fourteen

Changes

It has been said that the only constant in life is change. Most fluctuations are minor, the inevitable ebb and flow of life, but some circumstances forever impact our lives and our perceptions. My life was evidence of that fact as adjustments periodically disrupted the comfortable rut into which I'd settled. One such change would bring an unexpected grandchild to my family circle. It was Geri who called me with the happy news because, apparently, Chuck didn't want to deal with my questions. Specifically, what in the hell was he thinking?

Neither of them was in a hurry to marry, which I accepted with resignation. Daddy, on the other hand, was adamant that the couple wed. He and I were having one of our porch visits when I broke the news to him. As usual, Daddy didn't hesitate to give his opinion. "That boy of yours ought to marry that girl he's got in the family way. He's a grown man and needs to step up and take the responsibility to heart."

To circumvent arguing, namely that Chuck was a grown man for whom I couldn't make decisions, I changed the subject. "Are you feeling better since the doctor changed your blood pressure medication?"

Daddy folded his arms across his chest. "Yes, and I guess it's doing the trick, but I'm ninety years old, sugar. My mind tells my body what to do, but some days it won't oblige. I'm still mad as a wet hen about your sister taking away my car." He grew silent but had something else on his mind. "When do you think Chuck and whatever her name is will tie the knot?"

So much for changing the subject. I recognized that Daddy wasn't mourning the car he'd lost as much as his freedom and youth. I tried to soothe his ruffled feathers and patiently explained, "Pat didn't take away your car. After your last fender bender the doctor said it's too dangerous for you to drive, so we all made the decision to sell your car. Haven't we taken you everywhere you need to go and bought groceries for you? As for Chuck, I don't know if or when he will get married, Daddy, but my first grandchild is due in August. While I can't force Chuck to marry the baby's mama, I'll see to it that he provides for the child. By the way, her name is Geri."

He grudgingly admitted that he no longer had any use of a car. However, he was fixated on Chuck and his pregnant girlfriend. "Then they have several months to set a date and get married, find a place to live, and set up housekeeping before the baby is born. And if he gives you any trouble about marriage, you tell him Papa Joe said he should've thought things through before he scrambled into her bed. It's not like he's sixteen and didn't have sense enough to know better."

I continued rocking. "Yes, Daddy."

Basketball season was behind us, and baseball was in full swing. Neither Tom nor I missed a game, which included playoffs and tournaments. On the rare occasion when there was no weekend game scheduled, we threw our bags in the car and visited Savannah and Tybee Island or loaded bicycles onto the rack and roamed the Silver Comet Trail, stopping along the way to wade in the clear, cool waters of a refreshing stream. To the casual observer the four of us appeared to be a family, and we enjoyed spending free time with the boys.

Nonetheless, on the weekends when Thomas and Levi grudgingly stayed with their mama, Tom and I spent time together, some of it traveling. One such trip led us to my friend BJ's younger son's May wedding in Key Largo. We flew to Miami and rented a convertible for the drive to the islands. Although neither Tom nor I had ever seen Miami, we didn't waste time in the hot, humid, and congested city. We picked up the convertible, dropped the top, and left Miami in the rearview mirror as we headed south to our destination.

Granted, Key Largo proved to be as hot and humid as Miami but nowhere nearly as clogged with traffic. Our room at the Marriott on the beach was a welcome oasis, and we couldn't resist a nap on the king bed surrounded by a cool, quiet, darkened room. Afterwards, we showered and dressed in casual attire for the six o'clock rehearsal dinner at a seaside restaurant even though we weren't in the wedding party; BJ invited all the guests to attend. We enjoyed a delicious meal and the splendor of an orange and yellow sunset as water and sky became one. A small band was set up in a corner on the deck and provided music for those of us who wanted to dance in the moonlight.

It was after midnight before the party broke up, but Tom awoke early the next morning and roused me from slumber with kisses. I wanted to sleep-in but Tom opened drapes to reveal a beautiful day waiting for us. "Wake up, sleepyhead. We can sleep at home. Let's go downstairs for breakfast and then hit the beach for a couple of hours before it gets too hot. I thought since this is our only free day, we might drive down to Key West this afternoon and rent bicycles for exploring the island."

I pulled a pillow over my head and moaned. Sometimes Tom was like a Labrador puppy, affectionate, playful, and energetic. "How can you be so chipper this early in the morning, especially after a late night? Coffee, I need coffee."

He tugged the pillow from my grasp. "Easy. I get up before daylight because I have to drive to Atlanta for my job, so seven-thirty is late for me. Shake a leg, babe. Daylight is wasting, and coffee is waiting."

I had to admit I was glad I'd crawled out of bed when we found two lounge chairs available on the already crowded beach, which was a small-scale stretch of sand. A walk on the beach in Key Largo would have taken about ten minutes, roundtrip. I slathered on sunscreen and stretched out on the chaise when I noticed a group of women huddled together on a large beach blanket next to me. They apparently subscribed to the theory that it was five o'clock somewhere as they enjoyed frosty mimosas. Large, colorful beach hats bobbed in banter.

I didn't recognize any of them and concluded from bits and pieces of their conversation that they were there for the wedding, on the bride's side of the family who was originally from Boston. I'd been a loquacious child raised in the South, which meant I never met a stranger. I said to no one person in particular, "Did y'all have a good flight?"

My question elicited laughter from the group, and one of them wearing Jackie O glasses and the largest of the straw hats replied sarcastically, "Yes, and 'y'all' are evidently a part of the groom's family or friends. Did *y'all* have grits for breakfast?" Her comment prompted more laughter.

I overlooked her rudeness, but being raised in the South also meant I could handle myself when grownup mean girls stepped on my southern roots. "As a matter of fact, we are here for our sweet Chris. Jill is fortunate to marry such a handsome, kind young man who has chosen the Coast Guard as his career. As for grits, unfortunately, the hotel restaurant doesn't serve them—or sweet tea."

I paused to give the ringleader time to hand me a comeback, and she didn't disappoint. "Oh my, how will you ever survive without your grits and sweet tea?" Their sarcastic laughter spilled onto the beach.

I slid my sunglasses up so I could look her in the eye. "I'll manage. I doubt if any of you have ever read anything by Lewis Grizzard, so let me borrow a quote he was quite fond of: 'American by birth, Southern by the grace of God'. I slapped my sunglasses back to their resting place and said in a voice coated with saccharin, "By the way, *y'all* can kiss my ass."

Tom couldn't hide his amusement over my sarcastic southern charm but suggested we shower and change for the short trip to Key West, and I agreed. As we sped under blue skies and sunshine along Highway 1, over bridge after bridge that connected the Keys, the incident with the Boston bitches was lost in the scenery. But hell would freeze over before I would acknowledge them again. When we arrived in Key West we rented bicycles before enjoying lunch at a sidewalk café. Afterwards, we toured the island from Ernest Hemingway's home to the most southern point of the United States where Cuba rested a mere ninety miles away—ninety miles that separated Communism and freedom.

Tom and I ended the day by watching the sunset cast a warm golden glow over Mallory Square, and I was grateful for the trip's built-in leisure day. As an added bonus, the bride and bridegroom would be attending bachelor and bachelorette parties in their honor that evening which meant there was no reason to rush back to Key Largo. We strolled beneath the street lights of Key West hand in hand, with the sound of the surf and partygoers in the background. It was our last night when the beachside wedding took place, a ceremony highlighted by a lavender sunset.

Another trip took us to a Georgia beach: St. Simons Island, one of four barrier islands that made up the Golden Isles. Several of us couples rode motorcycles to the coast, but Pat said she wouldn't straddle Richard Gere that long. Pat had had the hots for Richard Gere ever since the movie, *Pretty Woman.* Admittedly, it was a long haul, but I was game and climbed onto the back of the Harley Tom bought from an elderly man. The gray-haired man admitted that old age had robbed him of his ability to handle the bike, and he reluctantly passed the keys to Tom. He told us both to enjoy the ride but from the misty look in his eyes, I realized he meant for us to enjoy the ride that is life. And we were definitely enjoying our lives.

We discovered the tranquility of Gulf Shores, the natural beauty of the Outer Banks, the cobbled streets of St. Augustine, and the majestic mountains of Asheville. The Great Smoky Mountains bordered what was known as the Tail of the Dragon, an eleven mile stretch of road located at Deals Gap and filled with over three hundred curves. It was a playground for motorcycles where wind in our faces and flickers of sunlight added to the pleasure of the ride.

One weekend trek took us to historic St. Marys in Georgia where we ferried over to Cumberland Island. We watched as wild horses roamed freely on the mostly untouched island. Another time we hiked dozens of trails that led to gorgeous waterfalls when we visited the Highlands in North Carolina. Tom said he'd never met a woman with a suitcase tied to her ass, but the adventurous escapades gave us time to get to know each other better and to be sure of our love. We were happy, but neither Tom nor I wanted to rush into anything.

When my trips interfered with helping out with Daddy, my sisters took over for me, mostly because, according to Joyce, I was the spoiled baby. She never got over being displaced as the baby in the family by my unexpected arrival as the seventh child when she was almost eight. I'd outgrown such pettiness and accepted that she and I would never have the close relationship Pat and I shared. Joyce and I had a fractious family connection at best but loved each other enough for her to pitch in when I wasn't available, as I'd done for her on occasion.

Sadly, Daddy's advanced age made it increasingly difficult for him to stay home alone. His doctor had no choice but to recommend we admit him to the local nursing home where he could be cared for on a twenty-four hour basis. It was not a decision to be made lightly, and a family meeting was held to discuss alternatives. Daddy was purposefully absent because his suggestion to the news of a necessary fulltime caregiver had been that one of us would have to move in with him. As I had adamantly declined the invitation Daddy extended after Barry's death, he invited Joyce and her crazy-ass husband to live with him, a fact I reminded her of, but she vehemently vetoed that notion. "No way in hell. I have a husband and a home, and I'm not giving up either to take on Daddy twenty-four/seven. We'll have to work out something else." She glanced around my family room. "Maybe he can move in with one of you. Sheila, you're single and the obvious choice."

I was surprised Joyce didn't jump at the chance to change her pitiful circumstances but not surprised she saw me as the answer to our problem. I calmly replied, "Yes, I am single, but I also have a job that I can't afford to give up. Besides, Daddy and I could never live together even if my home were three times the size. Lord only knows how Mama lived with him for sixty years."

Donnie and Jerry remained silent, and although Gene had contributed to Daddy's financial support, there was little he could do from his home on Merritt Island. Even though Daddy liked Florida—especially fishing—and there was enough room for him, Gene had already made it clear that he and Vern were in no position to move Daddy in with them. Gene's stance on the matter was irrelevant since Daddy wouldn't want to move that far from home. Short of having Daddy as a permanent house-guest, our long-distance brother said he would agree to whatever the rest of us decided.

Pat offered a solution, but it wasn't ideal. "Joyce you don't have a job, so if you could stay with him during the weekdays, the rest of us could alternate nights and weekends."

We all held a look of panic. Donnie disrupted our silence. "Shelby and I are retired and enjoy our freedom, so I'm not about to commit to some kind of rotation timetable that will bind us to caretaking. And let me bring up the fact that none of us is medically qualified to care for an aging parent. I don't even know CPR." He motioned around the room. "I'm willing to bet that y'all wouldn't know what to do either in the event Daddy suffers a stroke or heart attack. There's always the possibility he could fall and break a hip, which would mean the nursing home. I'm not going to take on that responsibility. Sorry, but I'm out."

The subject of team tagging Daddy's care was taken off the table, and it was agreed that he would have to be admitted to the nursing home. The fly in the ointment was that Daddy would flatly refuse to go willingly. Therefore, the next topic of discussion was who would do the deed that no-body wanted to do. Both Joyce and Pat admitted they couldn't be the ones, as did Jerry. The process of elimination left Donne and me, and I wasn't going to dump the task on him alone. The two of us wavered on how to best handle a difficult decision, but came to the conclusion that there was no easy way around the fact that Daddy wouldn't willing go to the "old folks home." Pat mentioned that Daddy had another doctor's appointment in the upcoming week and volunteered to pick up the necessary papers from the nursing home that required the doctor's signature. With the matter settled

I promised to touch base with Donnie the following week, and my siblings scattered.

The day we dreaded arrived much too soon, and Shelby chose to join us. Daddy thought it was unusual for three of us to escort him to a doctor's appointment but never smelled a rat. The medical exam was brief, and the completed forms for the nursing home were discretely given to us by the nurse as we left the office. We helped Daddy into the car and he commented, "It's about lunch time, and I'd like to go to the Dairy Queen. Can't remember the last time I had a banana split."

I feigned enthusiasm. "Sure, Daddy. Whatever you want is fine with us."

The four of us had lunch at the fast food diner, and Daddy did everything but lick the dessert dish after he polished off the banana split. He wiped his mouth with a napkin. "Well, that was mighty tasty. If y'all will see me to the house, I believe a nap is calling my name."

None of us said anything as we made our way back to Bremen, to the street where the nursing home was located. Daddy noticed and said to Donnie, "Son, you turned a few blocks too soon. Why are you taking a detour?"

Donnie disregarded the question and eased up the hill to the parking lot of the nursing home. Daddy said with a laugh, "If you've got somebody you want to visit, I'd like to be taken home first. Don't want the staff to mistake me for a resident."

His laughter trailed off when I slid out of the car and walked around to Daddy's door, which I opened for him. "Daddy, we're here to check you in. You're too feeble to say home alone, and we don't have a choice."

Daddy looked at me, tears welling up in faded blue eyes as I took his arm and coaxed him out of the car where an orderly with a wheelchair waited patiently. "Sugar, I'd rather you bury me than to move me in here."

I struggled with conflicted emotions. "And I'd rather bury you, but you're not dead. Please, Daddy, don't make this harder than it already is."

His shoulders slumped with resignation, and he allowed the orderly to assist him in sitting down in the wheelchair. Pat and Joyce arrived with a suitcase carrying Daddy's essentials as we were getting Daddy settled in his room, with the promise to buy him a new television set. Joyce took one look at Daddy and began to cry like a baby, mascara running down her cheeks. I pulled her by the arm into the hallway and hissed, "Stop it! We mutually agreed that this is the only answer. Of course if you've changed your mind about moving in with him, we can load him up and leave right now."

With a few dramatic sniffles, she dried her tears and mumbled through her tissue. "No, I can't do that."

"Then paste a smile on your face and help us unpack his bags."

Jerry came in the room, which was becoming crowded, and promised, as we all did, that one of us would check on Daddy every day. Pat pointed to the phone on his nightstand and told him that she would bring his list from home with our home and work numbers so he could call us anytime he needed anything. There was an air of awkwardness as we hugged him goodbye and made our getaway into the fresh air and sunshine. It was not our finest moment.

Thankfully, Daddy adapted to his new living quarters and on most days was happy. One day when I ran by on my lunch hour to take him a Big Mac, he assured me he'd already eaten in the dining hall with his friends, several of whom he'd worked with in the men's clothing manufacturing company. "You know, this is not where I wanted to spend my final days, but overall it's not too bad. The food is pretty good, I have round-the-clock care, and if there's a fire these people will see to it that I'm gotten out of the building. You know I worried about that in my old house, that it would catch fire, and I wouldn't be able to get out in time."

"I remember, Daddy, but you don't have to be afraid here." The wall clock told me I needed to get back to the office. "I have to go now, but Jerry or Pat will be by after work. Is there anything you need them to pick up for you?"

"No, sugar, I have everything I need." His hand reached out and took mine. "I didn't mean to make it so hard on you and your brothers and sisters to bring me here. The truth is I'm better off, but I was too stubborn to admit it. So don't trouble yourself that you had to damn near drag me outta the car."

I stood to leave and kissed his forehead. A tender squeeze of my hand let me know I was forgiven.

Chuck and Geri found a small, two bedroom apartment that fit their budget and eloped to Gatlinburg where they spent a few days honeymooning. Daddy voiced his relief that Chuck had done the right thing by marrying the mother of his child. I, on the other hand, treaded lightly so as not to intrude in their lives, but I did offer to assist with the expense of a nursery. I also ventured so far as to throw a baby shower where long-time friends and family came to my door bearing much needed baby gifts. My heart wasn't in any of these activities because I was worried over how the young couple would make it with the added expense of a baby. But I loved my son and there was nothing to be done except make the best of the situation. I'd learned from more than one friend who'd alienated her son by issuing an ultimatum—only to lose said son. I wasn't willing to interfere to the point of fracturing the relationship between my son and me or pushing my new daughter-in-law away. I wanted only to be included in my granddaughter's life.

It was one a.m. on a Sunday morning when the phone rang, and I snatched up the receiver in a matter of seconds. It was Chuck who said in a strained voice, "Mama, we're here, at the hospital. The doctor said it's going to be a few hours, or more than a few, but I promised to call you when Geri was in labor."

"Thank you for calling. I'll be there in about an hour. Is Geri's mama there yet?"

"Not yet. She said that first babies are always slow and that she will be here in a few hours. If you do drive down, can you please go to Walmart and pick up a disposable camera? I left ours on the coffee table, and I think the Carrolton store is open twenty-four hours."

"Of course I will. I'll keep you company while we wait and maybe give moral support to Geri." I hurried to put myself together and debated as to whether or not to call Tom, but there was no need in waking him and the boys when the baby, in all likelihood, wouldn't be born until mid-morning or early afternoon. He would have more than enough time to arrive before the baby, Brenna, made her appearance.

Geri's mama arrived after eight and was wise not to have hurried to the hospital as I'd done. Tom made it to the hospital well ahead of the baby and took me to lunch at the cafeteria as I refused to leave the hospital. After hours and hours of labor and walking the hallways, we were ushered out of the delivery room, with the exception of Chuck. Tom was with me in the small waiting room adjacent to the birthing room when we heard a newborn's unmistakable cry. He hugged me and congratulated me on becoming a "Nana," the name I settled on after other considerations were tossed by the wayside.

After what seemed an eternity we were permitted to enter the birthing room. Nothing could have prepared me for the overwhelming love that flooded my heart and soul when it was my turn to hold my first grandchild. I held her perfection in my arms, and her tiny fingers wrapped around my pinkie. I was in love, a love I'd never before experienced, not even with the birth of my sons. Brenna looked very much like her daddy and was soft and pink and absolutely adorable. She was a precious angel whose little hands unknowingly held my heart, and she would forever be my grandangel. I snuggled her close and whispered a prayer that God would always be with her and guide her path. What I hadn't known to pray for was America, for His protection against unforeseen, unadulterated evil.

It was a mild, sunny September morning, the morning Thomas and I were on our way for a nine o'clock appointment with the orthodontist. At my suggestion, Thomas was reviewing notes for his Georgia History exam. The radio was on, but I wasn't listening because I was thinking about Tom's and my upcoming extended weekend trip to Colorado. We were flying out of Atlanta early Friday morning for Denver, where a rented car would take us to a cabin in Estes Park. From there we planned to ramble around the area until Monday's late afternoon flight home. Tom had never traveled to the West and was very much looking forward to the trip.

There was nothing out of the ordinary on that day, September 11, 2001. It was a day like any other. Until it wasn't. The announcer's stricken voice interrupted the flow of music and my thoughts to advise his listeners that American Airlines Flight 11 had crashed into the North Tower of the World Trade Center. It was first believed to be a catastrophic accident, but the tragedy that became infamous had just begun. Approximately fifteen minutes later United Airlines Flight 175 crashed into the South Tower. It was quickly determined that the collisions were not accidents but terrorist attacks, and chaos ensued as every flight was grounded. America was under attack by hijacked commercial airlines being used as missiles with designated targets.

When the sun set on that disastrous day, America mourned the loss of almost three thousand innocent people; another six thousand were injured. Alan Jackson aptly summarized the devastation in his song, "The Day the World Stopped Turning." Without a doubt the events of 9/11 left an indelible stamp on the landscape of our country—from politics, to the military, to First Responders to airport procedures. The tragedy robbed us of our innocence and forever changed the way we viewed the world around us. The attack was one of those moments in time when a person would never forget exactly where they were and what they were doing, such as those old enough to remember when Pearl Harbor was attacked or when President Kennedy was assassinated. Our collective sense of security, a faith that we were insulated from such malice was lost that day, and our core beliefs were challenged. It was a day etched in our hearts.

Comparatively, the adaptations Tom and I made for our trip were nothing more than minor inconveniences. Delta Airlines offered refunds or travel vouchers for a later date to any passenger who wanted to reschedule, but the Colorado trip was to celebrate Tom's birthday. We decided to keep the plans that were made weeks in advance. Nonetheless, our early morning flight was bumped again and again until we were finally allowed to lineup for a seven p.m. flight. A necessary but time-consuming wait to pass the scrutiny of beefed-up security where my razor and Tom's pocket knife were confiscated delayed us further. Despite those nuisances we were finally, and a bit anxiously, airborne.

Three hours later we picked up the rented Jeep and headed through the darkness to Estes Park where our cozy cabin rested by a large stream that sang over pebbles. As we'd eaten supper in one of the airport restaurants and were exhausted, we practically stumbled into the huge, four-poster bed where a down comforter welcomed us. It seemed I'd barely closed my eyes when I was awakened by sunlight that danced over the singing brook and announced the arrival of our first full day in Colorado. We didn't want to waste a minute and hiked a short distance on a mountain trail. An hour later we were amazed to find ourselves standing in pristine snow. A park ranger struck up a conversation and cautioned us to take it easy in the higher altitude. Our southern accents made it apparent that we were accustomed to hiking much closer to sea level, where the air wasn't as thin.

We heeded his advice and decided to drive over a portion of the Rockies, towards Durango, and stopped for lunch in Grand Lake, named for a large, crystal lake that attracted tourists. The quaint town was nestled in a valley modeled after a town of the Old West, complete with wooden boardwalks and saloons. On our second day another recommendation was made by an information guide at the state line when we drove north on Highway 25 and crossed into Wyoming. The man was tall and lanky and resembled an aging Smokey the Bear, wearing the same style hat and the addition of a tan uniform. Given our sparse surroundings, I asked the man if he could refer us to a local restaurant where we could celebrate my husband's birthday. His first suggestions were for eateries located in Cheyenne, but on second thought he provided directions to an old farm house on the outskirts of Laramie that had been renovated as a steak house. We walked around the capital city of Cheyenne before driving through backroads for miles and miles. We were rewarded with a delicious meal where the steak was fork tender and straw-berry shortcake was on the house in honor of Tom's birthday.

We drove back to Estes Park in the magnificent shadow of the mono-lithic Rockies, clothed in deep blue under the moonlight. Tom had to brake suddenly to avoid hitting a cow that led a herd across the two-lane highway. We both mistakenly thought a negligent farmer had failed to secure his cattle when I remembered noticing a brochure at the welcome center that warned tourists of the state's "open range" policy that allowed livestock to roam freely. Thankfully, a collision was avoided and we ar-rived safely back to our cabin where Tom built a fire to take the chill off our abode. We'd planned to finish packing but instead made love and drifted off to sleep to the crackling warmth of the fire. Packing waited until morning.

Our half-day plans were cancelled as it was necessary to arrive at the airport a full three hours before our scheduled flight to allow ample time for boarding. I scanned the cabin as I packed and mentally reviewed the last few days. It was a whirlwind trip cut short by a national tragedy that resulted in long lines and searches; nonetheless, it was one of our favorite trips. When we booked the trip we had no idea it would be "rut" season. Wildlife indigenous to the region was roaming, and we were able to see a variety of elk, mule deer, moose, and a herd of bighorn sheep in search of a partner for mating. Tom couldn't wait to take the boys on a similar excur-sion, and I suggested a two week trip the following summer, one that would include the Grand Canyon and Yellowstone National Park. Nothing would determine compatibility among the four of us like a two week road trip, which would make or break our collective relationship.

Doubt clouded my judgment, but my heart was already convinced that we were meant to be. Nonetheless, was Shelby right to question my sanity? No, I was perfectly capable of making relationship decisions. Or was I? Was the love between Tom and me what I'd longed for during the past few years of loneliness? It had been almost five years since Barry's death, but I still didn't know if I was ready for a marriage that wasn't yet on the table. I stopped deliberating on a possible proposal, snapped my suitcase shut, and hoisted my carry-on over my shoulder. Tom loaded our bags, and we were on our way to the airport well ahead of our four o'clock flight.

The Colorado trip was but one of our various trips filled with adventure, laughter, and lovemaking, but where was the road taking us? I was in love with Tom, and he'd made it clear that he felt the same about me. Even so, I had no idea what the future held for us—or if I was prepared for that future.

*Name changed

Chapter Fifteen

Blessings

I promised my late husband that when our grandchildren arrived I would love them enough for both of us, and I cherished my grandangel. Her parents allowed me to have her almost every time I asked, and I set up a makeshift nursery in one of the spare bedrooms for times when Brenna stayed overnight. Although Tom wasn't her biological granddaddy, he adored her, as did Thomas and Levi, and they all adopted her as their own. Our combined Christmas would be more special by the inclusion of a baby to love, and my heart was full the afternoon we decorated the tree and I hung a new ornament. It was a dated Hallmark collectible, a Mother Goose cradling an infant and labeled, "Grandbaby's 1st Christmas."

As I watched Tom tenderly place Brenna on his shoulder and sooth her fussiness, I thought about his kindness the past October, when I'd taken flowers to the cemetery on Barry's birthday. He'd insisted on accompanying me to our family plot in a rather isolated location and waited patiently as I arranged the flowers to my satisfaction. He pulled a few stray weeds and noted that we should have a load of gravel delivered to the plot and volunteered to help me maintain the gravesites. Tom was sincere and never wavered from his true colors. He was consistently considerate, thoughtful, and kind. We rarely argued, and when I was upset over nothing important, an apology and roses appeased my anger. Tom was a good man, and I could envision myself growing old with him—until he pulled the rug out from under those pleasant thoughts.

For whatever reason, Tom grew nostalgic as he rocked Brenna to sleep and asked, "Have you ever thought about starting over, you know, having another baby?"

I dropped an ornament that shattered on the hardwood floor and was relieved it wasn't one of meaning. "No, not for a minute, and have you lost your friggin' mind? You do realize that's my *grandchild* you're holding? Not only am I not interested in having another baby, my tubes have been tied, and Dr. Martin assured me the procedure was permanent. It was a choice Barry and I made when the boys were teenagers, a decision I've never regretted. If, however, you think you might want to start over then we need to part ways so you can find yourself a baby mama." I was sweating at the mere thought of having a baby at that point in my life. "Hell, Tom, if by some medical miracle I found myself pregnant, I'd hang out at the tracks and wait for the five o'clock Amtrak to blow through town."

He gently placed Brenna in her mesh playpen and turned to me. "Why? So you could jump aboard and leave town?"

"No, so I could jump in front of it."

Tom laughed and wrapped me in his arms. "I don't want a 'baby mama'—or a baby. I want *you*." He shrugged it off. "It was a stupid suggestion that I blame on Brenna's baby smell and how it felt to snuggle her sweetness. I promise to never bring up the subject again."

The moment of madness passed, and I breathed a sigh of relief.

It was a gorgeous spring weekend when Tom and I decided to visit one of our favorite places, the beautiful, tranquil mountains of North Carolina. It was a last minute trip when we'd realized we were both able to take Friday off and extend our weekend while the boys would be with their mama. I was a planner, but Tom preferred to fly by the seat of his pants and we were lucky to find a room on a weekend filled with arts and crafts festivals. We checked in at Betty's Bed & Breakfast located in Black Mountain and dropped our bags on the third floor. Our room was actually the renovated attic of a rambling old farmhouse that had been turned into one of several

B&Bs in the area. Tom and I used what was left of the day driving over a few of the many scenic roads of the Great Smokey Mountains until dusk dropped over the mountains. A velvet night filled with stars found us at a folk festival in historic downtown Asheville, listening to the twang of bluegrass banjos. The magical setting was infused with the citrusy scent of magnolia blossoms.

Dog-tired, we slept like logs and decided to spend Saturday outdoors again, in the fresh air and sunshine that splashed over the mountains. After a scrumptious breakfast of omelets and homemade warm-from-the-oven blueberry muffins, we dressed in light layers and tossed bottled water and snacks into a backpack before heading for the hills. Parking and picnic tables were located at Mount Mitchell State Park for the Black Mountain Crest Trail near the trailhead. The footpath was all but deserted as we made our way through wildflowers that nestled among spruce-fir forests. Rhododendrons, lady slippers, trillium, orchids, violets, and mountain laurel bloomed in pink, lavender, and white—colors that glistened with remnants of morning dew to create a bejeweled setting. We hiked in companionable silence, with only the sound of birds and wind that rustled treetops.

The strenuous hike was worth the climb as we reached the second peak, our goal, and relaxed on a large, flat rock that overlooked a winding river. The magnificent view and cooling breeze were our compensation, though time wouldn't allow us to complete the entire twelve mile hike before darkness settled over the mountains. We ate our granola bars and apples amid light conversation. Afterwards, Tom gathered up our trash and stuffed it into his backpack before he retrieved a small jeweler's box.

I pretended not to notice and wondered if he could hear my racing heart. The moment of truth had arrived, and I was both elated and terrified. For more than two years Tom and I had gotten to know each other, and our relationship had been carefree because at the end of the day we each went to different houses. But marriage, with all of us under one roof, was a whole different level of commitment. Was I ready to take the proverbial leap of faith and say 'Yes'? And was a good first marriage an indication that I would have a good second marriage?

The breeze kicked up and swept the mountain with much cooler air, and I was grateful for the warmth of the sun. Or maybe it was nervousness that sent chills over my body. Tom pulled a hoodie from his backpack and tossed it over to me. "You look cold, and I packed a sweatshirt. The temperature's usually cooler in the higher elevation."

I tugged the fleeced warmth over my head. "Thanks, Tom. I really appreciate how you take care of me."

He turned to face me and took my hands in his. "I want to always take care of you. You know, Sheila, I've loved several women during my life, and I've been honest with you about my past relationships. But for the first time in my life I'm *in love*. I'm in love with you, and I don't know how to say this other than to ask—"

My jumpiness interrupted him, "Oh, Tom, this is such a perfect, romantic spot. I never—"

It was his turn to interrupt, "Before you say anything I need to finish. I've thought about this proposal for months, and I don't want to blow it." He gently kissed me and continued, "I want to spend the rest of my life with you. I realize I'm not the first man you've been in love with, but I want to be the last one, the man who grows old with you." He slipped the small box from his pocket and flipped it open. "Will you marry me?"

A flawless, solitaire diamond was flanked on each side by two smaller diamonds. I was suddenly calm and very sure of my answer. "Yes, yes, Tom. I will marry you. And while you are in love for the first time, I'm in love for the last."

Wind whipped my hair and tears away from my face so that Tom could plant a lengthy kiss on lips that warmed beneath his unbridled passion. When he released me he slid the ring onto my finger. I commented on its beauty, and Tom explained, "The setting caught my attention because of the three stones. When you marry me you're taking on not only a husband but also two boys, and I hope you've had time to think that over."

I stared at the ring and smiled at Tom. "Yes, I have, and I love you more for accepting the responsibility of raising your sons. I might add that Thomas and Levi can't scare me, not after raising Brad and Chuck."

I rested my head on Tom's shoulder and as he held me close, I contemplated the hills and valleys in my life. When I was in the lowest of those valleys, not once did I imagine that I would marry an amazing man or that I would have a whole new family to love. I sat on the windswept mountain and noticed how the diamonds on both hands sparkled in the sunlight. The heart-shaped ring on my right hand embodied the love of my past; the engagement ring on my left hand held the promise of a new love.

My sons and the rest of my family and friends were thrilled with the news of the engagement, even Shelby came around to the idea. Daddy was relieved that I would have a man to stand by my side during my twilight years. Melba, Barry's mama, was overjoyed that I'd met another man with whom to share my life, and she and Carl accepted that my life had to go on. But it was Melba who carried the anguish of a mother who'd lost a child. I told her that everybody should be loved all of somebody's life and assured her that I would love Barry all of mine. She welcomed Tom into our family, and gave me the gift of her approval—and sexy lingerie.

Charlcie, on the other hand, was not happy in the least when we broke it to her. She folded her arms across her ample chest and suggested I keep my name instead of taking Tom's surname. "After all," she rationalized, "Your children and grandchild bear your late husband's name, and you won't be giving Tom another child. There's no doubt it would be better for everyone if you don't take *our* last name."

Tom said calmly, "Mama, do I need to remind you that you changed your last name when you remarried after Daddy's death? And you didn't have children with your second husband."

"You don't need to remind me of a damn thing, Tom. There's nothing wrong with my memory!"

I interjected, "No, Charlcie, I won't be having any more children, but I am marrying your son. As his wife, I will accept his name as my own."

She ignored my comment, and Tom patiently explained to his mama that whether or not I took his last name was none of her business. "Sheila made her decision without your interference." He walked across the room and planted a kiss on Charlcie's forehead. "Call me when you get the bill for your homeowner's insurance, and I'll bring you a check. Goodbye."

Tom was good to his mama, which Pat said was a sign of a good man. Despite his meddling mama, I still wanted to marry Tom—especially in view of the fact that my family could be considered a can of mixed nuts on any given day. On the ride home I started a conversation. "The first time I met your mama, she didn't hesitate to tell me that you needed a wife to help you finish raising her grandsons. So why is she so bitter about our engagement?"

"When she met you she was blowin' smoke up your ass, most likely to scare you off." Tom enlightened me as to why Charlcie was not happy about our plans to marry. "Her strategy was for me to stay single, finish raising the boys, and then move in with her to take care of her in her old age. In her opinion, you pissed on her picnic. My older sister died in a car accident years ago, and my younger sister left town and never looked back. It's easier for Mama to blame you than to believe that I had no intention of giving up my life for hers."

I was silent, but Tom knew my feelings were hurt because Charlcie hadn't welcomed me with open arms. He kissed the palm of my hand and dismissed her reaction. "I've fallen in love, and if Mama can't be happy for me, then so be it. Let's move on to another topic, for instance, have you given any thought as to where you want to live after we're married? I've got a pretty good nest egg that will make a good down payment on a house."

His unexpected segue caught me off guard. "What? I have no intention of selling my house and assumed we'd all live in it. After all, it's already accommodated a family of four, and I see no reason why it can't do so again. Of course, the boys' bedrooms will need to be redecorated and we should take them shopping for their new furniture. I want them to feel welcome in what will be our home."

Tom held up his hand in protest as he made a left turn onto the Highway 27 Bypass. "Slow down with the decorating Martha Stewart. If you don't want to sell your home and invest the money in a retirement account, that's fine. You can lease it to a nice family with references, but I'm not going to have every busybody in Bremen gossiping about how I'm living off you or that I can't afford to buy a house for us. Barry bought that house, and I would be uncomfortable living in another man's home."

"Is that what this is about? I hate to point out the obvious, but Barry no longer owns that house. We bought it together, and it belongs to me and I don't want strangers living in it. As for you 'living off' me, I guarantee you that's not gonna happen. I'll provide the roof over our heads, and you'll pay for everything from groceries to utilities to help with maintenance and whatever else the boys need. You've already bought a new SUV for us, and in a few years you'll have to buy cars for Thomas and Levi. As for gossipmongers, you haven't lived in this town long enough to realize that the first thing you have to do is disregard what anybody says about you. It's nobody's business where we live, and after a few days the subject will be old news." What I didn't share with Tom was that I'd paid off the line of equity I'd used to bail out the failed business or that my home was my security blanket. In the event that our marriage fell apart or if he died before me, I would always have a place to live.

He was silent as he merged into the right turn lane but shrugged his shoulders in resignation. "Ok, Sheila, if you're sure this is what you want, then we'll move in with you after we're married. Speaking of, have you already made those plans by yourself, too?"

"My first 'wedding' was in a courthouse with a Justice of the Peace officiating, so anything would be preferable. I've given it some thought, and I'll discuss things with you after I've done some more research. I'm considering a fall wedding, which will give us time to adjust to the idea of living together. We can also use the time to start moving some of your things to the basement and setting up rooms for the boys. I want y'all to move in as soon as we return from our honeymoon."

He'd already lost one argument so didn't tackle another but assured me that whatever I wanted was okay with him. "My daddy taught me the best way to a happy marriage is to learn to say, 'Yes, dear'."

Destination weddings were becoming increasingly popular, and after much wavering, Tom and I decided to combine our wedding and honeymoon in Jamaica. Even though it would be only the two of us at the ceremony, Charlcie wouldn't have the chance to wear black or make a scene at the church by lassoing her son or tripping me as I walked down the aisle. Plans were finalized as schedules were coordinated, details ironed out, and reservations made at the Sandals Resort in Ocho Rios. With help from friends I found the perfect wedding gown that was both elegant and simple. The dress was a creamy ivory floor-length, off-the-shoulder dress with an embroidered, fitted bodice and slightly flowing, chiffon skirt.

September arrived much too soon. Plane and resort reservations were made, as well as the date for our wedding, and the boys' rooms were set up and waiting for them. Coworkers Jane and Vanessa put together a surprise bridal shower for me, held at the office for the staff. Theirs was not the only surprise that day. Tom and I were doing some last minute packing when the doorbell rang, and I was delighted to see Brad and Valerie. They'd stopped by to congratulate us once again and to share some wonderful news of their own. Brad presented me with a small gift bag, and I retrieved a rather confusing photo in a silver frame that was engraved with the words, "I can't wait to see you, Nana!"

Tears sprang to my eyes as I realized the picture was a sonogram of my new grandchild. Hugs were passed around, and my happiness had no boundaries. I couldn't have dreamed of a more perfect wedding gift. My excitement over the baby, the wedding, and my life interfered with sleep, but I was so ecstatic when the alarm went off that not even a lack of sleep could mar the day. We hurriedly showered and dressed in order to allow extra time at the airport for security checkpoints. We boarded Air Jamaica for Montego Bay, despite preliminary weather warnings of an impending hurricane in the area.

The flight was uneventful and once we landed, a passenger van waited to whisk us to the Sandals Resort where our wedding waited sixty miles and three days away. Exhaustion caught up with me, and I dozed briefly along the route, which was broken up by a pit stop for cooling refreshments. The break also gave locals the opportunity to pedal their goods to "wealthy Americans." Those of us women with "tall hair" were warned not to agree to have our hair braided as the process took much longer than we would be told, and there wasn't enough time. Not only did I not think braided, beaded hair would be my best look, other than bottled water we didn't make any purchases. A dozen or so of us climbed in the van, leaving disappointed vendors behind.

As we continued along the coastal road I noticed that Jamaica was a beautiful tropical island, a sharp contrast from the destitution that was so painfully displayed on the other side of the window. Many of the shacks were nothing more than lean-tos where black kettles hung over a laboring fire. Barefoot toddlers wearing only ragged, oversized t-shirts wandered about barren, dirt yards; there was nothing that even resembled a toy to be seen. It was evident their lives were a constant struggle to survive. During the early years of my first marriage, Barry and I sometimes had difficulties making ends meet, but we knew our situation was temporary. We may have been young and as poor as a church mouse, but we had something those people didn't: hope.

The van halted and nudged my thoughts of the Jamaican people aside. Our luggage was unloaded, and we were greeted by a gracious hostess offering chilled towels and cooled champagne for our refreshment. We walked into the opulence of the lobby, and it was as if Tom and I had been transported to a different world from the one we'd encountered on our drive to the resort. Nothing about Sandals reflected the poverty indigenous to the island. Our room was tastefully appointed with island-themed décor, and there was a large balcony overlooking the turquoise waters of the Caribbean. I stepped outside and inhaled the sea air to clear my head and noticed several guests enjoying the pool in the last rays of the sun. Tom slipped up behind me and encircled me in his arms. I pulled him closer and realized that vague, restless, unnamed longing I'd felt for the past few years was gone. My heart was home.

We unpacked and strolled along the beach before going to bed early after a very long day. And we had a nine o'clock appointment with the resort's wedding planner to finalize details such as music, flowers, pictures, etc. We arrived promptly at nine, but the woman with whom I'd scheduled the appointment was late. When she showed up an hour and half later, Monique expressed no explanation or remorse for her tardiness or at having kept us waiting. When Tom pointedly checked his watch she explained that "island time" was not precise and that we should relax and revel in the beauty that surrounded us. "Mi deh yah, I am here. No worries, mon" was her only excuse as she pulled her notes from a file bearing our names.

We decided not to let her flippant attitude regarding appointments spoil our day and proceeded to select flowers, including a beautiful nosegay with a matching boutonniere for Tom, and which photography package we wanted. We'd already chosen the music to which I would walk down the pathway to the gazebo; our first dance would be to our song, "Amazed." The final order of business was the dinner menu, which would be served on the balcony of one of the restaurants, along with French vanilla cake garnished with chocolate curls and flowers—with specific instructions to box up the top layer and send it to our suite. Monique protested that it wasn't practical to transport the cake aboard our flight, but I intended for our newly blended family to share the cake together. And by damn we were going to do just that.

With specifics taken care of we put on swimsuits and hit the beach where the drinks were flowing, and the music was loud. I wanted to go for a cruise on the glass bottom boat, but my request was met with "No, mon, it is a storm in the sea." To emphasize the warning of an impending hurricane, the man pointed to where workers were boarding up the dozen or so stained glass windows in preparation for the angry waters of the Caribbean.

Thankfully, the squall churned miles away and would hopefully not disrupt the tranquility of the island. After a few hours in the sun, we retreated to the coolness of a beachside tiki bar where the bartender took one look at Tom and commented, "Yo, Kenny Rogers, you don't do well in the sun, mon." He popped the top on a frosty bottle of Red Stripe, made in Jamaica and the only beer served, and handed it over the bar to Tom, who despite the use of sunscreen did not "do well in the sun."

Two beers and a wine spritzer later found us showered and on the streets to do some exploring, despite that tourists were encouraged not to leave the "compound." Another honeymooning couple we met on the beach told us about a marketplace to buy souvenirs that was located a few blocks from the resort. We were barely a stones' throw from the resort when we were approached by a burly Jamaican offering to sell us "ganja" at a very good price, special for the Americans.

I paused in the street to ask what he was selling, but Tom placed his hand in the small of my back and directed me away from the man. "Keep walking. Don't look back, just ignore him."

"Why? He said his ganja was high quality and very reasonably priced. I don't know exactly what ganja is, but it might be something we're interested in buying."

Tom never slowed our pace. "'Ganja' is marijuana, and unless you want to be thrown into a Jamaican prison, keep walking."

That was all I needed to hear to increase my gait and head in the opposite direction. In a matter of minutes we reached the open air bazaar that was little more than a shanty town comprised of shacks filled with cheap knickknacks. We were immediately accosted by several vendors all claiming to have the best deals. I quickly dismissed them with a wave of my hand. I wasn't interested in any of their wares and intended to buy souvenirs in the resort gift shop. Tom, on the other hand, was bartering with a woman wrapped in bright colors and costume jewelry over a set of bamboo mugs. Her braids bobbed in unison with her headshakes, first no and then yes. Tom was so pleased with himself over his bargaining skills when he convinced her to drop the asking price of twenty dollars to a mere two dollars per mug. I didn't have the heart to tell him that because the handles were actually blooming, he wouldn't be able to take them through U.S. Customs.

We left the market and came across Jimmy Buffet's Margaritaville where we appreciated a refreshing frozen margarita but lost track of time. We raced the sunset to get ourselves back to the resort before darkness descended and realized that "island time" was contagious. The two of us enjoyed another excellent meal by candlelight with a view of the ocean. The waiter who served our coffee poured in just enough brandy to light the liquid and smiled broadly when Tom tipped him ten dollars. We returned to our room and went to bed early as tomorrow would bring another ad- venture. We were going to climb the falls of Dunn's River, and I looked forward to the outing.

Morning greeted me with gray skies and drizzle, so I called the front desk to confirm the excursion and was assured the van would be waiting in front of the hotel at ten o'clock. That's all I needed to know to give Tom a shoulder shake to wake him for breakfast. We grabbed our backpacks and threw in a couple of towels, snacks, bottled water, and our required water shoes. When we arrived at the falls, Tom pointed out that it wasn't neces- sary to take up luggage space by packing our own shoes because there were several vendors that rented them for a nominal fee. I looked at him like he had three heads. "Excuse me, but have we met? There's no way in hell I'm renting a pair of shoes that have been worn by everybody and his brother. Honestly, sometimes it's like you don't even *know* me!"

He conceded with "Yes, dear," and thanked me for sparing him the horror of wearing used shoes. Tom wore sarcasm well. We followed the guide along a trail that led to the midway point of the falls. As we pro- ceed to climb upwards, the leader advised us to use caution on the slip- pery rocks and to stay together. The sky held ominous clouds, and we collectively surveyed the falls and moved carefully over the wet boulders. When we reached the top, there was a small area where we took a break before we began the descent, which proved more difficult than the climb. Nonetheless, the treacherous trek was well worth it when we reached the bottom of the falls where the cascading river raced down the lush, green mountain and across the beach to greet the shore of the turquoise Caribbean. The adventure came to a close, and our group was reluctantly led back to the parking lot.

Once deposited at the entrance I realized the day trip had been more strenuous than I'd anticipated. We grabbed a quick bite in one of the casual cafés and retired to our room, showered, put on pajamas, and dropped into comfortable chairs on the balcony. The sky was dark and menacing, and the wind was wrathful as it blew white caps over the deserted beach. We hadn't heard the latest weather regarding the hurricane, no doubt not an accident. After all, there was no need to unduly panic the guests. Nonetheless, I was sure that if we were in imminent danger, we would have been evacuated and relocated inland or to higher ground in the mountains.

Unconcerned about the impending storm, I yawned and suggested to Tom that we turn in early since tomorrow was our big day, our wedding day. Tom smiled and eagerly followed me to bed where sleep was postponed before we slept entwined in each other's arms. I was awakened early in the morning by the sound of torrential rain and the banging of a stray shutter that had escaped its hinges. The bedside clock informed me that it was almost seven. I sat up and looked around the room and saw my wedding dress hanging on the closet's louvered door. Rain slammed against the French doors, but the reinforced doors held firmly against the onslaught. I turned on the television and found a local weather station that reported the hurricane was fifty miles offshore and was diminishing as it turned away from Jamaica. The rain, however, would bombard the island for the next twenty-four hours.

I clicked the t.v. off and accepted that we would be married in a downpour. There was nothing to be done about the weather, so I pulled the covers over my head and drifted off to sleep. An hour later Tom's soft kisses trickled down my cheeks and neck. "Good morning, my bride. Are you ready to spend the rest of your life with me?"

I rolled over and snuggled into the curve of his arm. "Yes, a hundred times, yes. I just wish the weather was better. I hate the idea of walking down the aisle looking like a drowned rat. Do you think the photographer can work some voodoo magic so the pictures will be okay?"

"Don't worry about the rain or how you're gonna look. This is our wedding day, and nothing else matters." He gave me a passionate, lingering kiss that made me forget about the rain. "We better get a move on. We need to shower and throw on something comfortable for breakfast before the day gets away from us. We can't be late for the five o'clock ceremony, no matter what the islanders say about time." He lovingly caressed my back. "You've made me happier than I've ever been, and I promise to cherish you every day that I live."

I snuggled closer. "Hey, save that sweet talk for the vows."

We held each other close, and I marveled that I'd fallen in love, something I never could have imagined only a few years ago. That was before I met Tom, an easy man to love. I pushed the comforter aside and hopped out of bed. "Looks like I'll be first to shower."

He smiled and chased me into the bathroom. "Nothing says we can't share a shower."

The day went by in a blur as we prepared to say our "I dos." Tom was dressed and ready by four, but I still had some final touchups to makeup; my hair was bound in hot rollers. I sent him away because I didn't want him to see me in my dress until I made my way to the altar. "Please go to the bar and have a beer. The wedding planner will meet you there in half an hour and escort you to the gazebo before she comes to get me. Hopefully, she'll have a very large umbrella."

"Stop worrying about the rain. You're going to be a beautiful bride."

"Thanks. I happen to be marrying a very handsome groom."

I kissed him and sent him downstairs to wait while I finished my makeup and pulled rollers from my hair. I carefully slipped the ivory dress over my head and donned pearl earrings and a matching necklace—my something "borrowed" from Pat. I turned to assess the image in the mirror. She was a far cry from the young girl who'd eloped decades ago. The woman who stared back at me had lived a life filled with challenges, joys, and sorrows. She was a survivor who stood glowing with happiness. I smiled and spritzed on perfume just as Monique tapped on the door, which I promptly opened.

"Oh, my, you look the way all brides should. You're radiant, Sheila. Are you ready to go? Your husband-to-be and the pastor are waiting in the gazebo."

I picked up the trailing bouquet of colorful island flowers, with its Bird of Paradise and orchid centerpiece and replied, "Thank you for the compliment. And, yes, I'm as ready as I'll ever be." Rain flowed over the balcony, and the surf pounded the shore. "I wish the weather had cooperated and sent sunshine instead of this deluge."

"Don't be sad about the rain, mon. The skies pour showers of blessings on your marriage."

I didn't know whether she believed that or if she was merely attempting to console me. It didn't matter, so I dismissed the weather and was met in the lobby by one of our witnesses who held an umbrella over me as we exited. He was taller than I and walked with me as I eased down the soggy pathway strewn with rose petals. Shania Twain's "From This Moment" wasn't the traditional wedding march, but the song Tom and I selected held special meaning for us both as we left our broken roads behind to begin a new life together.

Thomas and Levi were disappointed at not having been included in the Jamaican trip, but Tom reminded them that we'd taken them on an adventurous two week trip out West the past summer. As they weren't the only ones unable to attend the wedding for various reasons, family and friends planned a reception for the weekend after our return as man and wife. At least, I hoped we were married. When I made the arrangements, I'd requested a Baptist minister to perform the ceremony. Nevertheless, as we'd sat in the bar waiting for a dinner table the night after our wedding, my husband had pointed out a resemblance between the minister who married us and the bartender. "Do you think the guy making drinks is the same man who married us?"

Exasperated, I'd replied, "Really, Tom, I don't think a Baptist minister would be moonlighting as a bartender." I argued that perhaps they were brothers or the likeness was nothing more than a coincidence. Either way, we'd been given a marriage certificate after the ceremony, along with the top tier of the small wedding cake that I carried on our flight home amid protests from the flight attendant. I assured her that the cake had gone through the scanner at security and that I would strap the cake in the empty seat beside me. Tom, on the other hand, was relieved of his prized bamboo mugs before we boarded.

Other than that minor difference of opinion there were no other problems, and we landed in Atlanta where we'd left our car at a park 'n go so as not to inconvenience anyone with a dreaded trip to the airport. It was Saturday morning, and we had much to do before greeting our guests at the Lion's Club golf venue where the reception in our honor was to be held that evening. The "fairies" had done a fantastic job in arranging everything from mailing the invitations to food, including a second wedding cake. Flowers, decorations, and a disc jockey completed the soirée. The happy occasion was a large gathering of friends and family where gifts, hugs, and wishes for a long and happy marriage were bestowed upon us. Unfortunately, neither Tom's mama nor sister was in attendance, although they were on the guest list. I was disappointed that they snubbed our attempt to include them but didn't let their absence detract from our celebration.

After the party we helped with cleanup before Tom, his sons, and I left for home. It was after eleven, and I was ready for bed. I yawned pointedly and speculated as to why none of them made any pretext of going home until the realization hit me that they *were* home. I'd lived alone for years, but what had previously been my home was now our home. I stood and stretched and suggested we all hit the sack, and the boys said their goodnights and went to their rooms. Tom grabbed a bottle of wine and two glasses and led me to the seclusion of the porch for a private, wel-come home get-together before we settled into what became a routine of normalcy.

As expected, there was an adjustment period. I'd forgotten how much laundry four people required and how much food growing boys consumed. Thomas and Levi had been taking turns doing the laundry when it was the three of them, but I made a deal with them that I would do the laundry if they would take responsibility for keeping their rooms clean. It helped that Tom was supportive, such as when I asked Thomas to take out the trash. He scowled and weighed his choices until his daddy sternly admonished, "Don't make her ask you twice."

Thomas took out the trash without complaint, but I later overheard him ask Tom if all women were as bossy as I was. Levi had the same question, but before Tom could say anything, I entered the family room and snapped, "Listen you two, if you did what you were supposed to do without me asking, then I wouldn't have to constantly remind you to pick up after yourselves. Until you do, you'll just have to tolerate my nagging. One day, when you're married, you'll both thank me. So will your wives."

Undoubtedly, part of my grumpiness could be blamed on hormones. My first husband and set of sons had to cope with my severe PMS and monthly mood swings, and it seemed my second family would have to endure the fluctuating hormones of perimenopause. In one of my unreason-able outbursts Tom tried to calm me down to no avail, and I yelled, "As a man, you have no idea what it's like to go through menopause!"

His response was quick and to the point. "The hell I don't! I've walked every mile of that road with you, so don't tell me I don't know about the hot flashes and night sweats and temper tantrums. There are days I pull in the driveway and don't want to get out of the truck. Between your roller coaster hormones and the boys' raging puberty hormones, I dread going in the house because I never know what kinda storm is brewin'."

To be fair, he had a point. I apologized and made an appointment with my gynecologist to discuss the transition through unfamiliar territory. Dr. Martin ordered bloodwork to verify my hormone levels and prescribed a low-dose combination hormone replacement treatment. Thankfully, by the time the holiday season arrived, I was feeling much better and the uncomfortable symptoms and fit flingin' had, for the most part, subsided. Our Thanksgiving and Christmas as one big family were special occasions as we celebrated our blessings and the beginning of a New Year. A year that brought heartbreak and happiness to my life.

Chapter Sixteen

Life Is a Journey

It was a bitterly cold January afternoon when Jerline called me at my office to ask a favor. "I hate to bother you at work and to ask you to take a day off, Sheila, but could you possibly go with Jerry and me to see the oncologist tomorrow? We were called this morning and told an appointment has been scheduled in the morning to go over Jerry's latest scans."

"An oncologist?" I was aware that my oldest brother was having some medical issues and had been undergoing tests, but the "C word" was never mentioned. "Yes, of course, I'll go with you. Is the oncologist at Piedmont, or was Jerry referred to another facility?"

"Thank you. It's just that I'm a bundle of nerves about this latest round of test results, and you've been down this road before. We'd both feel better if we had someone with us, you know, in case the news is bad. And, yes, the office is located near Piedmont. Jerry plans to drive, but we need you for moral support and to ask questions that may not occur to us."

"I'll do what I can to help. After the many times you were there for me during Barry's illness, I'm indebted to you both. What time should I be ready to leave?"

"His appointment is at ten o'clock, but considering the traffic Jerry wants to leave by eight-thirty. Thanks, Sheila." Her voice was muffled through her tears as she whispered, "Please pray for him. And for me. I'm not strong like you, Sheila."

Strong like me? Clearly, she'd forgotten the days when suicide was preferable to my pain. There was no need in reminding her of what she might be facing so I said, "Absolutely. I'll see y'all in the morning."

Dawn tiptoed through the blinds after my restless night of worry. I stared at the ceiling and recalled Jerline's comment about handling adversity and what she'd said when Barry died. My sister-in-law conceded that I was stronger than she could ever be should anything happen to Jerry. She confessed that she wouldn't be able to live without him, a confession I'd resented at the time. I'd wanted to scream at her, to demand to know why she thought she wasn't capable of burying her husband when I'd buried mine. I pushed those negative thoughts aside as I put on a pot of coffee, showered, and dressed. I prayed for my brother and that the news wouldn't be as bad as Jerline feared.

Unfortunately, it was worse. The doctor entered the exam room and introduced himself to each of us. He shook Jerry's hand and looked him in the eye. "I'm sorry we have to meet under such circumstances, but you were referred to me for a second opinion." Sleet began to fall and pinged on the window. Jerry, Jerline, and I remained silent as we waited for him to continue. "I don't enjoy being the bearer of bad news, but it is my responsibility to be honest with each of my patients." He cleared his throat while we waited with tension that was tangible.

Jerry quietly prompted, "What is it you have to say, doctor?"

He pushed his glasses onto his forehead and let out a heavy sigh. "You have stage four liver cancer, and there's nothing that can be done. I'm so very sorry."

Jerline visibly shrank into a huddle of hysteria, and I tried to console her but needed to find out more from the doctor who had, in effect, signed my brother's death certificate. "I don't understand. Why can't you recommend radiation or chemotherapy or a liver transplant? There have to be treatments to consider."

Jerry remained silent, and Jerline whimpered in the corner. The doctor addressed me. "Because the cancer is too advanced for either radiation or chemo to be successful. As for a transplant, cancer patients are not viable candidates. As I said, there are no treatment options available." He turned his attention to my stunned brother. "I suggest you get your affairs in order, sir. The reality is that, at best, you have six months to live. We can, of course, control your pain with morphine. I truly wish I could offer you hope, but I'm being honest when I tell you that there's nothing medically we can do. To tell you otherwise would be misleading."

Jerline was unable to deal with the devastating news. She retrieved a bottle of Xanax from her purse and was eatin' like M&M's. Jerry hung his head in abject resignation. While I was all too familiar with the cruelty of cancer, I refused to accept the facts we were given and pleaded with the apathetic doctor to offer alternatives to acceptance.

He brushed my pleas aside with an air of arrogance, as if Jerry were no longer his concern. "I've already told you there isn't anything I or anyone else can do for your brother."

"That can't be the end of this discussion. Surely there is another oncologist who can recommend some kind of treatment. What about a partial liver transplant? He has an identical twin brother who lives in Florida, and even though Gene has had some health problems of his own, I'm sure he'd be willing to donate a portion of his liver to save his brother. If he's not physically able to have the surgery, then test me. I'm his sister, and I'm young and healthy."

"I'm sorry, but the diagnosis is final. Even if you were a match, it would be too little too late. The scans indicated that the cancer is present outside the liver."

With that, he gathered the charts and left us alone. I didn't expect the news to be good, but nor was I prepared for the finality of the diagnosis. Jerry's knees buckled as he slid from the exam table, and his voice wavered. "Sheila, I don't think I'm in any shape to drive us home, and neither is Jerline." He pulled car keys from his pocket and handed them to me. "Do you mind driving?"

I fought with tears that begged to be released and took the keys. "No, not at all. We'll make you comfortable so you can rest. Jerline can sit up front with me."

The three of us made our way to the covered parking lot. Jerry stretched out in the backseat, and pulled a blanket up to his chin. I helped Jerline into the passenger seat where she slipped into a Xanax coma. I slid behind the steering wheel and adjusted the seat and rearview mirror for a drive home that seemed interminable. Jerry never spoke a word, and I stared cautiously out the window as the wipers fought to keep sleet off the windshield. We finally pulled into their icy driveway, and I helped them to their den where Jerline dropped onto the loveseat, and Jerry collapsed in his recliner. I lit the gas logs to knock the chill out of the room, turned on a small lamp, and sat in a rocker beside him. There was a serenity about Jerry, and I wondered if he'd suspected what the doctor confirmed. An hour passed with the ticking of the grandfather clock and they both fell asleep, a blissful respite from reality.

There was nothing else to be done. I locked the door behind me, pulled my jacket tighter against the icy pelts, and walked the half mile to my home where the tears were allowed to flow freely. Once I'd composed myself I began calling my brothers and sisters, who'd left messages on my machine inquiring about the outcome of the tests. Afterwards, I called Tom who was sympathetic and offered to leave work early, but I assured him that wasn't necessary and that I had to notify one more person. With a heavy heart I bundled up against the cold and made the short drive to the nursing home to tell Daddy that his son was dying.

I entered the darkened room where Daddy was dozing in the recliner as an old John Wayne movie blared from the t.v. I picked up the remote and turned off the distraction of gunslingers. The silence awakened him, and I flipped on a bedside lamp. He was momentarily disoriented but found his voice. "Hey, sugar. What are you doing here this time of day? Shouldn't you be at work?"

"Yes, Daddy, but I needed to take the day off. I went to Atlanta with Jerry and Jerline to see the oncologist."

"Oncologist? That's a cancer doctor, ain't it? What did he have to say?"

I didn't realize that a ninety-one year old man could hold his breath. "It's not good news, Daddy." I grasped his wrinkled, withered hand. There was no easy way to say it, and I blurted, "Jerry's dying. He has maybe six months at the most."

Daddy exhaled and tightly clutched my hand. "How's he takin' it?"

"I think he's accepted his fate and seems to be at peace with it. He asked about another opinion, more tests, but the oncologist assured him that if any other doctor gave him hope, it would be false hope. Jerline's a train wreck."

Daddy released my hand and asked me to help him to the bed where he lay lifeless, and I couldn't begin to grasp what he must've been feeling. It could be the same sense of loss and longing, a longing to do something when there was nothing to be done, that I felt. It was several minutes before he spoke. "You need to call the preacher and have him add Jerry to the prayer requests. Don't know if God has a miracle for my son, but it won't hurt to pray for one."

"No, Daddy, it won't hurt. I'll call Curtis when I get home and let him know what's going on with our family and to ask for prayers."

Daddy shifted his weight and asked me to turn off the lamp. "You should be gettin' back to the house before darkness sets in, in case the roads freeze over."

"Yes, Daddy." I stood, kissed his forehead, and left him alone with his sorrow.

The sands of the hourglass flowed rapidly towards Jerry's impending passing as we waited helplessly for the inevitable, an outcome he'd accepted. He was spared the trauma of chemo and instead was prescribed morphine to control the ever-increasing pain. Despite the circumstances Jerry clung to his faith, put his affairs in order, and did his best to prepare Jerline for the arrival of Death. I didn't want to intrude on the couple's privacy but visited often and offered what little solace I could. For the most part my life continued to be busy and full with family and work. Time was relevant for all of us, and winter's slumber was awakened by the arrival of spring.

It was a spring that brought with it the renewal of life in more ways than one. I was at the office when Brad called sometime after ten o'clock to tell me that Valerie, who'd been on bedrest for the past few weeks due to a difficult pregnancy, was in labor early. Her obstetrician made the decision to perform an emergency C-section at noon, and I assured Brad that I would meet them at the hospital. My grandson would be a preemie, and I prayed he would be a healthy baby.

I hurriedly explained circumstances to my boss and that I had to leave for the day. I grabbed the phone to call Tom and share the news. His voice was tense when he answered, and he sounded stressed. "Hi babe, I'm about to walk into a job meeting. Can I get back to you later?"

"Actually, I'm on my way to the hospital. Brad called a few minutes ago to tell me that he and Valerie on their way. She's having an emergency C-section at twelve o'clock because Jackson is going to make his appearance early. Sorry I caught you at a bad time, but I wanted you to know and—"

"Oh, no, Sheila! I can't be there for his birth. Honey, I'm so sorry, not to mention disappointed. This meeting is important to the project, and the architect flew in from New York to review changes before the deadline. If I didn't absolutely have to be here, I would leave now."

"It's okay. Really, I understand. I know this project has consumed you, and you need to be there. I've gotta run, but I'll call you as soon as I can." I hung up the phone, called Pat to apprise her of the situation with a promise to call her later, and sprinted out the door.

The traffic was slow in Carrollton that time of day, and I was lucky to find a parking space at the always busy Tanner Medical Center. An elderly lady dressed in pink directed me to the correct floor, and her face lit up with a smile when I told her my first grandson would be arriving at noon. I waited impatiently for the elevator doors to open and hurriedly stepped into the hallway that led to the maternity waiting room. A nurse informed me that Valerie had already been taken back to the OR to be prepped and that Brad was with her. I found a vacant chair and picked up a magazine just as Valerie's parents, Roy and Sara, came in to join me.

The two of them were carrying on a conversation, so I returned to the hallway to pace and wait for Brad to come through the double doors with good news. The fast-paced clunking of work boots on tile caught my attention, and I glanced down the hallway to see Tom approaching, wearing a big smile. Surprised, I rushed to meet him, and he embraced me with a bear hug and questions. "Did I make it in time? Has the baby arrived? How's Valerie?"

"What are you doing here? What about the mandatory meeting?"

He shrugged as if it wasn't a big deal when it was. "I was sitting there, taking notes, when it hit me that my grandson was going to be here at lunchtime and that I would miss the event for yet another mundane job meeting. So I excused myself due to a family emergency and hauled ass out of Atlanta." He checked his watch. "It's a quarter till twelve. Is he here yet?"

I threw myself in his arms and hugged him. "No, not yet. Dr. Martin is here so it shouldn't be much longer. Brad and Valerie, understandably, want some time with the baby before we'll be allowed to see him. Brad promised to update all of us as soon as the baby is here."

I linked my arm through his and walked him towards the waiting room where we were joined a few minutes later by my oldest son, a very proud daddy. Mother and baby were doing well, and when I finally got the chance to cradle my tiny, healthy, and perfect grandangel in my arms, the same sense of overwhelming love I had when I first held Brenna filled my heart and soul. There were also the same bittersweet tears that Barry wasn't there to hold his grandson.

Tom handed me a tissue as he wrapped his arms around both baby and me and whispered, "Don't be a baby hog. It's my turn to hold him. After all, Jackson and his Poppy are going to have to get to know each other, too."

My tears were suddenly tears of gratitude.

My bliss was short-lived when Jerline called a month later to tell me that hospice was called to offer assistance during Jerry's final days. One afternoon, at Jerline's request, I walked over to sit with him while she ran a few necessary errands. He was resting when I arrived, and I sat next to the hospital bed that was rented to keep him more comfortable. I thought he was sleeping when he stirred and asked for a sip of water and thanked me for the simple favor. We sat in silence for a few minutes, and I noticed a single tear that slipped down his cheek.

Prayers for Jerry were not answered, and I could find no words of comfort until I noticed his tattered Bible on the coffee table. Many of the pages were dog-eared, with several passages of Scripture highlighted, but the one that caught my attention as appropriate was the 23rd Psalm. I held his hand and began to read, "The Lord is my shepherd; I shall not want." By the time I finished with the words "…I will dwell in the house of the Lord forever," a sense of peace enveloped us both. That was the last time I saw my brother.

Daddy refused to attend the funeral, claiming that he was not physically able to go. Cindy offered to make arrangements for an ambulance to transport him from the nursing home to the service, but he declined. I suspected he was emotionally unable to bury his oldest son. Afterwards, Tom and I went to visit Daddy and found him staring out the window. He didn't acknowledge our presence for several minutes, and he never turned to face us. He eventually asked but one question: "Is it over?"

I walked to where he sat dejectedly and gently touched his shoulder. "Yes, Daddy, the service is over, and he was buried in our family plot, right next to where Mama was laid to rest." There was no need to mention that he would also be buried beside Mama. "Would you like us to stay with you for a while?"

His reflection revealed the moisture that glistened in his weary eyes, and late afternoon sunlight painted shadows across the traces of time, every wrinkle a story. Daddy's heartbreak was tangible, and I bent to hug him. He brushed me away and without a word, waved his hand in dismissal. I didn't want to leave him alone with his grief, but Tom put his arm around me and led me towards the hallway. I paused at the door and turned to see an old man, head down, frail shoulders shuddering with the weight of his tears.

While Jerry's death was expected, Jerline's was not. Two months after Jerry's funeral my neighbor, Ricky, called to tell me that an ambulance had rushed into the neighborhood. He followed it to its destination, which was my late brother's home. He thought I would want to know, and I thanked him. As it was late Tom and the boys were sleeping, and there was no need to disturb them. I hurriedly dressed, snatched up car keys, and dashed out the door.

When I arrived the ambulance was in the driveway, and a paramedic was working over Jerline's lifeless body. A woman in uniform saw me standing there, watching the surreal scene before me, and closed the doors of the emergency vehicle. I stood alone and motionless in the glow of rotating red lights that sliced through the darkness. Several minutes later the woman climbed out and asked me to move my car. I followed the ambulance to the hospital, as did Jerline's divorced son who lived with her and had called 9-1-1 when he found her unconscious on the kitchen floor.

Jerline died of a brain aneurysm a few hours later and once again our families gathered for another funeral to say the goodbyes we were denied. Death was cruel, whether it was anticipated or whether it caught us off guard, leaving us stunned and saddened. Experience had taught me that despite tragedy and heartache, life goes on. I mourned the loss of Jerry and Jerline and grieved for them, but my life moved forward with a predictable rhythm.

Summer fell into fall, and Thanksgiving was behind us. The Christmas season was in full swing, and I'd already shopped for my two grandangels who continued to fill my days with joy. My happiness was interrupted when Pat called to tell me that Daddy had been transported to the ER in Carrollton. I left the office to meet her at the hospital and to await the diagnosis. Pneumonia wasn't necessarily a death sentence, but Daddy's doctor didn't offer us much hope for recovery. "Your father is despondent, and his body is weak. I'll do all that I medically can, but you both have to realize that there's not much chance of improvement. At his advanced age, he will most likely continue to deteriorate."

We thanked the doctor and helped Daddy get settled in his room before we called Gene, Donnie, and Joyce to give our siblings the news. Gene was the only one of us who didn't live nearby, and had made the trip from Merritt Island only a few months ago to see his twin brother before he died and to attend Jerry's funeral. We promised to keep him in the loop, and the four of us coordinated our visits to sit with Daddy. A few days later it was my shift on a wintry afternoon when Daddy asked for strawberry ice cream, a favorite treat of his before he was diagnosed with diabetes a decade earlier. I left his bedside to oblige.

"Excuse me, nurse? My daddy is a patient in room 307 and has asked for ice cream. Do you have strawberry stocked in the patients' refrigerator?"

She ignored my question while she perused Daddy's medical info. "I'm sorry, but he's a diabetic and isn't allowed to have ice cream." She snapped the chart shut with finality. "Maybe you can bring him some sugar-free the next time you—"

"My daddy is dying, so his diabetes isn't really an issue. 'Next time' may not be a possibility." I smiled sweetly with eyes of steel. "If necessary I can get out on this frigid day and drive to Kroger for the ice cream he wants, or you can save me the trip by getting a container from the stash in the freezer. Either way, my daddy is going to have strawberry ice cream today."

She hesitated momentarily but realized I was dead damn serious. She stood and moved towards the mini-fridge. "All right, then. I believe we do have strawberry on hand. I'll bring a cup to his room when I have time."

My voice dripped with sarcasm. "Your compassion is a credit to your profession. Don't forget to bring a spoon."

The treat arrived within minutes, and while Daddy was able to only swallow a few bites he declared, "That's the best strawberry ice cream I've ever had. Thank you, sugar."

"You're welcome, Daddy. Try to rest now. Donnie will be here in an hour or so, and I'm sure you'd like to visit with him." I opened a book

I'd taken along to pass the time, but Daddy was restless, and I asked, "Is there anything I can do to make you comfortable? Do you need a drink of water?"

He remained silent, as if collecting his thoughts. "I'm an old man, and I'm tired. I've buried my wife and two of my children. Barry, too, who was like another son to me." He shifted his frail body, and I fluffed his pillow. "I haven't always been the man I should've been. If I hadn't been a drunkard, I could've been one of the best salesman any of 'em clothing plants ever had." He paused to catch his breath. "I could've been a better husband, better to all you kids, but I drank and hard liquor eats away at a man's soul from the inside out. Never knew what I was lookin' for at the bottom of a bottle, but it cost me a lot of years that should've been spent making life easier for your mama."

"We all have our regrets, Daddy." He'd been a functioning alcoholic for decades, but I barely remembered the man my older brothers and sisters grew up with so couldn't speak to those years. Instead I said the only thing I could think of to console him. "You gave up your vices years ago and repented. God forgave your sins, and you have to do the same."

As if he hadn't heard me he rambled on. "I'm afraid. Afraid to die, afraid of what's on the other side of death. Even though I've been saved and baptized and the Bible tells us not to fear death, I can't lay my fears aside."

I wasn't prepared for his anxiety about the afterlife. I was at a loss but then thought of one of our porch talks, which I recounted. I pushed my chair closer to the bed and took his fragile hand in mine. "Daddy, do you remember the time a few years ago, when you were still able to drive and were riding through the countryside?" He remained silent and I resumed, "It was a route you'd taken dozens of times, past our church and out by Great-Grandma Carroll's homeplace next to the old General Store."

He nodded. "Yes, I remember that day, the day I came up to a four-way stop and knew I was lost. I didn't know where I was or how to find my way home. I was scared."

"I know you were, Daddy, but then you prayed and asked God to show you the way home. You told me that you were suddenly surrounded by light, a brilliant white light you couldn't explain. And when the light vanished as suddenly as it had appeared, you were lucid and knew exactly where you were and how to get home."

He gave me a feeble smile and asked, "Do you think that's what heaven will be like, a white light guiding me home?"

"I don't know, Daddy. Nobody knows. We just have to trust that our faith will be rewarded."

His worry lines eased into calmness, and he was sleeping when Donnie arrived to take my place. It was Donnie who called a few hours later to tell me that our daddy had died quietly in his sleep. The official cause of death was pneumonia, but I often wondered if Daddy died of a broken heart filled with regrets.

The year of three funerals, as it came to be referred, passed, and months blew across the calendar like tumbleweed across the desert. Before I could blink Brenna and Jackson were in first grade and Pre-K; Thomas and Levi were in high school. Sports spun from one season to the next, and I sat in the heat, rain, and cold to show my support from the stands. Girlfriends came and went, as girlfriends had a tendency to do. Tom lectured both boys about safe sex and made it clear that should their carelessness result in a teenage pregnancy, they would be responsible for the baby. To which Thomas replied, "I know, Dad. Twenty minutes of sex won't be worth the consequences."

Twenty minutes! Bless his naïve, sixteen-year-old heart. Thomas had an accident of another sort, a minor car wreck in which the only casualty was a mailbox. He was banged up, as was his car, but he was alone and wasn't seriously hurt. My bonus boys, as I'd deemed them, didn't give us any major problems. Admittedly, there were a few bumps in the road, but we navigated those setbacks together as the family we'd become. Thomas and Levi were gentle souls, and even though I hadn't given birth to them, they were my sons.

Although, after our engagement I'd expressed concern to Daddy about starting over with a ready-made family. He consoled me with, "Aw, sugar, 'em boys will be grown before you can turn around" And they were. Thomas and Levi graduated high school and as neither was academically inclined, they made the decision to move in with some friends and to find their own paths. I strongly disagreed with that decision, but Tom pointed out that they were young men and, as such, could make their own choices. Others were not given an option regarding their fate, as Charlcie learned a few months later when she was diagnosed with stage-four breast cancer.

Tom was distraught when his mama elected to forgo the mastectomy, chemo, and radiation treatments recommended by her oncologist. Her argument to Tom and his sister was that she'd read the medical brochures that outlined standard treatment and side effects. Having personally witnessed the debilitating aftereffects of cancer treatments, a part of me agreed with Charlcie. The doctor assured them all that without those medical procedures, she wouldn't live more than six months. But Charlcie stood her ground and refused treatment. She hadn't made the choice to have cancer, but she made the choice on how, and pretty much when, she would die.

Four months later she was in the care of hospice and was literally lying on her death bed when she told Tom that she wanted to see me. It wasn't that I had no compassion for his mama, but she and I had had a fractious relationship at best. Despite that fact I'd offered to help in any way that I could during her illness, but my offer was disregarded, and I respected the boundaries Charlcie put in place. Therefore, I was surprised when Tom called to tell me that his dying mama had asked to see me and that I shouldn't waste time obliging her request.

I left immediately for the hospital and slipped into the darkened room where Charlcie's breathing was noticeably labored. Tom led me to her bedside and she smiled in the dim light as she reached for my hand and motioned me closer. I leaned over the bed rails until I could hear her whisper, "I'm sorry, Sheila, for treating you so bad all these years. You're a kind woman to marry a man with two kids, and I know you've been good to all of them. I never doubted that you loved my son, and I need you to forgive me for not accepting you as his wife."

Tears I didn't anticipate stung my eyes. "You have my forgiveness, Charlcie, but there's really nothing to forgive. We both love the same man, and I'm sorry if you ever felt that I was somehow taking your son away from you. That was certainly not my intention, and I never put limits on how much time Tom wanted to spend with you or questioned his financial assistance. I'm just sorry the two of us couldn't have crossed this bridge years ago."

Charlcie nodded her agreement. "Me, too. I know that's my fault, and I regret that we didn't become friends." She patted my hand affectionately. "Thank you for coming, Sheila, and thank you for loving my son and grandsons. And for forgiving an ornery old woman."

I left a while later so that Tom and Nita could have their mama transported home, where she wanted to die. I was awake the next morning before my alarm clock buzzed, waiting to hear from Tom. He called shortly after daybreak to tell me his mama was gone.

The funeral was, of course, as Charlcie had wanted it to be, and Nita and her family returned to their home in Warner Robins. Tom's homeplace was left to him and Nita, but his sister made it clear to Tom that she had no interest in moving back to the area; she wanted to sell the house and ten acres of land as soon as possible. Despite the fact that he didn't need a place to live, Tom immediately offered to buy Nita's share of their inheritance—an offer she readily accepted. Maybe owning a home was his security blanket.

Tom admitted that it had taken his mama's death to remind him that life was short and that our days were numbered. Perhaps it was that slap in the face by his own mortality that prompted him to pursue his dream of having a lake place and led us to what became known as "Poppy's Place." The recreational lot was large, with lots of shade trees, and included a dock that waded into the water and where brightly colored umbrellas protected us from the summer sun. Tom's first purchase was a pontoon big enough for all of us to glide lazily across the thirty-thousand acre lake.

His next purchase was a camper with bunk beds for Brenna and Jackson so they could spend some of their weekends at the lake where they created happy childhood memories. We toasted marshmallows around a campfire, fished, and swam; Tom pulled the kids behind the pontoon in an oversized towable while spray and sunshine bounced on their smiling faces. They couldn't wait to feed impatient ducks that quacked expectantly. Family cookouts included cornhole games, Frisbees, and water gun battles. Tom added a couple of jet skis to our inventory, and we spent hours chasing the sun.

My husband's long-held dream wasn't my dream, but I came to cherish those summer weekends when we escaped to the lake. Poppy's Place was a retreat where family and friends gathered under the cooling shade of oak trees, where a tire swing hung from a huge limb, and where a bright yellow picnic table held enough food for us and for anyone else who happened along. It was a peaceful, happy place where visitors lost track of time as they slowed down to savor the day. Laughter floated to the clouds, and colorful beach towels snapped in a breeze that threatened to pull them from the clothesline where they were hung to dry. Poppy's Place was where we sipped lemonade, swapped stories, and reminisced over shared experiences.

One such experience was the day a few of us were caught on the lake in the pontoon when an unpredicted thunderstorm arrived with a vengeance. White-capped waves rolled beneath gray skies, and an angry wind whipped across the water. No doubt friends Judy and Paul appreciated the memory more than the actual experience. But most days were pleasant.

Brad considered the jet ski to be a dirt bike on water, and he and Valerie loved to play under blue skies. But Chuck and Geri preferred the comfort of the pontoon. The lake became one of teenagers Thomas and Levi's favorite places for them and their friends. Denise, a friend who'd grown up enjoying a lake, liked to swim in the cool, clear water. Jan, on the other hand, shocked us all by actually getting in the lake. Of course, she planted herself on a float and clung to it for dear life. In contrast, Cindy and Kim enjoyed lounging on a float and soaking up the sun, but we'd learned to tie the floats to the dock, lest they drift too far—again.

The lake was also where I learned more about pontoons than I wanted to know. For example, the depth finder was located at the *back* of the boat. I discovered that bit of information quite by accident when Donnie and Shelby were cruising the lake with Tom and me. Shelby and I were sitting in the front and saw a sandbar just in front of us, so I asked Tom the depth of the water. He told me that we were at five feet, so neither Shelby nor I said mentioned the sandbar—until we ran aground, and the pontoon came to a grinding halt. Tom and Donnie had plenty to say when they had to push the pontoon out of the shallows with the emergency paddles onboard. Oh well.

Then there was the summer lake neighbors Tina and Dwayne put their pontoon in the water, and there was a snake napping in the storage cubby hole. When the stowaway was discovered, those on board screamed and bailed as if the boat was on fire. The snake didn't waste any time abandoning the boat, either. One of the guys who jumped off the boat attacked the slimy creature with an oar. I decided he was my new best friend.

Those and other stories had different versions that were retold every summer, but nobody tired of hearing them. What Poppy's Place lacked in grandeur, it more than made up for in treasured time together and lasting memories.

One evening after sunset and after everyone packed up and left their idyllic getaway, Tom and I walked to the dock where oversized, fish-shaped, Adirondack chairs waited for us to collapse. A full moon climbed over the cove, and a soft summer breeze whispered over the glistening, calm water that reflected the moon's glow. The campfire crackled in the background, accompanied by the sound of a crane that soared overhead and of frogs whose loud croaks announced rain was approaching. Tom reached for my hand, and we sat savoring the stillness of the night. It had taken a few weeks for me to realize that although I didn't think a lake place was what I needed, it turned out to be exactly what I needed.

Life unobtrusively carried us forward. The Grandangels were growing up much too quickly, faster than had my own children. Thomas and Levi left the limitations of Bremen to pursue careers in the oil fields of Texas where work was plentiful and there was money to be made for those willing to work. Thomas wasn't tied to Bremen and even though he'd had girlfriends that included two or three serious relationships, he decided that bachelorhood suited his rolling stone lifestyle. Levi, on the other hand, married Sarah, whom he'd met in high school, and they gave us the gift of a new baby.

I held his tiny perfection with a heart that didn't recognize genetics but overflowed with love for the third time. Despite that Levi was gone for weeks on end, and it was not the ideal living situation, he worked hard to provide for his wife and son, Cash. He'd learned responsibility and sacrifice from his dad's example, and I was proud of the young men the boys had grown to be. I also admired them for having the courage to follow the road of opportunities.

Our lives were content, and three years later Sarah gave birth to our fourth grandangel, a beautiful baby girl named Scoutt while living in Texas. Pat, Sarah's mama, was with her daughter when her granddaughter was born; Tom and I made the trip two weeks later so that I could fall in love with Scoutt. Eventually, Sarah and our youngest blessings moved back to Bremen because Levi was gone much of the time, and she felt the need to be close to family. And we needed them home. Tom and I were happy to have them home and never used the term "step" when referring to our grandangels; they were *ours*.

As I decorated the Christmas tree and hung the 2015, "Grandbaby's 1st Christmas" teddy bear for Scoutt alongside the three ornaments that preceded hers, I realized that my Christmas tree was also a memory tree.

There were the glittered silver bells and felt-covered reindeer from Barry and mine's first Christmas, ornaments from the 5&10 because that's all we could afford. Over my sons' protests I hung paper ornaments from their childhood days that they'd made in grade school and had proudly presented to me. I was fortunate to have traveled beyond the boundaries of my childhood and had collected Christmas ornaments from various vacation destinations. Tom contributed ornaments that intermingled with my collection and symbolized our blended family. The finishing touch was to carefully place several white doves, a red cardinal, and a green bird among the branches in memory of loved ones lost.

I stood back to admire the tree, which bore no resemblance to those artistically decorated trees by professionals, the trees that stood proudly in malls and department stores. Unexpected tears blurred the twinkling white lights as my life was reflected before me, my journey of joys and sorrows. I'd heard the expression, "I wish I'd known then what I know now" used often, but I was grateful I hadn't known what the future held for me. Thankfully, I was given only one day at a time, and my days unfolded in ways I never could have imagined.

Love was an integral part of my family, but sometimes love happened when it was least expected—whether it was a first love or a last love or another family to love. Regardless of how love found me, it carried with it the heartbreak of losing those I loved. It was an inescapable fact, but one that didn't diminish the happiness and love they each brought to my life. I was grateful for the common thread that connected us. It was a thread unbroken by death, which could come suddenly or bide its time.

My beloved sister Pat had a massive heart attack, which took us all by surprise. We gathered in the ER and waited to hear from the cardiologist on call. The young doctor finally emerged and informed Stanley, Pat's husband, that she'd survived the heart attack, but that there was too much damage to her heart for any chance of recovery. Her care was transferred to Piedmont Atlanta Hospital where there were multiple trips to the ER and hospital. During Pat's often extended hospital stays, one that included inserting a pacemaker that proved to be ineffective, Stanley, Kim, Cindy, and I coordinated our schedules so that one of us was always by her side. As painful as it was to watch her die, I cherished what time I had left with her, and we spent many long nights reminiscing over our shared past.

Among other things we discussed Francis, our oldest sister whom we'd lost to breast cancer decades earlier, when I was only twelve. Pat lived an agonizing year before she died, and losing her was as devastatingly difficult as had been the anguish of losing Mama. Two years later the last of my three sisters was gone when Joyce died from complications of her heart attack, which we were told was "mild."

The grief that inevitably followed the deaths of each of my loved ones was transient, and I accepted that broken hearts were a part of life. It was the ache of missing them that lingered. I missed Barry's love and our life together. I missed being able to call Mama and ask her for a recipe or about a long-lost relative. I missed Jerry and his humble spirit and his wife Jerline. I missed Pat's endless energy and her ability to take charge. Though Joyce and I never had the close relationship I had with Pat, I missed her. I missed my mother-in-law, even though Charlcie never bothered to sugarcoat anything. I missed Daddy and that he always spoke his mind—about everything. And that he called any time something was important to him.

There wasn't a Thanksgiving morning since Daddy died that I didn't wait for the call that wouldn't come. Yet my daddy's voice reached from the past to inform me of the time and channel where we could watch the Macy's Thanksgiving Day Parade. His predictable phone call always began with, "Sugar, 'em boys up yet? The parade is on! Don't miss it before it's over."

Daddy's annual advice proved to be a wise metaphor for life. And I don't want to miss a minute of the parade...before it's over.

Made in the USA
Columbia, SC
18 December 2019